ADVANCE PRAISE

"Dr. Courtney is a respected colleague with substantive experience working with young children and families. In this book she highlights a broad range of topics that together provide the foundation for offering concrete, kind, and trauma-informed help to children and families. She presents a truly integrated approach that combines contemporary knowledge about neuroscience, the brain, the body–mind connection, and the person of the therapist. Science currently points to treatment of trauma to include humanistic approaches that are expressive, multi-modal, creative, sensory, and promote the body–mind connection. The chapters reveal how processing and contemplating art and dreams, encouraging journaling, family play, yoga, neurofeedback, and other sensory techniques such as sound and movement, can produce self-regulation and a sense of release, communication, and competence. Dr. Courtney also discusses the history of touch in clinical practice, and you literally feel her passion about incorporating safe touch with parents and children in her attachment-based model called FirstPlay."

—Eliana Gil, Ph.D., RPT-S, ATR, Senior Clinical and Research Consultant, Gil Institute for Trauma Recovery and Education, LLC, Fairfax, VA

"Rich in theory, techniques, case examples, and research findings, this volume is an excellent resource for both beginning and experienced therapists for expanding their skills in working with infants, children, adolescents, and families. Highly recommended!"

—Charles E. Schaefer, Ph.D., RPT-S., co-founder and Director Emeritus of the Association for Play Therapy

"Organized around the humanistic perspective, *Healing Child and Family Trauma Through Expressive and Play Therapies* begins with a discussion of the theoretical landscape to set the stage for reviewing clinical applications of expressive arts and play therapies to assess and heal child and family trauma. Each chapter engages readers by incorporating numerous activities and case examples. This book is a must-read for novice and experienced practitioners working with the traumatized child and their family."

—Susan W. Gray, MBA, Ph.D., Ed.D., LCSW, University Distinguished Professor of Social Work Emerita— Barry University, author, and recipient of the National Association of Social Work Lifetime Achievement Award

HEALING CHILD AND FAMILY TRAUMA THROUGH EXPRESSIVE & PLAY THERAPIES

HEALING CHILD AND FAMILY TRAUMA
THROUGH
EXPRESSIVE &
PLAY THERAPIES

ART,
NATURE,
BODY,
STORYTELLING,
AND
MINDFULNESS

JANET A. COURTNEY

W. W. NORTON & COMPANY
Independent Publishers Since 1923

Note to Readers: Standards of clinical practice and protocol change over time, and no technique or recommendation is guaranteed to be safe or effective in all circumstances. This volume is intended as a general information resource for professionals practicing in the field of psychotherapy and mental health; it is not a substitute for appropriate training, peer review, and/or clinical supervision. Neither the publisher nor the author(s) can guarantee the complete accuracy, efficacy, or appropriateness of any particular recommendation in every respect.

For information about permission to reproduce selections from this book, write to Permissions, W. W. Norton & Company, Inc., 500 Fifth Avenue, New York, NY 10110

For information about special discounts for bulk purchases, please contact W. W. Norton Special Sales at specialsales@wwnorton.com or 800-233-4830

Manufacturing by LSC Harrisonburg
Production manager: Katelyn MacKenzie

Library of Congress Cataloging-in-Publication Data

Names: Courtney, Janet A., author.
Title: Healing child and family trauma through expressive and play therapies :
    art, nature, storytelling, body, & mindfulness / Janet A. Courtney.
Description: First edition. | New York : W.W. Norton & Company, [2020] |
    "A Norton professional book." | Includes bibliographical references and index.
Identifiers: LCCN 2019030138 | ISBN 9780393713756 (hardcover) |
    ISBN 9780393713763 (epub)
Subjects: LCSH: Art therapy for children. | Psychic trauma in children—Treatment. |
    Family psychotherapy.
Classification: LCC RJ505.A7 C68 2020 | DDC 616.891656—dc23
LC record available at https://lccn.loc.gov/2019030138

W. W. Norton & Company, Inc., 500 Fifth Avenue, New York, N.Y. 10110
www.wwnorton.com

W. W. Norton & Company Ltd., 15 Carlisle Street, London W1D 3BS

1 2 3 4 5 6 7 8 9 0

For Ezra, Jacob, Abigail, and Sophia, my dear grandchildren,
who make my heart melt at just the word "Mimi."
And
To all the children in this world who constantly remind us grown-ups that
imagination, play, and creativity are three of life's most valuable gifts.

Contents

Acknowledgments

I feel so fortunate to have so many supportive and caring people in my life. I am thankful to my dear loving husband, Bob Nolan, my best friend, for all his patience and support, and who reminds me of the importance of balance in my life. My late father, Richard C. Courtney, who sparked my creative spirit and instilled my desire to learn; and who did not answer many of my questions, but instead prodded me to "Look it up in the encyclopedia!" Warm hugs to my mother—a natural born play therapist—my brother, Allen, and sister, Carol, my sons, Jesse and Austin, and daughter-in-law, Stephanie for their love and support and being my cheerleaders through this process. My four grandchildren bring me so much joy as we play and giggle in some good old-timey games of Old Maid, hide-and-go-seek, or storytelling. My deepest heartfelt gratitude to Prem Rawat, founder of the Prem Rawat Foundation, for his vital humanitarian and peace education efforts throughout the world.

The late Dr. Viola Brody, my mentor and author of *The Dialogue of Touch*, was instrumental in helping me to understand the significance of caring touch and first-play experiences to lifelong healthy attachments. Her work supports much of the foundational basis for several of the chapters in this book. I have a heart full of gratitude to Dr. Joyce Mills for all her encouragement, and who taught me about the power of *story* in the healing process. I am deeply thankful to Dr. Eliana Gil for all her support and care, and who I look up to as an esteemed role model. It has been an honor to serve in leadership positions for the Association for Play Therapy and I am grateful to CEO, Kathy Lebby, and all the staff at APT for their dedication to the field of play therapy. I am especially thankful to Dr. Susan W. Gray, my former Barry University Dissertation Chair, and Dr. Nancy Boyd Webb, a valuable member of my dissertation committee. Dr. Phyllis Scott, Dean of the School of Work at Barry University, and the Barry faculty share my commitment to improving the lives of children.

I am grateful to Deborah Malmud, Vice President at Norton, who initially reached out to me to consider writing a book on this topic. I am deeply thankful to her skilled staff, Sara McBride and Mariah Eppes, as well as my copyeditors Bill Bowers and Julie HawkOwl, whose expert attention to detail and editing suggestions made this book much clearer and grammatically correct. I am honored to be connected to this community of professionals dedicated to the highest standards of authorship.

To my dear colleagues and friends, too many to mention, I give a heartfelt hug for your loving and caring support. Finally, I am indebted to all the courageous families and children I have had the honor to work with, and who have taught me the truest meaning of living an authentic life.

Preface

A REFLECTION ON CREATIVITY AND PLAY: MY FATHER

I grew up surrounded by art materials—paints, clay, paintbrushes, all types of wood, and wood carving tools of all shapes and sizes. My father was an artist and was known for his ability to create portraits in wood. He carved portraits of presidents and family members and did commissioned work for customers. His artistic skills served him well over the years. It saved his life in World War II when he was asked at the very last minute to stay behind and create entertainment posters for the troops as his regiment was sent to the Battle of the Bulge in the Ardennes Forest, and everyone in his unit was killed. Later he had a successful career in advertising as a marketing executive and was a strong advocate for ethics in business (Courtney, 1964). In the 1960s he started his own business marketing consultation company utilizing a creativity method called "Synectics" (Gordon, 1961). But in the end, it was his enduring ability to play—to create—that became a stabilizing factor in his last years of life.

In 2004 my father was diagnosed with Alzheimer's disease, and in the spring of 2006, as I was completing my doctoral dissertation, he came to stay with me for one month as my mother was overwhelmed with the demands of caregiving and needed respite. Along with my husband, older son (Jesse), and his wife (Stephanie) we each planned to take a week off from work to spend time with my dad. My younger son Austin, ten at the time, spent time with "Papa" after school. Prior to his visit, I gathered together my art materials, and an art therapist friend advised me to have him recopy some of his past completed art work. But it was this one moment with my father that caused me much contemplation and I share it here:

I drove into the hobby shop parking lot, and my father held my hand as
we walked to the door. Once in the store, he followed closely behind me
as I started to look around. Unexpectedly, he pounded his cane hard on
the floor to get my attention. I quickly turned to face him. My father cried
out, "Aren't you going to buy me a toy?" He looked at me searchingly in
his now-familiar confused, blank stare. I stood still a moment absorbing
the question, and tears came to my eyes as I responded, "Of course, dad,
of course I am going to buy you a toy. That's why we are here."

Because of my perspective as a play therapist, I valued and respected my
father's need to play. I dug out some of my son's old Matchbox cars and
gathered some miniature sand tray items from my office playroom. Throughout his visit, we had creative activities planned for each day. And he played
and we played with him. We gave him back rubs and pedicures, we sang
together, we made artwork, but he particularly enjoyed playing with toys—
and to our astonishment he improved. He was calmer and more relaxed,
he smiled often, and seemed less confused. I followed through with my
friend's suggestion and had him copy on paper some of his past woodcarving
artwork—which made for some very interesting images. We even gave him
small jobs to do such as sweeping the floor, snapping green beans, and folding laundry. He chuckled and laughed. He was happy. And within days, his
memory became clearer—he was telling us stories from his past that I had
never heard before.

   As I pondered my father's desire to play, I realized that the inherent drive
to *play* and *create*, at any age, is so elemental. The world-renowned psychiatrist,
Carl Jung, recognized the value of play, and as an adult he used play as an outlet to help elucidate his deep-seated thoughts and feelings. He wrote:

> I went on with the building game after the noon meal every day. As soon
> as I was through eating, I began *playing* [italics added], and continued to
> do so until the patients arrived. In the course of this activity my thoughts
> clarified, and I was able to grasp the fantasies who presence in myself I
> dimly felt. (Jung, 1963, p. 174).

A few months after my father was back home in Ormond-by-the-Sea, Florida,
he fell, and sadly he never recovered from his injuries. In September 2006, we

had a small memorial gathering to say our goodbyes, and we all contributed our gifts of creativity: My sister (an elementary school teacher) read a children's storybook, my brother recounted stories, my sons played guitar, and we sang songs we knew he liked: "Does anyone know 'The Church in the Wildwood'?" And I created an art and craft table, where I sat in honor of my father's creative endeavors and we crafted coquina shell crosses for all to take home as special memories. It was therefore due to his (and my family's) enduring, innate ability to imagine, create, and play—my father's default saving grace—that I have dedicated my life in service of understanding. It is that unifying inherent human resilience that is universally common to us all.

JOURNEY OF CREATIVE AWAKENING

As I write this preface, my mind turns to my journey of discovery as a social worker and as a play therapist. I reflect on the teachers on whose shoulders I stand who helped shape my career, and I get teary-eyed, for to take the role of student is a humbling experience. It all overwhelms me as I recount the hundreds of people who have helped shape who I am in this moment of time. Surely, to write a book on any topic of depth, we must synthesize all the sources of learning. So, it is here that I share a brief collection of my creative journey of awakening.

Beginnings

As a freshman at Santa Fe Community College in Gainesville, Florida in 1979, I landed a position as the secretary to "Unit 8," which was designated as the psychology and sociology department. Being connected to some brilliant and very skilled therapists turned professors opened a whole new world of exploration. Beyond my course work, I attended classes in yoga, body work, dance and movement, and groups on growing intuition, exploring spirituality, and seeking an inner peace meditation, which I still practice today. I joined a research group on biofeedback, learned hypnosis, attended healing sweat lodges, joined a children's theater group, and then later took courses in improv at Florida State University as I began my social work career. In graduate school and beyond, I attended years of gestalt human potential training to explore my own inner depths of being, as well as understanding body-centered practices of healing for clients.

The Work

My first social work internship was in a domestic crisis shelter, where I worked with children and families in crisis. It was my first exposure to working with traumatized children and families, for which I was little prepared. But I saw the depth of the pain, hurt, fear, and betrayal these families experienced as they sought safety from abuse. I also witnessed the complexity of domestic violence as some people returned to their abusive situations, only to return to the shelter soon thereafter. My intensive work on an adult psychiatric and substance abuse inpatient unit and then later a children's psychiatric hospital formulated my understanding about the tenuous fine line of human consciousness and the trauma-related ripple effect of mental illness upon the whole family and social system. It was at the psychiatric children's hospital and a separate children's agency in the late 1980s where I began my play therapy experience—mostly working by the seat of my pants—as there were few opportunities for play therapy training at the time. Armed with a few good books, my foundations in social work, a strong intuition about holding a creative space for children, and a well-stocked playroom—I had no idea how good I had it!—I worked with children incorporating play therapy in groups, family therapy, and individual counseling.

At this time I began my career specialty, working in infant mental health in foster care and adoption. Parallel to the current opioid crisis, there were thousands of babies nationwide entering foster care in the late 1980s and early 1990s born with neonatal drug withdrawal syndrome, predominantly due to maternal cocaine intake during pregnancy. This close contact with traumatized infants led me on a lifetime mission to seek out ways to bring healing to infants and children through the study of attachment theory and later a comprehension of neurobiological influences. My years of full-time private practice, teaching graduate courses in the School of Social Work at Barry University, and my doctoral research in developmental play therapy, attachment theory, and practitioner experiences of touch eventually supported further research into the clinical and ethical implications of touch in therapy sessions with children. Please see the book *Touch in Child Counseling and Play Therapy: An Ethical and Clinical Guide* (Courtney & Nolan, 2017). My therapeutic model, called First-Play Therapy (presented in Chapters 9 and 10), is an accumulation of all my years of education, training, research, and clinical experience.

The Parallel Process of Transformation

This book has been a labor of love. It has called forth much perseverance, grit, and countless hours to conceptualize just that one more paragraph, or being awakened from sleep with the "Aha!" of how best to articulate that sentence I was wrestling with and writing over and over prior to giving up and going to sleep at midnight, or to look up just one more supportive reference to make this book stand on a solid, credible foundation. For writing this book, composed with heart, has challenged and transformed me.

At a deeper level, to write a book about the healing of family and child trauma inevitably points back to self. And it calls to mind my own hard stories of trauma experiences, which I addressed on my personal journey of healing. I have also engaged many of the expressive modalities discussed throughout this book as faithful resources for healing: journaling, dream work, art, yoga, mindfulness, storytelling, nature, the body work of gestalt processes, and walking with mindful intention through the labyrinth. And I think of my own therapists who listened and cared for me unconditionally and helped me to see my potential, even when life felt so dark that I could not see it for myself. Those life learnings I see now as gifts of understanding, of courage, and of hope that I bring to the moment of meeting with another human being. For all of us here on this amazing Earth share in universal sufferings of grief, loss, and emotional, psychological, and somatic pain that take many different forms. In this, we can develop a deeper sense of compassion to hold a safe sanctuary of containment to hear the difficult and heartbreaking stories of children and families that need to be heard, without judgment and offered with an authentic kindheartedness to honor the healing journey.

Introduction

Welcome to *Healing Child and Family Trauma through Expressive & Play Therapies: Art, Nature, Storytelling, Body, & Mindfulness!* The inspiration for this book evolved over the past 35 years, during a long, fascinating journey of discovery in the fields of play therapy and expressive therapy. These two separate experiential fields of practice dovetail together perfectly to meet the unique developmental needs of children. Although my expertise is firmly grounded within the fields of social work and play therapy (I have a master's and a doctorate in social work and am credentialed as a Registered Play Therapist-Supervisor) I wanted to expand my horizons and find new ways to help, and heal, children. Although I do not have a degree nor am I credentialed in any of the expressive arts fields, I supplemented my play therapy knowledge by attending many expressive arts training sessions—including art, music, dance, drama, nature, body, journaling, gestalt—and obtained supervision and consultation to expand my expertise beyond my training and supervision in social work and play therapy methods. What I share in this book are many of the expressive arts interventions I learned from those years of exploration, which I then successfully integrated into play therapy sessions with children and families.

Although this book provides some general foundations in play therapy and the field of expressive arts, it is not exhaustive. This brings to light an important ethical consideration. Since all professionals are ethically mandated to practice within the boundaries of their educational backgrounds, training, supervision, and professional experience, readers are encouraged to seek out additional training and supervision from disciplines that are beyond their training. Therefore, any of the expressive arts, body and play therapy modalities presented in this book requires in-depth study and experiential learning, and readers are urged to seek out any topics that pique their interest and delve into deeper study and training.

This book is written to contribute to the literature by providing mental health practitioners from all fields, and graduate students, with creative ways to grow their therapeutic toolkits in work with infants, children, adolescents, and families. There are two parts to this book. Part I comprises Chapters 1 through 3 and provides the necessary foundations to formulate the framework related to the clinical applications found in Part II. Chapter 1 crosswalks between the two fields of expressive arts and play therapies to highlight the common underpinnings, as well as recognizing the shapers of both fields. It also recognizes the ancient forms of healing—storytelling, dance, music, play, nature, ritual—that our ancestors innately drew upon to heal from the vast traumas that confronted them.

Research since the 1990s has generated a broader understanding of trauma and the (brain)-mind-body connection, creating a paradigm shift in our thinking about best practice interventions in the healing of clients. Chapter 2 provides an overview of the current literature and research within the fields of trauma and neurobiology, and provides a basis for trauma-informed work as the topics of expressive and play therapies are explored throughout the book. Chapter 3 highlights the therapeutic elements that are foundational to the therapeutic process and further expounded in Part II of the clinical applications. It identifies seven stages of therapy that provide a framework for working with clients' emotional, cognitive, somatic, and sensory experiences to heal from trauma.

Part II comprises the expressive and play therapy clinical adaptations. Chapter 4 explores the field of art therapy, synthesizing the relevant literature on the topic and provides supporting therapeutic assessment and intervention strategies for working individually with a child. Chapter 5 provides work with the family through art assessment, and Chapter 6 expands on the family expressive and play therapy applications through puppet storytelling and structured art interventions. Chapter 7 draws upon the healing forces of the natural world to provide experiences of healing with children and families. Chapter 8 explores several healing interventions for children through mindfulness practice, journaling exercises, dream exploration, mindful labyrinth walks, and healing through body therapies, with a focus on yoga. Chapters 9 and 10 provide my own therapeutic model of FirstPlay Therapy conceptualized for two different developmental levels. Chapter 9 highlights FirstPlay Kinesthetic Storytelling designed, for ages two years and beyond, and includes a composite case of a child in foster care to illustrate this therapy in action. Chapter 10 presents FirstPlay Infant Story-Massage (birth to two years) in practice with a group of young mothers residing in a residential substance abuse treatment center with their infants, who were born with neonatal abstinence syndrome. The group case study demonstrates how the mothers were guided in FirstPlay interventions to provide reparative experiences of touch, and were supported to attach and bond with their infants.

Many of the expressive and play therapy techniques are presented with detailed steps of implementation found throughout each chapter so that readers can gain a clear understanding of how the assessment or intervention can be suitably utilized. Additionally, interspersed throughout each chapter are experiential activities so readers can also experience the modalities firsthand through personal learning and reflection. These experientials, called "The Practice," guide opportunities for readers to engage personally in the creative expressive and play therapy techniques presented in each chapter and thereby augment professional self-awareness and skill-building competencies.

The future, I predict, will become more interdisciplinary as we step out of our chosen, familiar disciplines to embrace the understandings of other professional fields of healing. My many years' experience working with children has shown me that they may resonate with only a few expressive and play therapy modalities. It has therefore been helpful for me to have a variety of therapeutic tools at my fingertips so I can quickly adapt to a child's needs within the moment. A child frozen in trauma may shun the idea of a movement process, but he may be willing to take his hand and hit a drum, or pound it in clay. That same child may decide that journaling is more a "girl thing," but he may be willing to engage in a nature-based expressive intervention. Having the know-how to adjust to the child's and the family's needs provides more opportunities to enrich healing. As we cross-fertilize knowledge between fields of practice, we all broaden our ways of knowing to bring healing to the hearts and minds of the children and families we serve. I am thrilled you found your way to this book, and I thank you for taking this journey with me.

Part I

EXPRESSIVE
AND
PLAY THERAPY
FOUNDATIONS

Chapter 1

EXPRESSIVE ARTS AND PLAY THERAPIES: A RETURN TO ROOTS

"There is something to be learned from our ancestors."

Bruce Perry, MD, Ph.D.

"The expressive arts are ancient forms being rebirthed to bring much needed integration and balance into our world."

Natalie Rogers, Ph.D., REAT

magine for a moment an ancestor who lived two or three centuries back, perhaps a long-ago grandmother. Imagine how very harsh life was back then: There were no modern medicines or vaccines to fight off infection, and many people witnessed friends and family who succumbed to disease. Tragically, many children died in early childhood, and mothers often died in childbirth. Locating clean water and proper sanitation was difficult, and traveling took days with horses that became lame or and sick. Shelter from the elements was painstaking to build, and people shivered in the frigid cold and sweated in the sweltering heat because there was no electricity. Life was extremely harrowing, as they were subjected to daily stress and trauma. The question arises: How did your ancient grandmother help heal herself—emotionally, psychologically, and physically—to overcome such challenges? Over the centuries, many cultures healed mind, body, and soul effectively in community, family, and individually through song, dance, visual arts, play, storytelling, nature, touch, dreams, spirituality, and ritual.

These expressive ways of being evolved in our human species over millennia and were very much a part of daily life and community. We built our own homes, carved our own tools, and hand-fashioned our own furniture. We planted seeds and farmed our own food and sculpted pots from clay. We spun wool for our clothes and shaped materials to protect our feet. We created toys for children to play with, and games for social engagement. We painted symbols on rocks and walls. We touched one another to heal disease. We spent extended time in nature and created rituals in saunas made with fire, water, and hot stones. We knelt in ritual and prayer and searched for insight in our dreams. We crafted our own instruments, sang our age-old songs, danced hand in hand, and told stories that were passed down through generations. These creative endeavors helped to strengthen family bonds and united communities together to support emotional, psychological, physical, social, and spiritual well-being.

While modern-day societies and family systems may have lost memory of their ancestral ways of creating and healing, in many cultures those traditions of healing are still very much alive. Consider the following example: A psychologist was hired by an American company based in an African nation to intervene with a tragic disaster that had occurred at the facility, resulting in the deaths of some of the employees. Trained in crisis intervention debriefing, the psychologist gathered the employees (all citizens of the African nation) in a room, where he opened the group for discussion of the incident. The room remained silent as they all sat still and stared blankly at the floor. The psychologist tried his best skills to engage and empathize with the group and the deep pain they must all be feeling. Still silence and a heaviness in the room loomed. Finally, one of the employees in the group spoke up and said to the psychologist: "You don't get it, do you?"

Puzzled by the question, the psychologist said, "Get what?" Again, the employee, now shaking his head and looking directly at the psychologist, repeated the statement: "You just don't get it!"

Exasperated, the psychologist said, "What? What don't I get?"

After a long pause, the one deemed group representative replied: "This is not how we heal. We heal through drumming. We heal through song. We heal through dance." Now enlightened, the psychologist sat back in his chair with a new insight for contemplation that totally changed his paradigm of how he practiced therapy.

While expressive and play therapies may be perceived as seemingly modern-day treatment methods, there is nothing new about them. They are ancient forms of healing—storytelling, art, dance, music, play, nature, ritual—that our ancestors innately drew upon to heal from the vast traumas that troubled them.

McNiff (2005) found inspiration from our "shamanic forebears" that used ritual and symbolic forms of expression to "heal the soul" (p. xi). Bruce Perry (2015) viewed our ancestral resilience from a holistic neurobiological perspective:

> "Our ancestors had to learn to cope with trauma in order to survive; somehow traumatized people had to find ways to continue to sustain family, community, and culture and move forward. These core elements . . . touch, the patterned repetitive movements of dance, and song—all provided in an intensely relational experience. . . . The most remarkable quality of these elements is that together they create a total neurobiological experience influencing cortical, limbic, diencephalic, and brainstem systems. (p. xi).

From a Jungian perspective, perhaps we are each individually touching into our cultural and societal *collective unconscious*—the part of our inner knowing derived from ancestral memory and experience that is common to all humanity (Jung, 1964). Perhaps within me, within you, we are tapping into our own inner wisdom of healing and resilience that has been passed down through the ages. This book will hold our collective traditional forms of healing and how they are currently adapted and utilized as contemporary therapies to support an organizing framework to work with children and families within play therapy sessions.

FAMILY & CULTURAL RESILIENCE

With the above section in mind, I invite you to take a few minutes to engage in the following practice exercise: Family & Cultural Resilience.

THE PRACTICE

Family and Cultural Resilience

With a partner, take a few minutes to reflect on the following:

1. Using your imagination, call to mind your ancient ancestors and think of all the ways they used their skills, knowledge, and wisdom to manage daily life, heal from illness, gather and cook food, make clothes, create containers for food, build homes, search for higher meaning spiritually and ritually, and help

themselves to overcome emotional and psychological trauma. You can even imagine relatives from different time periods.

2. Think about the family system and cultural background you were raised in. What were some of the core expressive and healing elements from your family and/or cultural background that supported your family's and community's sense of resilience?

The following sections will define the two separate fields of play therapy and expressive arts therapy, and some of the noted "shapers" of the respective fields.

THE FIELD OF PLAY THERAPY

Margaret Lowenfeld (1979), who originated the "World Technique" (the beginnings of Sandtray Therapy) in the 1920s, is credited as the first to use the term "play therapy," in a letter to the *British Medical Journal* in 1938 (Lowenfeld & Dukes, 1938). And, in 1939, C. H. Rogerson wrote the first book about the topic, entitled, *Play Therapy in Childhood* (Rogerson, 1939). However, it was not until 1982 that Charles Schaefer and Kevin O'Connor (1983) collaborated to form the first organization dedicated to play therapy, called the Association for Play Therapy (APT). APT offers a credentialing process to practitioners to become a Registered Play Therapist or a Registered Play Therapy Supervisor. APT defines play therapy as "the systematic use of a theoretical model to establish an interpersonal process wherein trained play therapists use the therapeutic powers of play to help clients prevent or resolve psychosocial difficulties and achieve optimal growth and development." Internationally, there are different associations of play therapy, as every country has its own standards for educating and licensing degreed mental health professionals. Many universities offer specialty tracks in play therapy. (See the Association for Play Therapy website for a listing.)

Play can be intrinsically healing, which is the whole underlying premise of play therapy. Play therapy for children is often likened to an adult's capacity to talk out their feelings and experiences, whereas children might play out their feelings. Landreth (2012) suggested that as we think of therapy for adults as the *talking cure*, we should then think of play therapy as the *playing cure*.

Play therapy is differentiated from regular play in that the therapist assists children to address their problems by building upon their natural means of expression—the act of play (Axline, 1969). Play helps to dissociate children emotionally and psychologically through imaginative play that supports a safe distancing for children to address their problems, modify behavior, express feelings, and develop problem-solving skills (Landreth, 2012).

Over the years, the field of play therapy has been challenged to prove its efficacy as a valid therapeutic intervention for children, and not just be deemed "willy-nilly" or "whistling in the dark" (Phillips, 1985), but to show its treatment effectiveness through rigorous research to demonstrate its efficacy as a valid treatment approach for a variety of different diagnoses and family problems (Bratton, Ray, Rhine, & Jones, 2005; Ray & Bratton, 2010). Much of the credit goes to the many professional members of APT who have worked hard to make this happen. The new discoveries in neuroscience, especially related to the research in trauma (see Chapter 2), have also provided evidence that healing requires modalities that are indeed multisensory-rich.

Currently, play therapy has grown to encompass a broad range of play therapy models, some originating from adult-oriented theoretical models that were then adapted to children, and other play therapy models that were generated specifically for children. For example, John Allan (1988) adapted Carl Jung's theories to Jungian Play Therapy, and Viola Oaklander (1988) adapted Gestalt therapy to the child population known as Gestalt Play Therapy. On the

FIGURE 1.1: Play Therapy Umbrella
SOURCE: COURTESY OF JANET A. COURTNEY; ARTWORK BY AMBER HOOPER

other hand, Viola Brody created Developmental Play Therapy as an original play therapy model, and Bernard and Louise Guerney developed Filial Play Therapy (1989). In the early years of child treatment (1920s–1960s) many of these approaches were broadly used to treat children irrespective of diagnosis. Over time, however, there has been advocacy toward a more Prescriptive Play Therapy approach as developed by Schaefer (2003), in which the therapy is matched to the problem and/or diagnosis. Refer to the play therapy umbrella as shown in Figure 1.1 listing a wide-range of play therapy approaches.

THE SHAPERS OF PLAY THERAPY—
(FROM A HUMANISTIC PERSPECTIVE)

Play therapy has a wide range of theoretical underpinnings, as shown in Figure 1.1. However, as you will discover later in this chapter, a common thread between both expressive arts therapy and play therapy is found in humanistic underpinnings. Since my training background is grounded in this theory and imparted throughout this book, the following section will only present the shapers of the field of play therapy from a humanistic lineage. For an overall history of child psychotherapy and play therapy, refer to Homeyer & Morrison (2008) and Landreth (2012).

The roots of humanistic psychology began with one of the first American books related to therapy with children, written by Jessie Taft (1933/1972), *The Dynamics of Therapy in a Controlled Relationship*, (which is still very relevant reading). Taft, a student of psychoanalyst Otto Rank, adapted his work with adults to children. Rank's therapy focused on the therapeutic value of the therapist-client relationship, and Taft labeled her approach with children Relationship Therapy (Taft, 1933/1972). She differentiated her method from that of her psychoanalytic contemporaries of the time, namely Anna Freud and Melanie Klein—who also had their own differences between the Vienna School and the Berlin/London School, respectively (a separate conversation). The reader can hear the humanistic voice within the following statement by Taft (1933/1973): "For relationship therapy, like life, utilizes the forces already within the human being" (p. 296).

Frederick Allen (1976), Clark Moustakas (1959), and Elaine Dorfman (1965) continued to develop Relationship Therapy with children by further de-emphasizing the importance of insight and awareness as goals of treatment, and instead reinforcing the importance of the relationship. Allen (1976) argued against the need to have to "recreate" a child or to take over the child's own responsibility for living. He expounded a strong respect for children's capacity to work on their own problems and advocated for a here-and-now (present, not past) relationship. Any interpretation given to the child was only concerned with those feelings and activities that emerged within the therapeutic relationship. Allen (1976) wrote: "It is my belief that it is the experiencing and being able to live with their feelings that has more therapeutic value than giving a child an understanding of the past" (p. 232). Clark Moustakas is credited with much of the early child therapy research (Landreth, 2012) as he sought to validate the effectiveness of play therapy outcomes. In the Relationship Therapy perspective, Moustakas (1959) believed that the ". . . alive relationship between the therapist and the child is the essential dimension, perhaps the only significant reality, in the therapeutic process and in all interhuman growth" (p. xiii).

Although Carl Rogers (also influenced by Rank) is mostly credited as working with adults, he first began his career from 1928 to 1940 on the staff of the Child Study Department of the Society for the Prevention of Cruelty to Children in Rochester, New York. His book, *The Clinical Treatment of the Problem Child*, provides one of his first writings related to nondirective techniques intended to be used with children (Rogers, 1939). Conceivably, the person who popularized Rogers's work related to children to the professional community was Virginia Axline, when she published her book *Play Therapy* in 1947; and later to a larger lay audience when she published the transformative case study of a young child in her 1964 book, *Dibs In Search of Self*. By the late 1960s, the term Client-Centered Play Therapy had gained a respectful following—and some practitioners even refer to Axline as the "grandmother" of play therapy. Many expanded the Client-Centered Play Therapy approach including Gary Landreth (2012) and Louise and Bernard Guerney (1989). Today the gold standard for training new play therapists is to require training in the foundations of Client-Centered Play Therapy as a "101" of core knowledge, which can then provide a springboard to other forms of theoretical models of play therapy. The main tenets of humanistic psychology are a relatively nonhistorical approach, less emphasis on the authority of the therapist, unconditional acceptance of the child, and a pronounced awareness of the process of the child's play in the here-and-now relationship with the practitioner.

Another gold standard of knowledge for those in training and new to the field of play therapy is to understand the therapeutic change agents of play, or what Schaefer (1993) first coined "The therapeutic powers of play" and further elaborated by Schaefer and Drewes (2014) in their book, *Therapeutic Powers of Play: 20 Core Agents of Change*. Based upon clinical practice and research, 20 core therapeutic healing powers of play were identified, falling under four categories, a) facilitates communication, b) fosters emotional wellness, c) enhances social relationships, and d) increases personal strengths. Moreover, the core powers of play are viewed as common across all models of play therapy, and Schaefer and Drewes promoted the adoption of a transtheoretical orientation. The reader is encouraged to discover more about the therapeutic powers of play that assist in answering the questions *how* and *why* play can produce healing change for clients, as set forth in the book by Schaefer and Drewes (2014).

THE EXPRESSIVE ARTS FIELD

While the overall field of play therapy might be easier to define and track, separating out the diverse fields that utilize art as a healing modality requires more sorting through. Richardson (2016) wrote that expressive arts is a "nascent therapeutic field" (p. 4) that is emerging in different forms globally. And, very much like the field of play therapy, McNiff (2005) described the great efforts it has taken over the years to position expressive therapies from residing on the "fringes" of psychotherapy to a recognized credible healing intervention.

Estrella (2005) wrote that expressive therapies are founded on the "interrelatedness of the arts" (p. 183). Overall, this field has been described by a variety of different labels, including creative therapies, integrative arts therapies, action therapies, experiential therapies, intermodal expressive arts, expressive therapies, creative psychotherapy, creative arts therapies, multimodal expressive therapy, and integrative approaches (Estrella, 2005; Malchiodi, 2015; Richardson, 2016). The National Coalition of Creative Arts Therapies Associations (NCCATA), established in 1979, identifies and brings together six art-based fields: art therapy, dance/movement therapy, drama therapy, music therapy, poetry therapy, and psychodrama. Each of these distinct fields have their own unique historical roots, pioneers, university graduate programs, and associations that provide annual conferences and have rigorous standards for credentialing of practitioners. NCCATA defines their association as an "alliance of professional associations dedicated to the advancement of the arts as a primary therapeutic treatment across a variety of rehabilitative, medical, community, and educational settings." Creative arts therapists are defined as "human service professionals who use arts modalities and creative processes for the purpose of ameliorating disability and illness and optimizing health and wellness." To learn more about each of the arts fields, refer to the appendix at the end of this book with links to the respective association websites. Additionally, some of these expressive arts modalities will be addressed further in the chapters found in Part II, Expressive Arts and Play Therapy Clinical Applications.

The International Expressive Arts Therapy Association (IEATA) was founded in 1994 and promotes expressive arts, including "visual arts, movement, drama, music, writing, and other creative processes to foster deep personal growth and community development." There are two credential tracks that professionals can apply: 1) Registered Expressive Art Therapists (REAT), for those with advanced education and training, and 2) Registered Expressive Arts Consultants/educators (REACE) for those professionals who use expressive arts in education and the medical health field, but do not hold a mental health degree. In addition to the professional art fields acknowledged by the IEATA and NCCATA, Malchiodi (2015) expands the definition of "expressive therapies" to include "bibliotherapy, play, and/or sandplay within the context of psychotherapy, counseling, rehabilitation or medicine" (p. 12).

The Shapers of Expressive Therapies

When we turn to the expressive therapies literature, we find a surprising revelation. Natalie Rogers, daughter of Carl Rogers, has been at the forefront of the expressive therapies movement, where she integrated her father's concepts and also her mother Helen Elliot Rogers's talent as an artist to Person-Centered Expressive Arts. Rogers (1993) was fascinated by what she called the "creative connection," which she described as the "interplay among movement, art, writing, and sound" (p. 4), which stimulates self-awareness and can often occur at the nonverbal level. It's not surprising, then, that her father early on wrote an article entitled, "Toward a Theory of Creativity" (Rogers, 1954). Although she passed away a few years ago, her legacy in the field lives on.

Shaun McNiff, who initiated the first intermodal expressive therapy graduate program in the United States at Lesley University in Cambridge, Massachusetts in 1974, wrote that he first heard the term "expressive therapy" when he worked at a state mental hospital in Massachusetts. McNiff's (2009) foundations rely heavily on the work of Carl Jung and Jung's emphasis on the active imagination process, symbolic expression, and openness to turning toward different modes of expression to heal. Drawing upon our shamanic forebears from all parts of the world, McNiff proposed that art itself is the medicine.

Paolo Knill, Ellen Levine, and Stephen Levine, in their book, *Principles and Practice of Expressive Arts Therapy: Toward a Therapeutic Aesthetics* (2005) sought to define expressive arts therapies as its own "discipline unto itself" (p. 119). Intermodal expressive therapies, as developed by Knill, has its own theoretical framework rooted in imagination and play that is "characterized by an inter-relatedness among the arts" (119). Knill, Levine, & Levine (2005) help to distinguish the varied expressive arts fields related to their preferred senses. For example, the visual arts are visual; music is auditory; dance is sensorimotor; literature and poetry are auditory and visual; and theater is auditory, sensorimotor, and visual (p. 122).

Some expressive arts therapists (and play therapists too!) are integrating ecotherapy into expressive arts modalities, and perhaps in the future the expressive therapies literature may reflect more of this trend (see, for example, Atkins & Snyder, 2018; Kopytin & Rugh, 2017). This integration may also include the American Horticulture Therapy Association. Currently, the Appalachian State University in North Carolina offers a nature-focused expressive arts therapy curriculum under the department of Human Development & Psychological Counseling, founded in 1985 by Dr. Sally Atkins as shared here:

> At Appalachian our philosophy of expressive arts therapy is inextricably linked with the natural landscape in which we live and work. We live in the ancient mountains of the Southern Appalachian Range, among Native ancestors and remnants of the earth's oldest forests. Four rivers are born in this land, including what is believed to be the oldest river on the continent of North America. This is the landscape that shapes our daily life and inhabits our souls. Nature's cycles of creation, elaboration, destruction, and regeneration provide the model for creative process in art and life (expressivearts.appstate.edu/program, last para).

Perhaps it is within the child trauma literature where expressive arts therapists and play therapists find the most collaboration. This coming together could be credited to the wealth of neuroscience research and literature related to trauma that has emerged over the past 30 years, pointing to the need to approach trauma through more sensory-somatic oriented ("bottom-up") and right-brain interventions, as discussed in detail in Chapter 2. Cathy Malchiodi, an art therapist and expressive arts therapist and developer of trauma-informed expressive arts therapy, is a widely recognized leading expert on the expressive therapies as a healing treatment approach in childhood trauma (Malchiodi, 2015). She has also founded a nonprofit organization, Art Therapy Without Borders (ATWB), dedicated to using art therapy through education, research, and global networking specifically for art therapy initiatives. Another leading figure in the area of childhood trauma is Carmen Richardson (2016), founder and director of the Prairie Institute of Expressive Arts Therapy (PIEAT). The PIEAT approach sets forth a four-phase model of intervention, including understanding the child's world; cultivating safety and resources; processing trauma; and reclaiming, reframing, repairing, and reorienting (Richardson, 2016).

INTEGRATING EXPRESSIVE ARTS THERAPIES INTO PLAY THERAPY: A PRESCRIPTIVE APPROACH

In the expressive arts therapy field, there has been long debate about specialization to one single arts-based approach (music therapy, dance therapy, poetry therapy, drama therapy, art therapy) versus practitioners who choose to mix art modalities to enhance healing. Part of the debate stems from concerns that practitioners may spread themselves too thin, because mastering even one art takes a lifetime (Knill, Levine, & Levine, 2005), bringing to mind the old saying, "jack of all trades, and masters of none."

Conversely, many child therapists and play therapists have long held the wisdom that therapeutic modalities should be selected based upon the child's and family's assessed needs. Schaefer (2003) originated Prescriptive Play Therapy, which considers approaches that are most appropriate pertaining to a child's individual psychosocial and presenting problems (Schaefer & O'Connor, 1983). Schaefer & Millman (1977) conceptualized: "Rather than attempting to force a child into one all-purpose therapeutic mold, then, therapists are now trying to individualize, to fit the remedies or techniques to the individual child" (as cited in Schaefer & O'Connor, 1983, p. 1). Gil (1991) encouraged that each child must be "sized up" and assessed for which type of therapy method is best suited related to a child's diagnosis or problem and advocated for an "integrative approach" (Gil, 2015b). Webb (2019) described it as matching a child's problem to technique following a thorough assessment.

To be clear, expressive arts therapies are not play therapies, as Malchiodi (2015) reminded:

> It is important to clarify that although some practitioners define art, dance/movement, music, or drama therapies as play therapies (Lambert et al., 2007), creative arts therapies and expressive therapies are not merely subsets of play therapy and have a long history as distinct approaches in mental health and health care. (p. 13)

Neither are play therapies a subset of expressive arts therapies. McNiff (2005) sees the collaboration of fields as connecting "sister disciplines" that "affirm the creative space" that unites every form of experiential therapy. What is understood is that there is a mutual sharing of expertise between the fields, with those identified as expressive therapists crossing over to learn from play therapists (Malchiodi, 2005), and many play therapists—and child therapists—have turned to the expressive therapies' literature and training conferences to discover innovative ways to integrate expressive arts into play therapy and child counseling sessions (see for example, Degges-White & Davis, 2018; Dhaese, 2011; Green & Drewes, 2014; Malchiodi, 2005, 2015). I fit into this second category.

FIGURE 1.2: Humanistic Perspective
SOURCE: COURTESY OF AUTHOR; ARTWORK BY AMBER HOOPER

Humanistic Foundations: A Common Thread between Play Therapy and Expressive Therapies

Humanistic foundations are a common thread between play therapy approaches and expressive arts therapies, and because my training is firmly grounded in the humanistic paradigm, I will expound on some of the essential ingredients of the theory here. That said, recognize that practitioners from both fields integrate a wide variety of theoretical foundations, as shown in Figure 1.1 for play therapy (refer also to Crenshaw & Stewart, 2015 for a thorough compilation of theoretical foundations in play therapy). In the field of expressive arts, the literature cites several theories, including Jungian, crystallization theory, polyaesthetic, psychodynamic, humanistic, cognitive, developmental, systems, narrative, and solution-focused, among others (Knill, Levine, & Levine, 2005; Malchiodi, 2015; McNiff, 2009).

Carl Rogers and Abraham Maslow have both been credited as the "founders" of humanistic psychology (Bankart, 1997). Reflective of the literature, the terms humanistic psychology, client-centered, person-centered, nondirective therapy, and relationship therapy have often been used interchangeably. Essentially all speak to closely tied theoretical beliefs, with the importance of the therapeutic relationship paramount to the healing process. One of the chief principles is an underlying belief that human beings have an innate propensity toward growth, and the therapist's respect for a client's inner capacity toward self-efficacy and self-determination is central to the theory (Maslow, 1968; Rogers, 1965). The following statement by Axline (1969), a student of Rogers, summarized this therapeutic stance well:

> There seems to be a powerful force within each individual which strives continuously for complete self-realization. This force may be characterized as a drive toward maturity, independence, and self-direction. It goes on relentlessly to achieve consummation, but it needs good "growing ground" to develop a well-balanced structure (p. 10). . . . Nondirective therapy is based upon the assumption that the individual has within himself, not only the ability to solve his own problems satisfactorily, but also this growth impulse that makes mature behavior more satisfying than immature behavior. (p. 15)

Natalie Rogers described her person-centered work in expressive arts therapy as being "empathic, open, honest, congruent, caring," recognizing the individual's "worth, dignity and the capacity for self-direction." (Rogers, 1993, p. 3). In the same manner, Landreth (2012) advocated that the child-centered play therapist believes in the child's intrinsic motivation toward self-actualization, which moves toward improvement, independence, and maturity of self. He further emphasized that "the relationship, not the utilization of toys or interpretation of behavior, is the key to growth" (p. 86). Therapy therefore focused on the present, living experience, and Landreth made several distinctions, including focusing on the "present rather than the past," "the person rather than the problem," and "feelings rather than thoughts or acts" (p. 86). The humanistic stance is also found to include the qualities of authenticity, compassion, nonverbal and verbal processes, heartfelt presence, intuitive processing (right hemisphere), witnessing, alternative states of consciousness (trance), unconditional love, process oriented, attuned listening, here and now, multisensory experiencing, instilling hope, metaphoric and symbolic utilization, imagination, creativity, and play, among others (see Figure 1.2).

More Common Threads: Imagination, Play, and Creativity

When I cross-walk between the two fields of expressive arts and play therapy searching for common threads, three interrelated concepts stand out loud and clear: imagination, play, and creativity. In reviewing the literature on these three constructs, I find that many authors agree with one thing—they are difficult to define. As these constructs lay a foundation for all the chapters in this book, this section seeks to explore a working definition of these topics. As the reader will learn, the three interrelated constructs of imagination, play, and creativity have been purposely shown in order, as they each build upon the others, with first the emergence of imagination, then the outward manifestation of play that then materializes into creative form. Additionally, these three constructs are predominantly right-brain functions related to emotional expression (McGilchrist, 2009; Schore & Schore, 2012).

Imagination

The well-known contemporary American poet, Mary Ruefle (2017) wrote: "It is impossible for me to write about the imagination; it is like asking a fish to describe the sea" (p. 5). Formal definitions usually define imagination as holding an inner mind "image" or a visual picture. However, in education, we often try to find the strengths of our students by figuring out if they are predominantly auditory, visual, or kinesthetic learners. Paolo Knill (2005) reminded us that we often "neglect" to recognize all the aspects of multiplicity that are experienced within imagination. He asserted that imagination should not be limited to just visual images, but pointed to all the multisensory components of imagination. He wisely broadened our framework on imagination: "In fact, isn't it true that humans typically imagine not only visual images, but also sounds and rhythms, movements, acts, spoken messages and moving pictures—even tastes and tactile sensations" (p. 121). In connecting the sensory components of the arts back to the field of expressive arts therapy, Knill (2005) highlighted that, "imagination is thus truly intermodal" (p. 121). McNiff (2009) recognized that childhood imagination is central to the foundation of expressive arts therapy. Images can arise in many forms, and Siegel (2018) encouraged that we can tune into this through sensation, feeling, and nonworded worlds to gain a window into our inner self.

From a whole other perspective, Marks-Tarlow (2018) examined the importance of imagination as core to our ability to have empathy for another. She wrote, "Through inner channels of re-presentation, humans can see deeply through the eyes of another." She highlighted how imagination plays a "central role" in the healing of trauma, which she believes has been highly undervalued. Likewise, through the therapist's own imagination, she or he maintains the ability to hold a hopeful future vision for the client, even when they cannot see it for themselves. She wisely wrote that the therapist's ability to ". . . imagine an open and different future for that person is an important service. By holding hope in the face of another's hopelessness, we allow patients to 'lean into' our open perspectives until enough support, insight, and wisdom becomes internalized and supported" (p. 157). Wow! Think of that, such is the gift of imagination!

Play

Finding a unifying definition of play in the literature is not easy, and many authors admit to the difficulty. Stuart Brown and his colleague Madelyn Eberle (2018) in their chapter "A Closer Look at Play," wrote "It's hard to describe play succinctly" (p. 27). And Fred Rogers, who was well known for his acclaimed children's television program *Mister Rogers' Neighborhood*, used play materials such as puppets to help grow children's sense of self-efficacy (and so much more). Rogers (1986) wrote, "There's something about play that makes it very hard to define" (p. 3). Schaefer (1993) proposed an explanation for the play definition conundrum, "One reason play is difficult to define is that it changes form as young children mature" (p. 1). Of course, play is ever evolving beyond childhood into adulthood. Erickson's 1950 definition of play has often been quoted: "play is a function of ego, an attempt to synchronize the bodily and social processes of self" (as cited by Schaefer & O'Connor, 1983, p. 2). Schaefer (1993) viewed play as being intrinsically motivated from a sense of enjoyment with the "process of play being more important than the end result" (p. 1). He further conceptualized that out of play, creativity and innovation are sparked, as the child's play imposes new and novel meaning on objects and events. Schaefer & Peabody (2016) set forth a highly agreed-upon definition of play as, "An activity with the following key attributes: freedom from constraints of reality, positive affect, flexibility, intrinsic motivation, inner control, and a focus on the process of the activity rather than the outcome" (p. 23). What is clear, as Brown & Eberle (2018) explained, is that play is very ancient and has evolved over time to supply us with adaptive strengths that are key to our survival.

Creativity

Again, to seek out a definition of creativity is challenging. Fred Rogers (1986) proposed that ". . . creativity has to do with rearranging known pieces into new forms. And has to do with problem solving. Rearranging and solving . . . those are two important aspects of play as well . . ." (p. 7). *The Oxford Learners Dictionary* defines creativity as "the ability to use skill and imagination to produce something new or to produce art."

To advance our understanding of creativity, once again we return to a humanistic perspective and Carl Rogers, in his 1954 article, "Toward a Theory of Creativity." Here, he sought to put forth a theory of creativity, which he believed grew from a source of novel construction: "This novelty grows out of the unique qualities of the individual in his interactions with the materials of experience. Creativity always has the stamp of the individual upon its product" (p. 250). He further defined creativity as ". . . the emergence in action of a novel relational product, growing out of the uniqueness of the individual on the one hand, and the materials, events, people, or circumstances of his life on the other" (p. 251). Rogers also saw creativity as the "same tendency which we discover so deeply as the curative force in psychotherapy—*man's tendency to actualize himself, to become his potentialities*" (p. 251).

Play can therefore be viewed as a direct expression of imagination that manifests into novel creativity. In the introduction to their book, *Play and Creativity in Psychotherapy*, Marks-Tarlow, Solomon, and Siegel (2018) wrote that play and creativity (and I would add to this imagination) "speak to the heart and soul of what all psychotherapists engage in" (p. 3).

Putting it all together

For the purposes of this book, imagination, play, and creativity will be defined thus: Play is the curative and pleasurable externalized action (the doing) of imagination (inner visioning). And creativity is the novel product or art produced as a result of imagination and play that ultimately activates our highest potentiality of self-actualization. In other words, play is the outward channeling and manifestation of a child's inner imagination that creates a novel and creative outcome that drives growth and resiliency. Imagination, play, and creativity are our inherent curative forces that are a mainspring of therapeutic growth for children, and I playfully refer to them as the core *trifectas* of healing.

IMAGINATION, PLAY, AND CREATIVITY

With the above section in mind, I invite you to take a few minutes to engage in the following practice exercise: Imagination, Play, and Creativity.

THE PRACTICE

Imagination, Play, and Creativity

Take a moment to engage your imagination and envision yourself creating something new and novel in your life—something that inspires you and brings with it a sense of happiness and satisfaction. Allow your imagination to flow. Once you get a good sense of what you'd like to do, write it down. Now consider how you might take a *first step* to channel that novel inspiration into a playful or creative action: Gather some art supplies, collect earth items from a nature walk, or write a poem. Keep planning your steps of action to see your imaginative idea work its way into a playful and creative endeavor.

Imagination, play, and creativity are vital to the treatment of childhood trauma through post-traumatic play utilizing expressive and play therapies. In the next chapter, we will explore child trauma and how the field of neurobiology has expanded our understanding of what the child is experiencing from a whole body perspective.

Chapter 2

TRAUMA, NEUROBIOLOGY, AND THE CREATIVE HEALING PROCESS

"Trauma only makes sense in the light of evolution."
Stephen Porges, (2018, p. 66)

Sadly, children have always been the most vulnerable to life experiences of trauma—abuse, neglect, and abandonment—and until the last century they were granted few protections. In ancient times, infanticide for both legitimate and illegitimate children was common, and beatings and abuse were acceptable, as children were viewed as not having souls—they were born in sin, the evil needed to be beaten out of them—according to a viewpoint prevalent in Western society. "Boys were castrated as preparation for the brothel, or to have their testicles sold to make magic potions. Girls had little value. The selling and sacrifice of children were also practiced" (Committee on Child Psychiatry, 1982, p. 9). Today, despite many societies' great efforts to protect children, one can quickly learn by scouring the day's vast news outlets that many children around the globe continue to suffer. The knowledge of such continued abuse of children feels overwhelmingly grim, and for those of us who have dedicated our lives to the prevention and healing of childhood abuse and neglect, there is no time for complacency. It is clear that we still have our marching orders. The United States Centers for Disease Control and Prevention website listed the following reports (note this is only for the United States and does not represent numbers globally—refer to the World Health Organization: https://www.who.int):

- There were 676,000 victims of child abuse and neglect reported to child protective services (CPS) in 2016.

- It is estimated that one in four children experiences some form of child abuse or neglect in their lifetimes and one in seven children has experienced abuse or neglect in the last year.
- About 1,750 children died from abuse or neglect in 2016.

Trauma can take many forms in childhood, from loss of a parent, accidents, abuse and neglect, illness, hospital procedures, bullying, violence in schools, divorce and separation, natural disasters, and trauma related to abuse, neglect, and abandonment. The impact on children's emotional and psychological health is substantial, including, anxiety, fear, depression, aggression, and withdrawal. Terr's landmark book *Too Scared to Cry* (1990) described her analysis of the effects of trauma on the children who were kidnapped on their school bus in Chowchilla, California and had survived. Prior to that time, the long-term effects on children had rarely been studied and often minimized by the lay society. She noted that after World War II, children's subjective experiences were often summed up as "children will forget their bad time" (p. 10). This mindset exists partly because children experience and manifest their deep hurt and pain very differently than adults. Currently, the old myths that children do not experience the effects of trauma have largely been dispelled (with the exception of infants—see the discussion in Chapter 10) and this is particularly credited to the neuroscience revelations of the 1990s (Schore, 2012), and to rigorous research studies, such as the Adverse Childhood Experiences study, commonly known as the ACE study.

The ACE study included 18,000 participants and was instrumental in providing evidence that early life trauma can have a detrimental effect throughout childhood and into adulthood. In brief, the ACE study revealed strong correlations among the number of risk factors children were exposed to in relationship to later life stress and dysfunction within families (Vincent, et al., 1998). In this study, childhood trauma influenced health and well-being throughout the lifespan, with higher risk of early death; disrupted neurodevelopment; social, emotional, and cognitive impairment; adoption of health-risk behaviors; and disease, disability, and social problems. The ACEs were categorized into three groups: 1) *Abuse:* emotional abuse, physical abuse, and sexual abuse; 2) *Household challenges:* mother treated violently, household substance abuse, mental illness in household, parental separation or divorce, criminal household member; 3) *Neglect:* emotional neglect, physical neglect.

To learn more about the ACE study, visit the Centers for Disease Control and Prevention website at www.cdc.gov.

CHILDREN EXPERIENCE TRAUMA DIFFERENTLY THAN ADULTS

The National Child Traumatic Stress Network (NCTSN), which was established by an act of Congress in 2001, defines children who have suffered traumatic stress as "those who have been exposed to one or more traumas over the course of their lives and develop reactions that persist and affect their daily lives after the events have ended." Terr (1991) divided childhood trauma into two basic types: Type I (single event, such as a hurricane or car accident) and Type II (multiple experiences of trauma, such as family violence or physical or sexual abuse). Depending on the type of trauma and multiple symptoms a child may display, some children may meet the criteria for post-traumatic stress disorder (PTSD) as defined in the fifth edition of the *Diagnostic and Statistical Manual of Mental Disorders*, or DSM-5 (American Psychiatric Association, 2013), which also distinguishes the unique developmental needs of children as separate from those of adults. NCTSN identified several childhood reactions to trauma, paraphrased here to include intense emotional upset; depressive symptoms or anxiety; behavioral changes; difficulties with self-regulation; problems forming attachments; loss of previously acquired skills, attention and academic difficulties; nightmares; difficulty sleeping and eating; and physical symptoms and pains. Older children may use drugs or alcohol and behave in risky ways.

How children experience and heal from trauma can be very different than the ways adults do, and children will often play out their trauma, worries, and feelings as an evolved adaptive measure of protection (Brown & Eberle, 2018; Panksepp, 2018; Schore & Sieff, 2015). Play is like our body's natural immune system, which kicks in when we're under threat of disease. Similarly, when children are exposed to traumatizing experiences, play becomes their emotional and psychological immune system and kicks in to help mediate painful experiences. I've often heard play likened to a natural emotional antibiotic for children. The following example highlights just how differently children process through overwhelming emotions and information compared to adults: A mother related to me that when she told her four-year-old daughter that her grandmother had died, her daughter sat still and silent for a few moments, and then abruptly got up and said, "*I think I will go play now.*" Erikson (1963) observed the role that *solitary play* provides in emotional healing and described it as an ". . . indispensable harbor for the overhauling of shattered emotions after periods of rough going in social seas" (p. 221). Levine & Kline (2007) identified several differences between child and adult trauma, including brain development, level of reasoning, incomplete personality formation, and dependency, as well as varied attachment relationships, restricted motor and language skills, and limited coping skills (p. 40).

Perry (2006a) explained that *developmental trauma* (sometimes known as *relational trauma*) is caused by traumatic life experiences that occurred within the context of interpersonal relationships, such as those categorized in the ACE study. These types of trauma can alter the brain, resulting in enduring emotional, behavioral, cognitive, social, and physical problems. Infants and very young children are often neglected in discussions of trauma. Many people perceive that infants and children are unaffected because they do not retain a conscious memory of the trauma. However, this myth of infancy is a serious oversight, as we know those trauma experiences are part of the implicit memory. Van der Kolk (2014) advised ". . . whatever happens to a baby contributes to the emotional and perceptual map of the world that its developing brain creates" (p. 56).

Post-traumatic play

The phrase *post-traumatic play* was coined by Terr (1991), who identified four characteristics related to childhood trauma: 1) visualized or perceived memories of the traumatic event; 2) repetitive behaviors; 3) trauma-specific fears; and 4) changed attitudes about people, life, and the future. She later expanded the characteristics to include 11 categories (Terr, 1981). Gil (2017), a leading expert in the field of play therapy, viewed childhood post-traumatic play as a form of *child resilience* and identified two main types as *dynamic* post-traumatic play—when the play is observed as positive or therapeutic—and *toxic* post-traumatic play, when play is observed as "stuck" or posing a danger of retraumatizing the child. Gil (2017) further set forth four variations of post-traumatic play, including: 1) the use of objects to represent a trauma; 2) symbolic posttraumatic play that disguises the trauma specifics; 3) post-traumatic behavioral reenactments, with the child playing alone; and 4) reenactments by the child attempting to engage others. Gil (2017) also distinguished several observable differences between what she labeled *dynamic* versus *toxic* post-traumatic play, also known as *stagnant* post-traumatic play (Gil, 2006). When play is dynamic, it is observed as positive and more fluid. The play has variations and changes with more affect availability and becomes less rigid over time. When play is observed as toxic, the play does not change and the affect and body remain constricted, while the interactions with the therapist may remain limited. She cautions that stuck toxic play can pose a "danger of retraumatizing the child" (p. 5). Gil (2017) also noted that the post-traumatic play extends beyond what we might think of as traditional engagement of play activities, and emphasized that ". . . play surfaces in art creations, in sand tray scenarios, in stories, in miniature work, and in children's behaviors with others" (p. 58). In other words, posttraumatic play shows up within varied modalities that may be deemed as expressive arts modalities.

At this point, I would like to advise and caution the reader that treatment of post-traumatic play takes considerable depth of training, study, preparation, and supervision, and the reader is encouraged to seek out and obtain specialized training and engagement with varied reading materials, as this area is beyond the scope of this book.

Many of the case studies presented in this book can be defined through the lens of play defined by Gil.

DOWN THE NEUROBIOLOGICAL RABBIT HOLE

It is easy to get lost in the abundance of literature and research in the field of neuroscience. It's a fascinating journey and in the words of Bonnie Badenoch (2008), it's about "getting comfortable with the brain" (p. 191). The advances in brain research since the mid-1990s have generated a broader understanding of the (brain)-mind-body connection as the field of psychology moves to embrace a bio-psycho-social-cultural (and spiritual) *paradigm shift* of healing with clients (Schore, 2012). When describing the neuroscience of the brain, Kestly (2014) suggested we think of it as the *embodied brain* versus imaging a brain in our heads. The new revelations in neuroscience have been especially valuable to the understanding of trauma and form the basis of the following sections in this chapter. Badenoch (2018a) related the embodiment of trauma as:

Trauma is an embodied experience, touching all the neural pathways in our bodies: our muscles, the brains in our bellies and hearts, our autonomic nervous systems, our brainstems, our primary emotional-motivational systems, our limbic regions and neocortices, and reaching down to even finer systems at the level of our cells and genes. (p. 12)

Now, a note of disclaimer as we move forward for the rest of this chapter. As my doctoral degree is in social work and I specialize in play therapy, it is clear that I am not a neuroscientist. Therefore, what I am sharing in this section is a synthesis of what has been most eye-opening and helpful in informing my practice, and most pertinent to the cases presented in this book. Another role in understanding the wealth of the neuroscience literature is about giving us all a shared common language that helps us to feel met. In that, what has spoken to me are the matters of interpersonal neurobiology; neuroplasticity; the triune brain; explicit and implicit memory; polyvagal theory (fight, flight, and shutdown) and neuroception; the window of tolerance; and right and left mode processing.

THE PLAY CIRCUITRY

In a discussion on play, it is fitting to turn to the social scientists. In his land-mark book *Play: How it Shapes the Brain, Opens the Imagination, and Invigo-rates the Soul*, Brown (2009) discussed his studies of highly violent, antisocial men, all of which pointed to a startling discovery: Most had childhoods of play deficiency. His studies, conducted in the 1960s, led him to a lifetime of explor-ing the essential role of play in human existence, seeking to understand such questions as: What is play? and What is its role in emotional health? He con-cluded that suppression of a strong drive to play, which is seated in the survival centers of the brain, over time can inhibit "healthy social development and can impair judgment and emotional balance" (p. 30). He used the analogy that just as sleep deprivation can lead to a cortical imbalance contributing to impaired judgment, so too can play deprivation have a similar effect.

Another social scientist, Jaak Panksepp, known for his studies in affec-tive neuroscience research, found through animal brain scans that all mam-mals have a shared neural circuitry within the subcortical brain (i.e., mainly noncognitive) that make up seven basic emotional states: SEEKING, FEAR,

RAGE, LUST, CARETAKING, GRIEF, and PLAY (Panksepp, 2009). (Note that Panksepp capitalizes these concepts for recognition that these are separate affective functions.) In relationship to the importance of play for children that supports pro-social brain maturation, Panksepp (2018) emphatically stressed that: "Without abundant PLAY and SEEKING, the mental health and positive creativity of our children will be compromised" (p. 249). Specifically, he advocated that children need "open spaces" for them to be allowed natural physical play (without toys). Theresa Kestly (2014), in her book, *The Interpersonal Neurobiology of Play*, provides an excellent working model of how she integrates Panksepp's emotional systems within a play therapy context.

INTERPERSONAL NEUROBIOLOGY

Interpersonal neurobiology (IPNB) is well acknowledged in the child psychological fields, including play therapy and expressive arts, and there is a strong desire to integrate interpersonal neurobiology knowledge into our work with children and families (Badenoch, 2008, 2018b; Chapman, 2014; Kestly, 2014; Malchiodi, 2015, to name a few). Siegel (2012) wrote that Interpersonal neurobiology (IPNB) started with an interdisciplinary group of more than 40 colleagues who met over a period of four years to explore the connection between mind and brain and what it means to be human. Siegel (2012) defined IPNB well in the following passage:

> IPNB embraces everything from our deepest relational connections with one another to the synaptic connections we have within our extended nervous systems. It encompasses the interpersonal power of culture and families, as well as insights into molecular mechanisms; each contributes to the reality of our subjective mental lives. Based on science, IPNB seeks to create an understanding of the inter-connections among the brain, the mind, and our interpersonal relationships. (p. 3)

Having roots in attachment theory, this new framework of IPNB assists in our understanding of how the mind, body, and brain are shaped by our interactional relationships with others. In particular, the IPNB model provides a neurobiologically informed basis for how changes can occur within the right-brain-to-right-brain emotional interactions of attuned resonance that occur between the therapist and client over the course of treatment (Schore, 2019). Cozolino (2014) related that interpersonal neurobiology seeks to understand the "workings of experience dependent plasticity" and focuses on "the neural systems that organize attachment, emotion, attunement, and social communication" (p. xvii).

THE AMAZING NEUROPLASTIC BRAIN

Siegel (2012) informed us that the nervous systems at the bottom of the skull have about 100 billion neurons with "trillions of supportive 'glia' cells!" (p. 15). Wow! These neurons have dendrites where electrical impulses are sent down the "dancing fingertips" (as I call them after seeing dendrite videos) that extend outward at the ends to create a *synapse*, which links to other neurons. The synapse is the connection that links neurons together and is experience dependent. That is, the brain is not static, but rather it "continually changes its synaptic interconnections in response to experience" (Siegel, 2012, p. 15) throughout a person's lifetime. This calls to mind the oft-quoted truism set forth by Donald Hebb (1949): *Neurons that fire together, wire together*, often referred to as a *use-it-or-lose-it* (as cited by Siegel, 2012, p. 22) phenomenon of brain development. Neuroplasticity speaks to the resilience of the human brain and its ability to transform itself. As described by Doidge (2007), the breakdown of the word neuroplasticity is neuro for "neuron" related to the nerve cells in the brain and nervous systems, and for "plastic," meaning "changeable, malleable and modifiable" (p. xix). Herein lies the hope—our inner resiliency—as the brain can "modify wired-in painful or frightening experiences by activity within the mind and *between* minds" (Badenoch, 2008, p. 11). This speaks to the importance of the therapeutic healing reciprocal relationship—a core theme in interpersonal neurobiology. Cozolino (2014, p. 394) identified four factors of therapy that enhance neuroplasticity: 1) a safe and trusting relationship with an attuned therapist; 2) the maintenance of moderate levels of arousal; 3) the activation of cognition and emotion; and 4) the co-construction of narratives that reflect a positive, optimistic self.

The Triune Brain

Paul MacLean (1990) theorized that we have three brains (reptilian, paleo-mammalian, and cerebral cortex) that have evolved over millions of years, with each one created on top of the other and all connected by nerves. The oldest brain, the brain stem—also known as the "reptilian," "lower," or "primitive" brain—is responsible for sensorimotor function for survival, movement, five-sense perception, and regulatory functions, especially sensation. In Perry's (2006a) neurosequential model for treating abused children, he advocates for treatment methods that help to "regulate the brainstem's sensitized and dysregulated stress-response systems" (p. 50). The next brain in the middle is the paleomammalian brain, home of the limbic system, deemed the "emotional brain" and is responsible for attachment, motivation, feelings, and the integration of memory. Within the limbic system is the amygdala, which van der Kolk (2014) metaphorically refers to as our internal "smoke detector" and is a means for us to detect danger in the environment. External sensory information is received in two directions, one "down," to the amygdala (our unconscious brain) and the other to the frontal lobes, to conscious awareness. If a threat is detected, it activates our autonomic nervous system (ANS), which mobilizes for a whole-body response, releasing the stress hormones cortisol and adrenaline.

The cerebral cortex is the last brain to evolve, includes the frontal lobes, and is not fully developed until a person reaches the mid-20s. All information from the different parts of the brain travels to the frontal lobes, which sit behind the forehead and help us to make sense of the world. This is known as our "thinking" brain, with the most cells and synapses, and is responsible for advanced reasoning, problem solving, and language. Van der Kolk (2014) likens this brain to a "watchtower" that monitors experience and decides whether a situation is safe or dangerous. What is relevant to those who have experienced trauma is that it can increase the "risk of misinterpreting whether a situation is dangerous or safe" (pp. 61–62). This is especially true for young children, who have minimal life experience, limited coping skills, and immature cognitive and perception abilities. Pertinent to the discussion of the triune brain is the concept of "top-down" processing, which refers to the influence of the more evolved brain structures on the forebrain structures. This is in contrast to "bottom-up" processing, which refers to the influence of the more primitive brain development on the higher level brain.

Memory

We have two types of memory: explicit and implicit. Explicit or declarative memory begins around age two. It is our familiar conscious memory that helps us to make sense of time and space and to recall events in our life. The second is our implicit memory, which begins during the later months of pregnancy. Implicit memory assimilates our emotional and sensory experiences at an unconscious level. Siegel (2012) advised that traumatic experiences are mostly encoded in the implicit memory, and it is also within the implicit memory where the healing of trauma can reside (Badenoch, 2018b).

To illustrate implicit memory, I will provide a personal example: I always enjoyed ice skating as a child. In my conscious, explicit, autobiographical memory, I recalled where my friends and I skated on Hoot Owl Pond, how I bundled up warmly, and even what my skates looked like. More than 30 years later, I had an opportunity to skate again. I remembered the body movements of skating forward, however after about 20 minutes of skating and confidence building, something unexpected happened that took me by surprise. My body's implicit memory began to take over, and suddenly—without conscious awareness or plan—my body swerved around and I started skating backwards. Looking down at my legs and feet, I thought: "What? What's this?" I was actually pretty good at it, but I had no conscious memory that I knew how to skate backwards. It was a joyous, exciting moment of surprise! As my left brain began to take over the internal conversation of puzzlement, I soon fell. Now that I was down on the cold ice, another earlier, implicit life memory emerged: my inner 11-month-old little girl, who had just fallen on the floor from trying to learn how to walk. What did I do? I immediately stood back up and skated backwards again!

REMEMBERING A POSITIVE IMPLICIT MEMORY

I invite you to take a few minutes to engage in the following practice exercise, Remembering a Positive Implicit Memory.

THE PRACTICE

Remembering a Positive Implicit Memory

With my example of the ice skating experience in mind, think of a *positive* or *happy* moment when an implicit memory may have unexpectedly emerged. What do you remember about the memory? Where were you? Who was with you? What were you doing? If appropriate, share the memory with a partner.

SOCIAL ENGAGEMENT SYSTEM, NEUROCEPTION, AND CUES OF SAFETY

"A felt sense of safety is the bedrock of healing trauma," writes Badenoch (2018a, p. 9). Porges (2018) stated that the social engagement system of safety emerges from a face-heart connection that coordinates the "heart with the muscles of the face and head." This further functions to regulate bodily states of growth and restoration and for face-heart connection . . . via facial expression and prosody" (pp. 55–56). Neuroception is a term Porges (2018) introduced to define the neural unconscious processes of how we distinguish risk in the environment to determine if something is safe, dangerous, or life-threatening. So how do we distinguish safety? He proposed three conditions that must be present to feel safe (pp. 61–62):

1. The autonomic nervous system cannot be in a state that supports defense.
2. The social engagement system needs to be activated to downregulate sympathetic activation and functionally contain the sympathetic nervous system and the dorsal vagal circuit within an optimal range to (homeostasis) that would support health, growth, and restoration. And,
3. Cues of safety (e.g., prosodic vocalizations, positive facial expressions, and gestures) need to be available and detected via neuroception.

Porges advocated that *cues of safety* are a "profound antidote for trauma," (p. 61) that can be sent through facial expressions and voice to calm agitation. Lindaman & Makela (2018) discussed how the cues of safety are integrated into TheraPlay (an attachment-based relational play therapy model) sessions with children. This integration is demonstrated in this following passage about a five-year old client, "Again, I used my ventral vagal-mediated eye contact and prosodic voice to trigger Nora's neuroception of safety" (p. 242).

POLYVAGAL THEORY: FIGHT, FLIGHT, SHUTDOWN, SAFETY

Porges's (2018) polyvagal theory has been pivotal to the understanding of trauma processes, which provided a neurophysiological model for understanding trauma experiences. His theory provided a map for how mammals could "shift from an aggressive fight or flight state to a calm state that would promote intimacy." From an evolutionary perspective, Porges identified that mammals have two vagal pathways: one that produced a calm state and social communication (the social engagement system), and the other related to immobilization of defense reactions. The social engagement system was accessible during states of trust and safety. However, when trust and safety are not present or even *perceived* that way, it can enable our ancient defense mechanisms of fight, flight (hyperarousal) or shutdown (hypoarousal).

This shutdown, self-protective mechanism, sometimes labeled as freeze, allowed mammals to become inanimate in face of danger, resulting in collapse, fainting, immobilization, and dissociation. This is the way our human nervous system evolved to survive in dangerous and life-threatening environments. When children are in a highly aroused or shutdown state it is difficult for them to process information. Concentration and focus are impaired, and learning is compromised, which leads us to our next section about the *window of tolerance*.

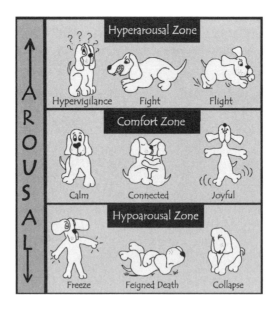

FIGURE 2.1: Window of Tolerance Chart
SOURCE: WITH PERMISSION FROM AND COURTESY OF BONNIE
GOLDSTEIN, PH.D., ARTWORK BY TERRY MARKS-TARLOW, PH.D.

THE WINDOW OF TOLERANCE

Perhaps one of the most widely utilized contemporary metaphors to understand trauma is the "the window of tolerance" (Siegel, 2012), which can help us to "distinguish between a regulated and dysregulated nervous system" (Kestly, 2014, p. 33). It speaks to our ability to manage different emotional states of arousal, which can vary from person to person. The concept provides a metaphor to visualize the activity of the autonomic nervous system's branches: hyperarousal and hypoarousal. At the top end of the window, when we feel safe, we normally experience high levels of autonomic arousal, such as an elated conversation with a friend about an exciting job opportunity. However, a state of hyperarousal can be triggered when we feel unsafe or when danger is perceived, and this can trigger mobilization of the fight-or-flight response.

At the lower end of the window, a perceived threat can trigger the parasympathetic branch of our nervous system into a state of hypoarousal (old dorsal vagal), immobilizing a response of freeze, faint, or fold. We can also have immobilization without fear (Porges, 2018). We can naturally feel lower levels of arousal, such as walking in a state of contemplation along a beach and listening to the waves. Variations in how individuals experience the window of tolerance are dependent upon several factors, including the individual's innate temperament, their early life experiences, and a myriad of mediating-in-the-moment factors, such as their state of mood, the context of a situation, who is present, lack of sleep, hunger, and so on.

Within the middle optimal range of the window lies the homeostatic emotional social engagement system. In healthy play, children know how to modulate their play to stay within the optimal range. Russ (2004) cited a study by Golomb & Galasso (1995) with a group of preschoolers they monitored for affect during the children's pretend play. They observed that if a pretend play situation was considered negative, a child would mediate that by imaging, for example, a friendly monster. And if the pretend play was positive, they would embellish the theme to enhance enjoyment. They concluded that children "monitor and regulate affect in play so as not to exceed a certain threshold while still having enough emotional involvement to play" (as cited in Russ, 2004, p. 14). As we work with traumatized children, their play thresholds may show up differently in relationship to the child's individual window of tolerance. (See the Window of Tolerance chart in Figure 2.1.)

The window of tolerance is expanded by the resilient factors of imagination, play, and creativity (as discussed in Chapters 1 and 2). With traumatized children, these three resources assist the children to expand the window of tolerance to encompass a wider range of emotional states. Through the safety of play, children can bump up to the edge of the window to what is emotionally and psychologically tolerable, and explore a divergent range of perspectives within a temenos of containment. Additionally, we can help to assist children to regulate their resilient nervous systems with self-regulation interventions, such as mindfulness practice, breathing exercises, movement and music, clay, art, and storytelling—essentially what we will discuss in Part II. Parents and caregivers who are safe attachment figures also act as external regulators for children, providing a calming and nurturing presence, including caring touch experiences (Courtney & Nolan, 2017). Including parents within sessions, such as the family play therapy sessions demonstrated in Chapters 5 and 6, is crucial to the healing process.

Left and Right Hemispheres

Perhaps it's in this neurobiology discussion about the differences between the right and left hemispheres of the brain where I become most enlightened, because it provides an understanding for just why the expressive arts and play are so crucial to the healing process. If you study the image in Figure 2.2, it's easy to see the brain differences, in that the right brain is known as our creative, intuitive, experiential, and emotional side, whereas our left brain is described more as our logical, linguistic, and linear brain. Siegel & Payne Bryson (2012) informed us that the right brain is more influenced by the body and lower brain areas and intuits communication nonverbally through facial expressions, eye contact, gestures, and posture and is interested in the "big picture—the meaning of an experience—and specializes in images, emotions, and personal memories" (p. 16). It is also the home to our implicit memory (Schore, 2012).

The Imprint of Trauma on the Right Brain Hemisphere

During an intake session with a mother, she relayed her frustration that her teenage daughter insisted she "can't remember" the details of what happened

FIGURE 2.2: Left Brain and Right Brain Hemisphere
SOURCE: SHUTTERSTOCK 692090629

in the car accident she was involved in. Van der Kolk's (2014) research with brain imaging showed that when participants in the study listened to their pre-recorded scripts in which they retell a traumatic event, scans of their brain revealed activation in the limbic area—the emotional part of our brain, which was expected. However, what was most surprising was a deactivation in the left frontal lobe of the cortex, in a region called Broca's area. This region, as van der Kolk (2014) explained, is known as one of the speech centers. He writes, "Without a functioning Broca's area, you cannot put your thoughts and feelings into words" (p. 43). This is the reason why many trauma victims may find it difficult to put their experiences into words. Additionally, scans revealed another region, called Brodmann area 19, which is in the visual cortex that registers images when first encountered. This may explain why, when trauma victims are triggered by something from the past, the "right brain reacts as if the traumatic event were happening in the present" (p. 45). Trauma encodes in the right side of the brain as images and sensations, not as language, making it difficult for victims to put their painful experiences logically into words. To return to the mother frustrated with her daughter who could not remember the details of the accident, it then made perfect sense to educate the mother about how trauma encodes in the brain.

Left to Right Brain Hemisphere Integration

Ideally, it is desirable to support the two brain hemispheres to work together, and for children to eventually become "horizontally integrated," as Siegel & Payne Bryson (2012, p. 22) put it. Horizontal integration is that delicate back-and-forth dance between the two hemispheres of a right-to-left-to-right progression. This helps to find a balance for children related to implicit and explicit memories and processes. Kestly (2014) provided an excellent example and diagram for the progression using a right-left-right progression, in an intervention she developed called "the neurobiology of the storytelling brain." Supported by the work of McGilchrist (2009), Kestly wrote that the ". . . language of the left hemisphere needs to be returned to the right hemisphere through metaphor where the storytelling becomes reconnected to the bodily foundation of meaning-making" (p. 123). Metaphor is the language of the right brain hemisphere (McGilchrist, 2009).

Mirror Neurons—Adopting the Other Person's Point of View

Mirror neurons, discovered in 1994 by a group of Italian scientists, are identified as specialized cells in our cortex that fire when you watch another person perform an action (Ramachandran, 2011), and that are also connected to a network of "resonance circuits" (Badenoch, 2008, p. 31). They assist us to have empathy for others—one of the most important attributes a practitioner brings to the healing process. McGilchrist (2009) advised that empathy, self-awareness, and identification with others are also connected to the right-brain hemisphere, and from a neurobiological perspective, "When we put ourselves in other's shoes, we are using the right inferior parietal lobe, and the right lateral prefrontal cortex . . ." (p. 57). Mirror neurons can help us to adopt another's point of view, and those firing neurons in our bodies can also help us to see our own selves as others see us—"an essential ingredient of self-awareness" (Ramachandran, 2011, p. 128). However, van der Kolk (2014) cautioned that mirror neurons highly impact traumatized individuals, as the dynamics of trauma can involve "not being seen, not being mirrored, and not be taken into account." And treatment methods need to "reactivate the capacity to safely mirror, and be mirrored, by others . . ." (p. 59).

TRAUMA AND THE EXPRESSIVE AND PLAY THERAPIES: HEALING THE RESILIENT NERVOUS SYSTEM

Trauma is a whole-body, sensory-based experience, and we therefore must attune to what we see, hear, taste, touch, and smell. As such, treatment modalities need to be multisensory and rich to reach clients at the varied sensory levels. Children's immature nervous systems are highly sensitive and can often be triggered into states of hyperarousal or hypoarousal, leaving them vulnerable to a range of emotional states of fear, aggression, and worry; disruptions in family and peer relationships; and an inability to focus or concentrate, interfering with academic performance. Intervening through play and expressive arts modalities can help to stabilize arousal states and can assist to expand children's emotional and cognitive windows of tolerance. Perry (2006a) wrote that, "dance, drumming, music, massage—patterned repetitive sensory input will begin to provide the kinds of experiences that may influence brainstem

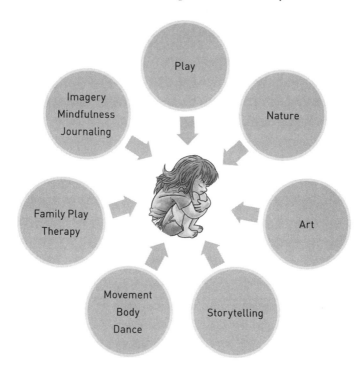

FIGURE 2.3: Healing the resilient Nervous System through Expressive Arts and Play Therapy

SOURCE: AUTHOR & INNER IMAGE: SHUTTERSTOCK 489913369

neurobiology to re-organize in ways that will lead to smoother functional regulation" (p. 38). Richardson (2016) highlighted how expressive arts assist in the healing process:

> Expressive arts have the ability to access implicit memory, which is coded in sensations and imagery, and offer nonverbal processes to express these iconic portrayals through dance, drawing, sculpture, or the sound of a drum. . . . the ability of the arts to offer containment and distance, along with playful elements, can assist children with accessing memory without creating too much arousal." (p. 40)

THE EXPRESSIVE ARTS AND PLAY

I invite you to take a few minutes to engage in the following practice exercise: The Expressive Arts and Play.

THE PRACTICE

The Expressive Arts and Play
Think of each of the expressive arts and play modalities found in Figure 2.3. Write down at least one memory of a time when you engaged each of the modalities throughout your lifetime, and list them below.

Play:

Storytelling:

Movement/dance:

Music:

Family Play:

Journaling:

Mindfulness/imagery:

Art:

Nature:

CASE OF DANNY: "I DON'T LIKE IT WHEN IT'S TIME TO SAY GOODBYE!"

This case example demonstrates how children can express trauma differently than adults, and shows just how very quickly children can cycle through the defensive states of protection of flight, fight, freeze, and fold. It also demonstrates how a therapist can learn to ground and anchor to provide a corrective emotional and relational experience for a child.

Internal Working Template of Loss and Abandonment

Loss and abandonment were two predominant themes in five-year-old Danny's life. He was removed from his parents' home due to abuse and neglect and placed in foster care. Danny was referred for play therapy when he was three years old. At the time of referral, he had been placed in and removed from five different foster homes. Therapy was held at the daycare facility where I had a makeshift playroom and brought with me toys, a sandtray, and art materials. Trained also in Developmental Play Therapy, I implemented varied relational "developmental games" taught by Brody (1997ab) and "first-play" interventions (Courtney, Velazquez, Toth, 2017). (Refer also to Chapters 9 and 10.) And at other times, the play sessions were nondirective; following Danny's lead in client-centered play therapy, where many of the themes he played out related to loss, abandonment, fear, and aggression.

About a year into Danny's therapy, his father was granted supervised visitation. Now, at age four years, Danny was physically strong, with dark brown eyes and thick brown hair that appeared always tousled, as if it had never seen a comb. The foster system began visitation with his father at a relative's home. After two visitations, I was called by the foster worker, who advised that they were having problems with the visitation, as Danny would angrily refuse to leave the house when it was time to return to the foster home, yelling, kicking and screaming, and then running to hide.

At our next session, Danny initiated a game of hide and seek. The room supplied to me at the daycare was an unused break room that held several empty cabinets. That day, he instructed me to close my eyes and count to ten, as he wanted to play hide and seek (an older developmental stage of peek-a-boo) (SAFETY). He hid in one of the cabinets, and I had to guess where he was.

Hmm . . . I wonder where Danny is? I opened one cabinet, "No, not here." I heard a giggle. Then another cabinet, "No, not here. I know he's close . . ." Another giggle. When I "found" him I would shout with delight, "Oh there you are! You are here! I'm so happy to see you. You are here!" and he laughed and giggled.

Since I had been seeing him for almost a year, we had solid and trusting relationship. He knew he could count on me for consistent responses of genuine acceptance to recreate corrective emotional experiences with a caring attachment figure in his life. He did not talk about his father, nor did I ask. As part of a regular routine, I advised him that it was getting time for us to say goodbye, and that he would be going back to the classroom. Unexpectedly, he yelled, *No! No!* (FEAR). He quickly bolted out the door and ran down the long, empty hallway toward the exit and parking lot (FLIGHT). I ran after him, calling his name for him to stop. My mind flashed on my recent conversation with his foster care worker and his reactions to the visitation. As this part of the building was empty, there was no one around as a backup to help. This is one of those therapist's worst-case scenario catastrophic fears that a child would run out of the building and into the parking lot unsupervised. It was a very scary experience.

I caught his arm right at the entrance door. As I held his arm, he kicked me in the leg, and then I blocked his fist before he hit me (FIGHT). We were now facing each other, both of us in a state of hyperarousal (my heart was pounding). Relieved that he did not get out the door, I said firmly: "This is not safe! It is my job to keep you safe." I let go of his arm and consciously tried to calm and ground myself (an ability I credit to my years of mindfulness practice). My heartfelt feelings of care for Danny came to the forefront, and I felt my own body begin to relax. I said again, in a softer voice: "I'm here to keep you safe."

Remembering again his deep pain of loss and separation, I felt a sense of loving compassion for him and understood his conflict. The mention that it was time once again to separate from someone he cared about, where he had no power of choice, produced an implicit memory of loss, which triggered a feeling of fear and panic. He was reenacting—he was showing me in real time—what was happening in his visitations with his father, and all his other experiences of separation. He was showing me how deeply painful it was to end our time together.

Danny was now frozen, looking at the floor (FREEZE). I said calmly, in a quiet voice: "Tell me that you don't like it when it's time for us to say goodbye.

He looked up from the floor and immediately began to soften and said in a soft, quiet voice, "I don't like it when it's time for us to say goodbye." At that, he leaned in toward me and just collapsed into my arms and offered up a silent cry (FOLD). He laid his head on my shoulder, and I held him. We both remained quiet. Nothing needed to be said. I felt his deep agony and offered up my love and care just to embrace him and allow him a space of safety and security. It was enough not to say anything. He continued to rest his head on my shoulder and held his arms around my neck. He remained still as he calmed, and allowed me for 20 minutes to hold him. It was the first time he had ever allowed me to hold him, and I wondered how long it had been since someone had truly just hugged and held him. By the time we were back at the classroom, I put him down, and he silently looked at me and said goodbye. He was now back in the homeostatic window of optimal range arousal. I was told that his next visitation with his father went very differently.

Processing the Encounter

Since infancy, Danny's experiences related to attachment figures and relation-ships were marked by separation, loss, and abandonment—his internal work-ing model. The mention of ending the session triggered his implicit memory of feelings of anxiety and fear related to loss and abandonment. Although it was a safe part of our routine to say goodbye at the end of the session, he *mis*-neu-rocepted a sense of threat (not uncommon in traumatized clients) as his deep-rooted feelings of fear and abandonment surfaced, which can be correlated to his recent contact with his father. Bowlby (1988) advised that when children feel a threat of abandonment, it can create intense anxiety that can also arouse *anger*, which he viewed as understandable and a "basic human disposition" (p. 30). Our time to end the session matched his internal template of *people I care about leave me.*

When I finally caught Danny, he was in a state of hyperarousal that then triggered a fight response. I was also in a state of hyperarousal, and at the same time, I became conscious of the need to calm and modulate my own internal emotional state. I feared a catastrophic outcome of him bolting out the door and into the parking lot, where perhaps an unalert driver in a car could have hit him. My own fears were heightened, as there was no one present to assist with safety in the environment. In the moment, I was able to return to myself to calm and monitor my feelings, reactions, and breath and was able to then provide *cues of safety* to him through my composed, soft voice tone. I was able to attune with empathy for what he was going through. As I relaxed myself through a conscious slowing of my breath, I began to mirror to him a calm state of somatic resonance. This quote from Stewart, Field, & Echterling (2016) may capture what was happening in the moment: "When the therapist models a calming presence, mirror neurons connect the two intersubjective experiences of therapist and client, granting the client greater capacity for self-regulation" (p. 9). When Danny began to calm, I was able to put feelings into words to help him identify what he might be feeling. In our reciprocal relationship, a foundation of trust and safety had been built during the therapy process. Conceivably, when I held him and his head was resting calmly on my shoulder, it is possible that our breathing and brain circuits may have synchronized.

THE CASE STUDY OF DANNY

With the above case study in mind, I invite you to take a few minutes to consider the following practice questions on The Case Study of Danny.

THE PRACTICE

The Case Study of Danny

Taking the role of the therapist in this case, answer the following questions:

- In retrospect, understanding now how Danny would react to the message that it was time to end the session, what would you decide to do or say differently to Danny to prepare him for the session ending and to instill cues of safety?
- How would you have handled the situation in the moment if Danny had kicked or hit you? What would you do? What would you say?
- How would the understanding of neurobiology, as discussed in this chapter, inform your interactions with Danny?
- How would you advise the foster parents to handle the visitation with his father?
- What would you do or say to Danny when you see him at the next session?

FINAL THOUGHTS

I hesitate to write the following, as it may appear as if I am negating all that was discussed in this chapter, but that is not the intention and I ask for your understanding. Here goes: Beyond all our new knowledge about the fascinating inner workings of the mind and body and all the neuroscience research that has been done and yet to be done, does it really change the healing process of what we have long known about our theoretical foundations, assessment methods, our essential therapeutic skill set, the stages of therapy, or the therapeutic powers of play? I contemplate this question for myself: Would I have handled that challenging situation with Danny any differently if armed with all the neuroscience understanding discussed in this chapter? For me, the answer is no. It was my years of education in the field of social work, my advanced training and practice experience in child counseling and play therapy, my experiences of supervision and mentorship from some very gifted practitioners, my years of daily practice of mindfulness, and all *my* therapists who helped me to feel seen with love and compassion that ultimately informed the way I handled the situation. Michael and Luke (2016) concur with this viewpoint, writing, ". . . neuroscience does not reinvent the therapeutic wheel" (p. 47). At the same time, I agree that my understanding of neuroscience matters has indeed strengthened my knowledge in understanding the inner workings of the body-mind emotional and relational connection. For example, in the case of Danny, my comprehension now of the neurobiological processes at play related to his experiences of trauma, enhances my understanding that his nervous system responded in the most protective way available to him in the moment. Does knowing about the inner workings of mind (brain) and body make me a better practitioner? Indeed, the answer is yes!

In the next chapter, we will explore some of the foundational therapeutic ingredients necessary in the healing relationship, as well as a model related to the stages of therapy.

Chapter 3

THE ESSENTIAL INGREDIENTS OF THE HEALING PATH

"We try to understand not in order to offer a rash cure to a rashly diagnosed society, but in order first to complete the blueprint of our theory."

Erik H. Erikson, *Childhood and Society*, p. 16

FOUNDATIONS OF THE THERAPEUTIC ENCOUNTER

This chapter provides a foundational blueprint to the therapeutic process in working with children. It builds upon the humanistic foundations in Chapter 1 and the awareness of childhood trauma in Chapter 2, and provides a working knowledge related to the clinical case applications found in Part II. In any type of therapeutic work with children or adults, the work needs to stand on solid ground. We need to understand the how and why of what we are doing, which then translates into steps of action within therapy sessions. This process takes a tremendous amount of assimilation and practice! Granted, some of these foundations may be included in graduate programs, which prepare students in all matters concerning therapy skill building. However, when providing trainings to practitioners in expressive and play therapies, I frequently hear: "I never learned about how to work with children in school." Often in university core course curriculums, children's courses may be left as electives or not offered at all. Although by no means exhaustive, this chapter provides some guidance, recommendations and foundations in child therapy that I have found helpful in my own practice.

CHILDREN ARE OUR TEACHERS: OPENING OURSELVES TO THE PLAY PROCESS

As adults, we often forget our own younger child-selves and our innate ability to play—of course there are different types of play—but I am referring to luscious, imaginative play. It has been a privilege, as an invited guest of sorts, to witness the amazing unfolding of hundreds of children's inner landscapes of imagination transposed to outer worlds of play and creativity. Children have reminded and taught me how to play again. Forgetting our own ability to engage in imaginative play puts us at a disadvantage when working therapeutically with children. Waldorf educator Marjorie Spock, sister to the renowned pediatrician Dr. Benjamin Spock, suggested that the reason for our lack of understanding with children is that the consciousness of children is very different from that of adults—and we forget that. She enlightened:

> Adults no longer remember their own state of being during early childhood, and few are able to observe children with sufficient keenness to gain a really searching insight into a consciousness so different from their own; the education to which most of us were subjected has done little to sensitize us to the phenomena of other individuals' inmost experience. Moreover, we habitually conceive children as sharing our own state of being. (Spock, 1985, p. 58).

My therapeutic skills have been enhanced not just through schooling and training, but by the multitude of children that I have worked with. Most important, children have taught me how to be an attuned and present play participant.

Play Therapy 101: My First Child-Teacher Lesson

One of my first child clients in play therapy was Sam, an eight-year-old boy. As trained, I followed a client-centered, nondirective approach. During our first session, he picked out a few toy character figures for me to play with, and he chose his own figures. The scene setup was that we were soldiers at war, and we were not on the same side. I was tracking his play and observing him for themes, which revealed anger, conflict, good guy, and bad guy. Then one of his soldiers shot one of mine. He said, "I shot you."

"Yes, I see my guy was shot," was all I knew to reply (I was not getting it).

Seemingly annoyed, he said, "So, your guy is dead!" in a tone that had an air of *this lady knows nothing about how to play!* And then he directed me, "So die!"

Oh yes, of course, my character needed to fall down and be dead, so I then placed my character face down on the playroom floor. I sat very still and quiet, with my head lowered. I knew well enough that if a child tells you in a play therapy session that your character was shot and killed, then that character needs to remain dead until the child tells you otherwise. While "dead," sitting with my head drooped and body hunched over, I listened intently to his character dialogues as he continued to play out the war scene.

Within a few minutes, he finally said, "Okay, your guy can get up now." And that was my first child-teacher lesson in play therapy basics.

To work with children at the level of play and expressive arts takes a tremendous amount of trust in the process, and a lot of letting go of control. We need to allow children in our presence permission to explore, change directions in the middle of a play process, safely express aggression and anger, drop glitter on the floor, hide under a table, or tear up a painting they just created. On the part of the therapist, it takes immense patience, spontaneity, and flexibility of mind. At the same time, it is essential that practitioners get back in touch with the playful side of themselves. There is an old truism that *we teach best what we most need to learn.* When I think of that for myself, perhaps I was drawn to work with children and the field of play therapy because I needed to learn to remember how to play. Perhaps my years of schooling, memorizing, test taking, and literature reading—all predominately left-brain hemisphere processes—had left me stiff and rigid. And the field of play therapies and expressive arts provided an avenue to free that stuck part of myself.

REMEMBERING YOUR CHILDHOOD PLAY

I invite you to take a few minutes to engage in the following practice exercise: Remembering Your Childhood Play.

THE PRACTICE

Remembering Your Childhood Play
Take a moment to consider the following reflective questions.
- What kind of things did you play when you were a child?
- Can you recall your play materials (dolls, trucks, coloring books)?
- Where did you play?
- Who did you play with?
- Within your play, can you remember the stories or themes of your play?
- What messages from others were you given about play?

About Hope, Change, and Action

Hope

Levine & Kline (2007) wrote this hopeful message about trauma and children: "Regardless of the cause, the good news is that not only can trauma be healed, but oftentimes also prevented . . ." (p. xxi). I'm sometimes asked if a child can heal from trauma, attachment-related disorders, anxiety, or other types of issues a child may be confronted with (refer to the ACEs in Chapter 2). My first answer is that inner growth and healing is a subjective experience. No one but that individual who is traveling on a healing journey can know whether they are feeling less burdened, happier, or more connected to others. I then place myself in that child's shoes. If I was in deep pain, lonely and confused, how would I want someone to answer that question for me? If I see only darkness, what do I need to hear? Then the answer for that child becomes crystal clear: Yes, of course children can heal from trauma . . . life can get better, and their inner emotional life can change. We can hope that life will get better for all the children and families we are working with.

However, in some situations hope without action means very little. There is a saying, *"Hope is the rope from which we stand."* This means we can stand around and "hope" that things will get better for children. We can *hope* that domestic violence will stop. Or *hope* that the abuse of children will end. But without action to take steps to make life changes, then very little will. No one understands this concept better than the environmentalists, from whom I first heard that quote while sitting at an Esalen Institute seminar hosted by Rex

Weyler, an original founder of Greenpeace International, and Nora Bateson, daughter of Gregory Bateson. As Weyler stressed, it is not enough to sit around and *hope* that our endangered whale populations survive—or any other species for that matter, including humans! We must take practical action steps to raise consciousness to promote change. (This took place at an Esalen Institute seminar in Big Sur, California on June 30, 2012.) Metaphorically, we need to *climb that rope*! So there is an advocacy for children to bring about change, as well as guidance to children and families through the steps of change.

On the other hand, as discussed in Chapter 2, children process and heal from trauma very differently than adults. Of course, the process of active change differs from child to child, related to a wide range of mediating factors, including the child's developmental age. We also consider the agents of change, as discussed in Chapter 1 (Schaefer & Drewes, 2014). However, as those who work with children well know, the beautiful unfolding process that is witnessed within a therapy session of a child's transformative play might not necessarily translate into practical environmental change—much to the chagrin of the hopeful caregivers and teachers (and the therapist's own hope, too!) Taft (1933/1973) described the dilemma well:

> From my viewpoint, then it is not possible to think of one's contacts with a child as justified by the possibility that he will work out verbally or in action the traumas of his infancy. . . .He will and can do only one thing: that is, undergo whatever new experience is permitted in the living present in relation to the analyst. If that has depth, significance, and a constructive taking over of will on the part of the child then he will have gained something therapeutic for himself, even though neither parents nor school teachers appear to profit by the results in behavior. (pp. 106–107)

THE THERAPIST'S OWN WORK

A book about the healing of children and families related to trauma must address the therapist's own preparation of self to be an attuned empathetic presence. In working with traumatized children, we will learn about a wide range of devastating and tragic situations that children have experienced, from heartbreaking details of physical and sexual abuse, sometimes by close relatives, including children sharing how they witnessed their father severely beat their mother. How we receive, take in, and respond to hearing children tell their painful stories has a huge impact on their overall recovery. Additionally, vicarious trauma is a high risk for therapists when working with traumatized children. We need to become as clear a channel as possible. Taft (1933/1973) believed in the importance of the therapist as an instrument of change: "In my opinion the basis of therapy lies in the therapist himself, in his capacity to permit the use of self which the therapeutic relationship implies as well as his psychological insight and technical skills" (p. 19).

To then gain the therapeutic capacity and skill to *permit the use of self* in sessions with clients, therapists must do two things: First, they must develop their therapeutic skills through training and practice, and second, they must *do their own work*. Many authors determine that growing practitioner self-awareness can happen in three ways: 1) personal therapy; 2) training courses that include experiential personal reflection; and 3) supervision. Yalom (2002) strongly advocated that therapists need to get themselves into personal therapy and related this for several reasons, including the need to understand what it feels like to be in the seat of the client. It also provides an opportunity for therapists to discover their own "blind spots" and to get familiar with their own "dark side" (p. 41). Cozolino (2014) referred to this as the "heroic journey" as therapists come "face-to-face with their own demons and brokenness" (p. 130). From a humanistic perspective, Rogers (1965) identified that therapists need to address their own struggles for personal growth and integration and that, "He [the therapist] can be only as 'nondirective' as he has achieved respect for other in his own personality organization" (p. 21). And, returning to the window of tolerance concept discussed in Chapter 2, we need to also be aware of our own thresholds and patterns of hyper- and hypoarousal states.

One area of potential countertransference for therapists is in the area of touch, as their own experiences of touch can highly impact the therapeutic relationship. Touch can immediately trigger physiological memory reactions that a therapist might not consciously be aware of, which could then generate reactions by the therapist that could potentially retraumatize a client. In my co-edited book with Robert Nolan, *Touch in Child Counseling and Play Therapy: An Ethical and Clinical Guide*, I wrote: "Perhaps more than any other area of professional countertransference inquiry, it should be considered a priority that practitioners explore how their own life experiences related to touch can potentially impact their behaviors and actions in their work with children" (Courtney, 2017, p. 12). Research outcomes of a nationwide survey of play therapists' attitudes and experiences related to touch in sessions with children revealed the need for therapists to obtain training in touch to grow clinical and personal self-awareness (Courtney & Siu, 2018). In the Developmental Play Therapy training model, Brody (1997b) developed a wide range of experiential exercises related to touch that therapists practiced during the training. She believed exposure to these touch-based training exercises assisted therapists to develop an empathy for what the child might be experiencing, as well as identifying potential countertransferences (Courtney & Gray, 2011, 2014). Additionally, the reflective supervision model is a good way to help therapists to identify their own thoughts, feelings, and uncomfortable reactions that may arise within sessions, including issues of touch (Grobbel, Cooke, & Bonet, 2017).

TIME AND SPACE

Regardless what population we serve, we are all limited by the constraints of time, whether it is the amount of time we have during an individual session, or the overall time we see a client from the beginning session to closure. In some cases, we may only know a child for one session, and others for a few weeks or months. For still others, it may be an ongoing relationship for years as the client returns to process the next bump in the road. In some situations, we are limited by external forces, such as funding for services, managed care, or agency policies that dictate how long we can see a client. Taft (1933/1973) saw that time represented not only the limitation of the therapy encounter, but the "inevitable limitation in all relationship" as viewed from an existential perspective of coming to terms with our limited human condition from birth to death. She wrote, "Time represents more vividly the necessity of accepting limitation . . . and symbolizes the whole problem of living . . . [the client's] relation to the growth process itself, to beginnings and endings, to being born and to dying" (p. 12). Ultimately, having some sense of what to expect during that time and space as we journey together with children and families is paramount to the therapeutic process—for that we need an organized framework of reference.

Stages of Therapy: A Road Map

We all need a road map, especially if we are going to navigate in unfamiliar territory. Thank goodness for voice-directed phone map apps that recently guided me into and around downtown San Francisco, or else I would have been very lost! To engage this metaphor of a road map, think of each new client—a child, teenager, family, and so forth as a new territory of sorts. This means that when you first meet them you are new to each other, so there are a lot of unknowns. Where do you begin in this limited time and space you have in front of you? How do you know where you are going? And how do you recognize it once you are there? Our theoretical models help us to navigate the in-session hourly time period—with a beginning, middle, and end. But what exactly is happening within that time and onward from session to session? What are the road signs that can help guide us on the way?

In my social work training, we were presented with varied stages that our adult clients move through in therapy. However, working with children and their progression through the stages of therapy is very different than working with adults. And I see this as a neglected area of discussion within our teaching objectives. One of the first play therapy trainings I attended was with Carol and Byron Norton in 1991. At that time, they presented a model of the stages of play therapy they identified as: 1) exploration; 2) testing of limits, which they later reframed as testing for protection; 3) dependency; 4) growth and integration; and 5) termination (Norton & Norton, 2008). This model gave me an initial road map of understanding that provided a clearer picture of what was happening and how the child was progressing overall (or not) within the therapy time together. I was so struck by the power of this road map that when I taught a course in social work practice with children, I created a midterm assignment that followed the progression of Axline's (1964) case study in her book *Dibs In Search of Self.* In this assignment, I asked students to find supporting examples within the book that identified the varied stages of therapy. It was a good learning assignment to help ground the theory into practice through a case example.

Over the years, I began to fill in the gaps of those stages of therapy as I gained a clearer clinical sense of what I was observing and what was happening as my child clients progressed through the therapy stages. From that, I identified seven Stages of Therapy (refer to Figure 3.1) categorized as the following: 1) Saying hello; 2) Temenos; 3) Reliance; 4) Resourcing; 5) Integration; 6) Action; and 7) Saying goodbye. Note that these stages are further organized into phases as follows: *Phase I:* Beginnings, "being courageous," saying hello and Temenos; *Phase II:* "The work": reliance and resourcing; *Phase III:* "empowerment": integration and action; *Phase IV:* "Futuring," saying goodbye. The rest of this chapter will present the stages of therapy and elaborate on the identified characteristics for each category. Although these stages and the characteristics under each category are presented in a linear progression, recognize that these stages of therapy can be recursive, and children may move back and forth between the stages at any given time. There are several mediating factors, including trauma experiences as discussed in Chapter 2, that can influence what is observed within each stage of therapy. Note that the stages of therapy presented in the next sections are considered as a positive or *dynamic* type of play progression, which may look very different from post-traumatic *toxic* play (Gil, 2017) as addressed in Chapter 2. It is from these stages of therapy related to dynamic progression that can then act as a standard of comparison to play that may be observed as stuck, stagnated, or toxic.

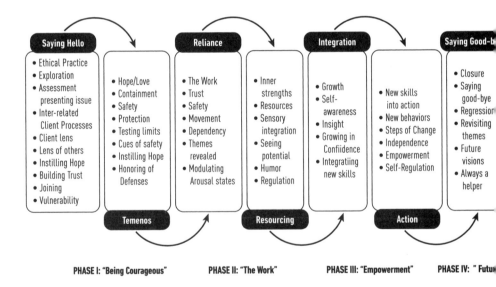

FIGURE 3.1: Child's Journey through the Stages of Therapy Process

CLIENT JOURNEY THROUGH THE STAGES OF THERAPY

Phase I: Beginnings "Being Courageous": Saying Hello and Temenos

Saying hello and Temenos are identified as comprising Phase I, as they spark the beginning phases of treatment and the importance of creating a safe environment to address the wide range of psychosocial dynamics, including establishing trust and safety, which is the foundation of all therapeutic work.

Saying Hello

The stage of "saying hello" is about figuring out *who we are in relationship to each other*. It's all about getting to know each other within a reciprocal therapeutic relationship. This is when we gain understanding about the presenting problem from both the child's and parent's perspectives, and this happens through intake and assessment, which are discussed in detail in Chapter 4. It is identified to include: exploration; presenting issues and assessment; building trust; understanding the interrelated client processes; client lens; lens of others; instilling hope; and ethical practice. This is also a time when we join the family system from a human ecology and family therapy perspective, and we establish ethical practice related to informed consent and clinical boundaries. We also draw upon what we know of interrelated client and family processes to view the client holistically from a psycho-social-emotional-bio/physical-cultural-spiritual perspective. We must step into the child's and family's shoes to understand their hearts and minds and to see life from their perspective. It is the beginning of instilling hope, and establishing foundations of trust and safety, without which we are going nowhere. It takes tremendous courage for a parent to pick up the phone and ask for help. It takes courage to open up to a stranger and speak our innermost thoughts and secrets, and for that reason I have labeled this phase of therapy "being courageous." This is because some see seeking help as a weakness. It is just the opposite, it is a very humbling and vulnerable place to be as clients are entrusting their hearts to us.

Temenos

There is a Zen Buddhist saying: "When we are thirsty, we want water, not a bucket." But we need the bucket to carry the water. Metaphorically speaking, we need structure and containment (the bucket) to carry the water, which is meant to represent the therapeutic healing space. Temenos is a Greek word used by Carl Jung to describe the sacred, safe, protected, and creative welcoming space that surrounds the therapeutic relationship. A mother remarked, as she walked into my office for the first time, "Oh goodness, I will never be able to get my son out of here!" Winnicott (1971b) called the therapeutic space the *holding environment*—a place where children can be free to express themselves in play without pressure of expectation on the part of the therapist to judge or interpret. This is the bedrock for a child to develop an internal sense of "I" or core self within (Brody, 1997b).

Temenos also addresses the concept of containment and structure. In a personal story shared with this author by Viola Brody, she retold a story from when she was in graduate school at the University of Chicago, where Carl Rogers was one of her professors (personal communication, 2002). She stated that there was a point when the instruction in the classroom became so nondirective that, in her words, "The whole class just totally fell apart." To understand what had gone wrong, Rogers held an individual conference with each of his students to gain feedback and assess the problem. It was not until years later that Brody learned the outcome of those conversations, when she attended a workshop with Rogers. She was listening to the lecture in the audience when he confided that there needs to be *some type of structure* to the therapy session with a client, and that he came to that insight after a graduate class of his had come unraveled. After the workshop, Brody told Rogers, "I was one of those students." There is a lesson here for all of us. In therapy with children, the structure that contains the therapy may look like a ritual of opening, middle time of the therapeutic engagement, with a ritual of closing at the end of the session.

The research of Stephen Porges (2018) and the polyvagal theory (discussed in Chapter 2) have helped us to understand the crucial importance of the need for safety, which enables play and intimacy. Creating safety for the client in the therapeutic relationship is crucial, as it is the keystone of trust. In fact, Bonnie Badenoch titled a recent book chapter, "Safety *is* the Treatment" (Badenoch, 2018b). Temenos therefore encompasses containment and structure to create a sense of safety, trust, and hope. As an analogy, we can envision a sailboat representing a structured container afloat on the ocean, with the need for safety as representative of the wind that fills the sails. When the sails are filled, a sense of trust emerges that then moves the boat forward on its journey. If there is no wind (a foundation of safety), then that boat is dead in the water. Similarly, in the therapeutic encounter, if that child or family does not feel safe, then therapy will be at a standstill, or unauthentic. Therefore, all along through Phase I, we are instilling a sense of hope, safety, and protection.

The following is an example of how I instill a sense of safety within the environment that I learned from play therapist Joyce Mills (2015). When Tommy, age four, entered the playroom, he was very shy and withdrawn. I greeted him with my turtle puppet and told him, "When Sammy the turtle feels scared, he tucks away into his shell home, where he feels *all safe and protected inside*. And, when he is ready, he pops out to say 'hello.'" I demonstrated this with my puppet as I moved the puppet down to hide in the shell, and then popped the puppet's head out to say hello.

The tone of my voice is soft and caring, matching the child's behavior. It is utilized to instill a feeling of *safety and protection* for the client "inside." What I am saying to the child is that inside this playroom you will be safe and protected, and at the same time I am instilling that he has a *home* of safety and protection within himself. It also gives a child permission to be shy or scared—that's understandable. At the same time, it empowers the child to have control of readiness to connect.

This is also the stage where children begin an exploration of the playroom space. They are given permission to choose whatever they would like to play. Benjamin, on his first session, opened every drawer and cabinet in the room. He lifted the top of every container and board game. He sorted through the art cabinet and stared inside the dollhouse. He picked something up and put it down again. He finally settled on the Legos. Such was the beginning of this dynamic exploration and curiosity play. During this phase, some practitioners identify that children may test the limits of therapy, and it is within the boundaries of safe limits, such as, *Children cannot hurt themselves or the therapist*, that the work of childhood play in the playroom transpires. Another limit may include that the toys remain in the playroom, or as I explain it to children, "The toys live here, this is their home." Some therapists include limits that toys are not to be intentionally broken—or if a child wants to break the toy, we can talk about the reasons why and how the toy may be replaced, or not.

Phase II: "The Work": Reliance and Resourcing

Phase II is a time when children get into the crux of why they are in therapy and they are observed to rely on the therapy time together. We are past the majority of the assessment and information gathering that go with Phase I (although assessment is always an ongoing process). Children come to the appointment prepared, and they have a clear sense of what they want to do during the time. It is clear they have put some thought into their therapy "work" between therapy sessions, and walk into the playroom knowing exactly what they want to play or create. I liken this to the adult version of a client coming into the session and sitting on the couch and saying, "This is what I want to work on today." It's taking responsibility for our time together, and a feeling of movement is in the air. The themes of the expressive play content—whether through art, storytelling, or sandtray—become more pronounced. Children may even come to talk to you more directly about what's on their mind. The following is an example I recognized immediately as a stage of reliance: After several weeks of client-centered play therapy with Mark, age seven, and observing the themes of his play stories in the sandtray—that actually took flight all over the playroom—one day he arrived and paused at the doorway. Making direct eye contact with me, he announced with a steady voice of confidence: "*Today we are going deeper than we have ever gone before.*" I thought to myself: *Janet, this is important, stay vigilant to every moment.* This was indeed deep, deep work.

With all said above, this stage maintains a complexity. Because there are always periods of movement, but there are also periods of pulling back, retreating, slowing down, regression, defensive behaviors, and potentially negative content—even toward the therapist (such as the case example at the end of Chapter 2). All this leads to an understanding that we have evolved, over thousands of years, adaptive ways to protect ourselves emotionally and psychologically against anxiety and the myriad hurts and threats that come our way. Perry (2006b) wrote, "Our conscious memory is full of gaps, of course, which is actually a good thing" (p. 28). These protective defense mechanisms begin in early childhood and develop in more sophisticated ways as we grow. Some defense mechanisms are positively adaptive, such as humor, sublimation, and suppression, and some are more highly protective such as repression, displacement, and denial. Granieri, et al. (2017) defined defense mechanisms as "unconscious mental mechanisms that are directed against both internal drive pressures and external pressures, especially those that threaten self-esteem . . . ; they develop according to predictable sequences with the maturation of the child; *they are part of normal personality functioning*" [italics added] (Introduction).

It is crucial to understand that defense mechanisms are vital to healthy psychological and emotional functioning. They are what keeps us going when life gets overwhelmingly tough, and to reiterate: *They are part of normal personality functioning.* In that, we must respect children's defense mechanisms for the valuable function they represent, and resist the immediate urge to rush in and try to take those protective inner resources of defense away. Of course, we invite the child to partake in healthier forms of learning how to express themselves appropriately and modulate states of arousal. But understand that if we try to take away anyone's defenses when they are not 100 percent on board in willingness to let go of and change, those defenses can evolve into new forms of fervent resistance and protectiveness. It's just their nature—it's our human nature. For example, a therapist may feel satisfied that she had assisted in a deep "breakthrough" in a session with a child. Some powerful processing work might have happened. And play and expressive arts therapies have the power of producing deep inner work. However, at the next session the child may refuse to come, or there may be some excuse or reason why they do not want to attend therapy. We therefore need to be continually attuned to a child's will of self-determination. The same is true for adults (even more so), and since child therapists also work with adults, we need to hold this awareness at the forefront of our work with children and families.

Resourcing

Conjoint to the category of reliance is the parallel process of building upon the strengths of a client. This phase is characterized by the following processes of resilience, drawing upon the children's inner resources, helping children to see their highest potential. In many ways, this stage of therapy is related to the humanistic stance discussed in Chapter 1, which speaks to our innate drive toward our highest potential to self-actualize. This stage speaks to our inner resilience. Walsh (2006) defined resilience as our "capacity to rebound from adversity strengthened and more resourceful. It is an active process of endurance, self-righting, and growth in response to crisis and challenge" (p. 4). Gil (2017) viewed children's play as a form of *child resilience,* and Mills (2015) described the play process as tapping into the child's *"resilient inner core"* (p. 178). Therapists can help children to identify and find within themselves their own personal inner resources, strengths, and resilience. Additionally, it has been identified that one of the most outstanding features of child resilience is that the child has at least *one* caring and supportive person in their life who believes in them. It only takes one other person to help make a difference in a child's life, and sometimes the therapist may ultimately be that caring person who sees the child unconditionally. One way we try to tap into a child's resilience is through resourcing and drawing upon children's inner strengths.

As a case example of inner resilient resourcing, I worked with an 11-year-old boy, Robert, who was having test anxiety at school. He was terrified of taking the test and failing. Building upon his strengths, I asked him to tell me the story of a time in his life when he had felt afraid about something, but he was able to overcome it. He then shared that he was a roller skater and had entered competitions with other skaters. Robert retold the first time he skated off the deep dip of cement enclosure that he described was like an empty, deep swimming pool. He was showing me, with his hand moving up and down in the air, how he learned to do roller skating tricks. I asked him how he felt when he first skated off the edge. "Oh, that was very scary," he said. Then I asked how he felt about it now. "I love it!" he said, sporting a huge smile. Overcoming challenges is an inner resource—and Robert had a working memory of what it feels like to build a sense of mastery. I then asked for him to feel that joyful feeling of success (his inner resilience that he carries with him) and then to bridge that positive experience to the classroom before the exam to access the confident feeling of the skating activity. He shared later that he put this into action in real time prior to taking the test in the classroom. This now leads in to phase III, integration and action.

Phase III "Empowerment": Integration and Action

Phase III is characterized by integration and action, and is marked by a sense of empowerment. It is putting new skills and behaviors into action, taking steps of change, and where children are more in charge of how they respond and regulate their emotions. In this phase, children appear to have *grown* over the course of therapy. Some of the new insights now seem to have been synthesized and integrated. The new skills or ways to self-regulate that were learned in earlier stages of therapy are now more integrated, and children can access these skills and qualities at will to put them into action. Children are more confident and empowered to draw upon their new abilities when needed. For example, a child may know how to help himself calm by taking a breathing break before a test. Or a child may automatically take responsibility and act independently for a chore that the parent has been nagging about, such as taking the garbage can up to the house from the street without being asked, or folding the clean clothes and putting them away in drawers. It can show up as an automatic responsibility of action. Sometimes we may hear stories from parents or teachers that the child is putting into action some of the skills they practiced in the session.

Sarah, age four years, was referred for therapy from her school because she was often pushing other children on the playground. These interactions led to an isolation and loneliness for Sarah as she felt the rejection by her classmates. In therapy sessions, Sarah was playing school with all the playroom puppets and practicing how to use her new *"superpower words."* Her monkey puppet calmly says to my rabbit puppet that I am holding, *"Can I have a turn now on the monkey bars? We can take turns."* (Sometimes before I respond, I step out of my pretend role and I empower the child to advise me how she wants the rabbit to respond—so they can direct the play as they see it fits best with their imagination.)

In this case I asked, *"Sarah, how do you want the rabbit to respond? What do you want the rabbit to say?"* As I ask these questions, I always change from my play character inflection back to my normal speaking voice. In this way, the child is aware of the difference in my stepping in and out of pretend play.

Sarah replied, *"The rabbit says, 'No!'"* This was an indication that she wanted to practice putting into action her new assertiveness skills. Soon after this session, Sarah had a positive shift in her behaviors and interactions with her peers. Sarah was making new friends, and she was feeling more empowered about how she was able to put into action her new superpower words.

Phase IV: "Futuring": Saying Goodbye

This last stage of therapy is a very sensitive time, especially if the child has been in therapy with the therapist for a significant length of time. Attachments happen within a trusted and caring relationship, and this final phase can bring up new or renewed feelings of loss and grief. And be forewarned: Attachment is a reciprocal process, and it is not uncommon for the therapist to also feel a pang of loss when it is time to say goodbye. At the same time, it is a period of celebration—of graduation—as the child is now ready to transition out of therapy. When a child is given enough time to prepare for closure, and it does not happen abruptly (which can sometimes happen beyond the therapist's control), two curious scenarios are known to arise: regression and revisiting.

Sometimes, a child may show signs of regression, which can be observed as a change in behavior or tone of voice to a younger stage of development. But at this stage, it is short-lived compared to previous stages, when regression to an early stage of development could last a whole session (such as baby talk coming from an older child). This regression can be recognized as a normal reaction to the pending loss of relationship, an understandable form of grief anticipation, and should be acknowledged and processed within the session.

The concept of *revisiting* occurs when a child returns to some of the themes that were played out during earlier stages of therapy. It can also be a brief touching base with the play materials, as shown in the following example: Mary, age eight, had been in therapy for over two years. During the last session, she slowly moved around the playroom to the different play centers—very similar to what she did on the first session. However, this time it had an air of revisiting an old, good friend—of saying goodbye to each play item that she had a relationship with. She did this silently and independently, and I observed as a compassionate witness as she touched and paused at the sandtray, then the dollhouse, a board game, and the art materials, as if she was remembering and taking in all that had transpired. At the same time, she was coming full circle and saying goodbye. When she was done, she looked at me and nodded her head and said in almost a whisper, "Okay," in a knowing sense of "I'm good," "I feel complete." I put my hand to my heart and nodded in an understanding, heartfelt gesture—so she could feel my understanding, love, and respect. Our time together was coming to an end.

The time of saying goodbye is also about looking ahead and imagining the next steps of life beyond therapy, or what some have called, "*futuring*." The play themes that emerge in therapy may represent something new, fresh, or reconstructed, and might include the therapist as they work together for a cooperative purpose. When I was working with five-year-old Jon after a pretend fire that burned the town in a play scene, he invited me to reconstruct a *new* town together using Legos and blocks. We worked together gathering the materials and designing the streets for the police station, fire department, and grocery store. And, like the phoenix that rises from the ashes, a new hopeful future was envisioned.

There are several ways to mark closure, such as creating a "graduation certificate" or making up a song together that summarizes the highlights of the whole therapy progression, beginning with the first session and ending with the last. One of the most important things I want to leave the child with is for them to know that—no matter what situations may arise in the future—there is always someone out in the world they can find, who will listen. Someone who will care and guide. The child now has an internal working model of what truly being seen and heard looks and feels like.

THE STAGES OF THERAPY

I invite you to take a few minutes to engage in the following practice exercise: The Stages of Therapy.

THE PRACTICE

The Stages of Therapy

Consider the Stages of Therapy and list of characteristics for each stage found in Table 3.1: Saying Hello, Temenos, Reliance, Resourcing, Integration, Action, and Saying Goodbye. Now think of how these stages and characteristics may have emerged with a client you have worked with in therapy. Alternatively, consider how any of these stages have manifested in your personal, family, and social relationships. For example, think of the times in your life when you have had to say goodbye in relationships. Or how you created a family home with an environment of temenos.

We now turn to Part II, which will explore the clinical applications of expressive arts and play therapies in action.

Part II

EXPRESSIVE ARTS AND PLAY THERAPY CLINICAL APPLICATIONS

Chapter 4

THE ART OF
CHILD ASSESSMENT
AND INTERVENTION

"Drawing [is] a mirror and metaphor for the artist."
Betty Edwards, *Drawing on the Right Side of the Brain,*
(Edwards, 1979, p. 23)

INTRODUCTORY BACKGROUND

Early on in my career, one of the most valuable skills I added to my tool-box repertoire was learning how to integrate art therapy assessments and interventions into play therapy sessions. In that regard, I attended art therapy conferences and at the same time sought consultation and supervision with two accomplished registered art therapists, Myra Levick and Ethel Ludwig. Levick (1986, 2003) is considered a pioneer in the art therapy field and was a founder and first president of the American Art Therapy Association, in addition to founding one of the first graduate training programs in the field at Hahnemann/Drexel University in Philadelphia in 1967. As a consultant on my dissertation committee, Levick was instrumental in guiding the research design, procedures, methodology, and final analysis of my dissertation study, which was later published in the *Journal of the American Art Therapy Association* (Courtney & Gray, 2011). The late Ethel Ludwig (Ludwig, 2015) supervised and guided my understanding in completing a series of child-oriented art assessments that provided essential insight in my work with children. What I present in this chapter is an accumulation of my years of apprenticeship with Levick and Ludwig; my research related to the analysis of art drawings; my attendance at numerous art therapy conferences and readings related to the topic; and my experiences of implementing art interventions as an adjunctive modality in play therapy sessions with children for more than 30 years.

Formulating a Therapeutic Paradigm of Art in Play Therapy

One of the best words of wisdom given to me in my early stages of art therapy discovery was to "learn everything possible" about how drawings and art have been used to evaluate children and what I considered "normal" child developmental drawings compared to "warning signals" (Levick, 1986, 2003), or used as projective tools and assessments (Klepsch & Logie, 1982). And then, once this was assimilated, I needed to "forget everything I had learned!" This meant that, once I had synthesized a wide range of art foundations, and I finally sat down with a child and invited them to draw a specific task, I then needed to table my art-learned biases to the backseat of my mind. I was to then open myself to the uniqueness of that individual child's art process.

From a humanistic point of view, my primary aim was to establish a sense of healing therapeutic presence (Robbins, 1998) and to allow the child the creative space to work with the art materials as desired. It is a very intimate moment when children draw, paint, design, and make a craft, or work in clay. I mostly became interested in what children were trying to communicate about their inner world through their drawings: their personal thoughts, feelings, stories, symbols, and themes that emerged. Malchiodi (1998) described how many practitioners have evolved over the years their intentional use of drawings from directed purposes of assessment and evaluation to focusing on the importance of therapy with children:

> Psychologists, therapists, counselors, and others have long used drawings in less formal ways with children, ways that are not specifically designed to assess, diagnose, or evaluate the child, but to provide a way for the child to communicate issues, feelings, and other experiences and to explore, invent, and problem solve through self-expression. (p. 10)

One of the first "101" lessons related to children's drawings (or any client art for that matter) is that children's drawings are considered documentation. Period! This means that, unlike many parents' homes with refrigerators covered in their children's art, client drawings—as beautiful and profound as they may be—are confidential, related to the client, and cannot be put up on the office walls. Children's drawings fit perfectly within a play therapy setting, as art provides a way for children to use their imagination and express themselves nonverbally. This can be especially useful for shy or withdrawn children and teenagers, or children with speech and language difficulties. From a client-centered perspective, I always followed the lead of children in the playroom, and if a child was not interested in art or drawing—and sometimes they are not—I would plant a *seed thought* that they could let me know if that was something they would like to do at a different time. If they commented that they "can't draw" or did not know how, I might suggest: "Draw the ugliest picture that you could imagine." This gentle challenge often paved the way for children to engage in other art activities throughout the therapy process.

Working with children requires flexibility, and sometimes play therapy sessions are a dance of endeavors, from drawing at the children's table, to telling a story with puppets, to moving to the dollhouse, and then back to the children's table to work in clay. In this shifting of play modalities in the therapy room, one can observe that similar themes can emerge among the different modalities. For example, a child may draw an image of two characters fighting that then gets played out within the sandtray or dollhouse. I liken the process to adult clients in therapy changing topics to discuss different matters in their lives. However, a keen listening ear can discover the underlying similar patterns of life themes that intermingle from one topic to the next.

About Eye Contact

The practitioner's posturing while the child is engaged in drawing or an art activity is central to the outcome and brings to the forefront a crucial therapeutic consideration: *eye contact*. We often hear about the importance of making eye contact—and it is essential. The most critical time when we need to have someone engage us with warm eye contact is during infancy and early childhood. This is one of the reasons why apprehensions related to parental overuse of technology during the child's infancy and early years is so concerning (refer to Courtney & Nowakowski, 2018, 2019, and Aiken, 2016). However, when working with children impacted by trauma, how practitioners make and engage eye contact is of the utmost importance. Over the years, when working with children impacted by trauma, I was mindful how I made eye contact. Eye contact is a very intimate experience, and those impacted by trauma can suffer harrowing shame and guilt. Therefore, children need to have the respect and space to decide their own readiness for eye contact. For example, if a child was sitting at the table drawing, I would sit very still and set my eyes looking down at the table. I wanted children to decide for themselves the amount of contact they were comfortable with. I did this at an intuitive level. Peter Levine (2018) explained why this sensitivity to eye contact is crucial for traumatized clients, as it relates to the vagal shutdown, where they may perceive their external environment as a life threat. He noted:

> The avoidance of eye contact by prey, in the face of a lethal predator is seen throughout the animal kingdom. Direct eye contact by prey is very likely to incite a lethal attack. . . . The therapist should not initially try to engage eye contact. . . . However, after clients have shifted from states of hypoarousal and shutdown into states of hyperarousal and hypervigilance, it is possible to engage them with a limited degree of eye contact and prosody. [As clients] settle from sympathetic hyperarousal into relaxation and restored equilibrium, [they may] seek out and sustain soft eye contact . . . (p. 17)

Thus, the need to be sensitive to eye contact arises often when engaging in drawing or art activities.

DRAWINGS IN BEGINNING PHASES OF THERAPY: A WINDOW TO THE INNER WORLD

Assessment in any form must be viewed from a multidimensional perspective, meaning that a holistic child assessment must appraise several different viewpoints, including: interviews with the parents or caregivers comprising birth, developmental history, and significant life impacts; external sources such as teachers, health care providers, or other systems including foster care or child protection workers; an assessment of the child's individual play themes, an assessment of the parent-child interactions, and any initial drawings completed by the child. The following drawing directives can be collected during the beginning phases of therapy, and they assist as an adjunctive modality in my initial assessment, decision making, and treatment planning.

The following is a list of recommendations to follow related to the implementation of any drawings completed with a client. This is all part of the documentation.

Drawing and Art Procedure Guidelines

- List all procedures—everything you did or asked the child to do related to the drawing activity or directive. Include the art materials used (size of paper, crayons/markers/paints, and so on).
- Put quotation marks around the directive task questions *you* asked. (Example: "Draw a picture of you and your family doing something together," or "Draw a picture of your 'safe place' ").
- Take notes on what you observe related to the drawing, such as: "Drew mother in the picture first and the cat last."
- Put quotations around client responses (for example, Client: "We are at the beach.").
- Have the client sign and date the drawing.

The Squiggle Game

As a beginning engagement and joining technique and to get a child comfortable with the idea of drawing and sitting at the children's table in the playroom, I sometimes began with "the Squiggle Game." This collaborative therapist and child drawing activity was created by Winnicott (1971a), who deemed it a way to explore the client's intersubjective states of consciousness. In the drawing game, the therapist and child each take turns drawing a "scribble" that is first initiated by the therapist. The child is then asked to "turn the scribble into something." The child is encouraged to pick up the paper with the scribble and turn it in any direction desired until something emerges that he or she would like to create. Then the child creates a scribble, and the therapist turns it into something. The game assists to level the communication gap between therapist and child, and for the therapist to model vulnerability to participate in creating something, too. This back-and-forth engagement generates a beginning dialogue that is co-created by both practitioner and child. It also begins the assessment process of discovering the child's use of imagination, emerging inner resilience, capability of abstract thought, and discovery of spontaneous symbols that emerge from the scribble. Sometimes the squiggle game can be used as an icebreaker to engage resistant clients, as shown in the following case situation.

Case Vignette: "Such a Cute Puppy"

After attempting to engage an angry teenager who was court-ordered for therapy without much success, in the second session the therapist asked Tonya if she would be willing to try something that the therapist described as a silly drawing game, but kind of fun. With a sullen, drawn face, she shrugged her shoulders and said, "Sure." While she was sitting at the children's table with crayons and paper, it was explained that they would take turns turning a scribble into something. The therapist went first and drew a scribble. Tonya picked up the paper and thought about it, then picked up some crayons and went to work, taking her time with the drawing. She turned it into an adorable puppy dog. Amused with herself, she grinned, and for the first time made eye contact with the therapist and said "Here," as she handed the paper back in a playful manner.

Looking at the drawing, the therapist playfully spoke to the puppy in an animated and caring prosodic voice: "Thank you puppy. Thank you, cute puppy, for coming out and playing with me today." The therapist paused and looked up to see her response. Tonya smiled and nodded with a knowing awareness that the therapist was really talking to her. It broke the ice and helped to begin a relationship of mutual trust and respect.

THE SQUIGGLE GAME

With the above discussion of the Squiggle Game in mind, I invite you to take a few minutes to engage in the following practice exercise.

THE PRACTICE

The Squiggle Game
Find a partner to engage the activity of *The Squiggle Game*. Each takes turns drawing a scribble and then the other to make it into something. Take time to talk about the activity and what was drawn, and any possible meanings related to the shape or image that emerged. Practice a few rounds of the game.

TAPPING HUMOR AND RESILIENCE

One of the least recognized factors related to resilience is a sense of humor (Walsh, 2006). Children have varied styles of humor, and getting to know a child's unique sense of what is *funny* can add significantly to the joining process with the child in therapy. Trauma can hinder a sense of humor, and the brain regions used in processing humor can show decreased activity in those experiencing depression. Laughter releases the body's natural "feel-good" hormones, such as serotonin, and endorphins that regulate pain and stress (Shibata, Terasawa, & Umeda, 2014). Utilizing humor in sessions with children, when deemed appropriate, can support the healing process, and the recognition of a child's capability to have a sense of humor can be an indication of progress related to a child's healing. Goodyear-Brown (2019) viewed humor as a way to mitigate the dance toward and away from trauma content for a child, and also highlighted that humor can equalize the therapeutic relationship as follows:

> Laughter can become the great equalizer in a session, giving humanity to a therapist who may have otherwise been perceived as more of an expert or technician than a human being and helping counter the hierarchical relationship that sometimes occurs in therapy. (p. 182)

"Draw a picture of the funniest thing you can think of"

One way to survey for a sense of humor is to ask the child, "Draw a picture of the funniest thing you can think of." This can be something that children experienced as joyful or funny, or that made them laugh from a past or current memory, or they can use their imagination to make something up. It is open-ended. When they are finished with the drawing, ask if they would be willing to tell the story of the drawing, with a beginning, middle, and end. Encourage the use of multisensory experiencing in the story, such as any memories of smell, or what they were hearing. What did walking on leaves sound like? What did the air outdoors smell like? Was there music playing in the background? This expands upon the child's inner resources and resilience, and we can act as an attuned witness and mirror back to them what we enjoyed about the story. We can highlight our favorite part of the story. For example, "Mary, my favorite part of your story was when you climbed the tree and said you were making sounds like a monkey!"

SIDE NOTE: To add a little lightness and humor to the discussion, I am reminded of a joke: *"Did you hear about the new children's art museum?* Answer: *"Oh yes, the place is full of refrigerators!"*

KINETIC FAMILY DRAWING

One of the most revealing assessment drawing activities completed during the initial phases of therapy is the Kinetic Family Drawing developed by Burns and Kaufman in 1970 (Burns, 1987). They added the kinesthetic action component as they viewed the images resulting from the Draw-A-Family (D-A-F), developed by Hulse in the 1950s, as limited to drawings that consisted of stiff, portrait-style pictures, or a "linear row of static unrelating figures" (Burns, 1987, p. xvii). Their adaptation to the D-A-F proved groundbreaking, and can add valuable insight to understanding a child within the context of the family

FIGURE 4.1: Kinetic Family Drawing Talking and Thinking: Sophia, age 6 years, tells her story of "fun in the sun."
SOURCE: USED WITH PERMISSION FROM STEPHANIE CROWLEY AND SOPHIA

system that might not otherwise be known. The art directive is: "Draw a picture of everyone in your family, including you, doing something together—some type of activity." This action-based drawing sets up a springboard to develop dialogue between the people in the drawing.

Kinetic Family Drawing: Steps of Implementation

Step 1: Invite the child to "Draw a picture of everyone in your family, including you, doing something, some kind of action."

Step 2: Instruct children to "Draw the whole body." (Avoid stick figures.)

Step 3: When the child is finished, have the child identify each figure in the drawing.

Step 4: Have the child title the drawing.

Step 5: Have the figures and all portrayals in the drawing "talk" and "think." Do this by drawing "talking" and "thinking" bubbles for each figure.

Step 6: Next, guide the client to create the dialogue in the picture by assisting to fill in each bubble for what the family members are saying and thinking in the drawing. For example, let's say the child drew a picture of himself, a father, and a mother in the drawing. Each figure would then have a talking and thinking bubble above it. I give an option to the child if they would like to draw the bubbles, or if they would like for me to help. I then guide the dialogue in the bubbles by asking the child, "I see this is Mom. What would she be saying in the drawing? And, if you could get inside Mom's head, what do you think she is really thinking about?" The child can write the words in the bubble or can have the practitioner's assistance.

> **SIDE NOTE:** I was taught to add the talking and thinking bubbles by Ethel Ludwig during supervision. Having clients add the bubbles provided the most valuable insights into my work with children and families.

The Kinetic Family Drawing is also a powerful intervention to engage with all family members together. In this way family members are directed through all the steps listed above and are then invited to share their drawings with each other. It can be an effective form of assessment and intervention, as family members discover more about each other and learn to value the differences in family perspectives. (We will be discussing more about family play therapy assessments, interventions, and recommended guidelines in Chapters 5 and 6.)

As an optional directive—and to better distance a child from the emotionally laden presenting problem—the therapist can alternately ask a child to "Draw a picture of 'a' family doing something together" without the direction to draw the picture directly of the child's own family, as shown in the following case scenario.

Case Vignette: "Stop hurting me!"

In a play therapy session with Juan, age 10, whose parents were caught up in a bitter divorce and fighting for primary custody of him, he was asked to "Draw a picture of 'a' family doing something together." Sitting slumped over at a children's desk, he drew a tennis court. On one side of the court, holding a tennis racket in one hand, was a female figure ("the mother"). On the other side, also holding a tennis racket, was a male figure ("the father"). The faces of the figures looked angry and contorted. In the middle of the court was a ball. He fills in the talking bubbles with the mother and father both saying, "I'm gonna get you!" and in the thinking bubbles, "He's mine!" The therapist facilitated the following brief gestalt encounter process:

Therapist: "Can you share with me a little about this family in the drawing?"
Juan (staring at the picture, pointing to the tennis ball): "I am the ball in the middle."
Therapist: "If that ball could speak, what would it be saying?"
Juan: "Stop hurting me!"

In the above example, in a neutral environment, Juan was able to express for the first time his deep hurt and pain that emerged metaphorically through his drawing. Caught in the conflict between his parents, he did not honestly share with either of his parents his true state of suffering. The parents were both so preoccupied with their own complicated emotional turmoil that they were unable to fully recognize the extent of their aggressive actions toward each other and their impact upon their son's emotional well-being. Juan, loyal to both his parents, did not want to choose between his mother and father, who were both battling over custody and other affairs. The safe holding environment of the playroom and the kinetic family drawing intervention offered a haven of protection for Juan to express his true feelings.

DRAW A PICTURE OF EVERYONE IN YOUR FAMILY, INCLUDING YOU, DOING SOMETHING TOGETHER

With the above section in mind, I invite you to set aside some time to engage in the following practice exercise: Draw a picture of everyone in your family, including you, doing something together.

THE PRACTICE

Draw a Picture of Everyone in Your Family, Including You, Doing Something Together

This can be related to your family when you were a child, or your family in the present.

Step 1: "Draw a picture of everyone in your family, including you, doing something, some kind of action."

Step 2: "Draw the whole body." (Avoid stick figures.)

Step 3: Identify each figure in the drawing.

Step 4: Title the drawing.

Step 5: Have the figures and all portrayals in the drawing "talk" and "think." Do this by drawing "talking" and "thinking" bubbles for *each* figure.

Step 6: Fill in each bubble for what the people are saying and thinking during the action in the drawing.

When you are finished, take time to contemplate your drawing and allow any thoughts and feelings about your drawing to come into your awareness. Next, if appropriate, find a partner and share your drawing.

Draw Anything You Want to Draw

Another drawing directive that can assess for a child's resilience is to ask the child to "Draw anything you want to draw." When working with a trauma-tized young girl who had been sexually abused by a family member, I asked her to draw anything that she felt like drawing. She nodded her head and chose several colorful crayons and quickly drew an outdoor picture with several colorful flowers with a sun and open tree. The image exuded happiness. When I asked her about the drawing, she said it made her feel "happy" and that she liked flowers and being outside. To me it spoke to her inner resilience and made me understand, despite the betrayal of her trust with the extended family member, that she had an inner sense of how to help herself feel better, and nature appeared as one avenue.

DRAW A PICTURE OF THE FUNNIEST THING YOU CAN THINK OF

I invite you to take a few minutes to engage in the following practice exercise: Draw a Picture of the Funniest Thing You Can Think Of.

THE PRACTICE

Draw a Picture of the Funniest Thing You Can Think Of

Take a few minutes to consider "Draw a picture of the funniest thing you can think of." This can be a past or current memory, or something you make up. When you are finished, find a partner and, as much as makes you comfortable, *tell the story* about your drawing. Include in your story a multisensory grounding with your listener: "What were the sounds you heard around you? Any smells that came to mind? What were you seeing? Notice any changes in your affect and mood in your body when you tell the story. What does the experience of you telling your story have on your listener?" Ask for comments related to their experience.

ARTISTIC METAPHOR: INNER RESOURCE DRAWINGS

The artistic metaphor and Inner Resource Drawing are found in the Story-Play model developed by Joyce Mills (Mills & Crowley, 2014; Mills, 2015). StoryPlay is an adapted Ericksonian indirective model founded upon the principles of Milton H. Erickson. Ericksonian theory postulates that indirective positive messages embedded in a metaphorical story will activate inherent healing processes that can reach a child at a deeper level of consciousness (Lankton & Lankton, 1989; Mills & Crowley, 2014). Metaphors are processed in the right hemisphere of the brain as they bypass the conscious level and speak to the child's unconscious. Courtney & Mills (2016) emphasized: "Metaphors can act as symbolic bridges of personal connection inspiring solutions that strengthen a child's own inner resources and resiliency" (p. 19). Ericksonian methods thus focus on the problem in a quietly diffused way, lowering resistance. Mills (2011) noted, "Stories and metaphors convey a message and idea in an indirect yet paradoxically more meaningful way; bypassing resistance and opening the doorway to receptive communication" (p. 12). Erickson believed that healing occurs when we are in our most open, childlike state. Rosen (1989) wrote about Erickson's underlying thinking: "It is in this 'child state' that we are most open to learning, most curious, and most able to change" (p. vii). Drawing upon children's inner resources is the cornerstone of the artistic metaphor and inner resource drawings. In this way, what emerges from children's drawings and art is then utilized to bridge back to the child to reinforce and support change.

Mills (2011) identified that artistic metaphors utilize drawing strategies that serve the following purposes: 1) Dissociates the child from the problem; 2) depicts the problem and solution visually; 3) gives external expression to internal thoughts and feelings; 4) draws upon the inner resources and resilience of the child; 5) inner resources can then be utilized to reinforce and support avenues of change for the child; and 6) provides information for future storytelling metaphors.

The following Three-Step Artistic Metaphor is an Inner Resource Drawing that is a strength-focused way to draw upon children's inner resources of healing (Mills, 2011; Mills & Crowley, 2014).

Step 1: Draw a picture of the problem. (We can help young children to understand this task by using other words such as, worry: "Draw a picture of a worry.")

Step 2: Draw how the problem looks "all better" (This gives a vision of hope to the issue and can imply that wellness does exist).

Step 3: Draw what will need to happen or change to get from picture #1 to picture #2. Another way to frame the task: "Draw where in your life have you had the 'all better feeling.'" The third step is what is called the "metaphorical bridge," and is the healing symbol for activating resources and potentials.

Hurricane Disaster Aftermath: Art as Therapeutic Relief

I have utilized the above artistic metaphor steps successfully to intervene with several different problem areas, populations, and settings. As an American Red Cross volunteer, I implemented the Inner Resource Drawing with children and families in play therapy crisis intervention groups at several designated hurricane shelters in south Florida (Courtney, 2004). (Note that in 2004, Florida was impacted by four hurricanes—Charley, Frances, Ivan, and Jeanne—all in close timeframes, which significantly impacted the distress of the children and families in the shelters.) During the groups, I asked children to "Draw a picture of a worry they might be feeling." Note that I did not ask them to draw a picture of the "hurricane." However, this is exactly what the children drew—images of storm, chaos, and destruction. The open-ended instruction was meant to support children to draw whatever emerged for them related to how they felt in the present moment. After they drew the first drawing, I then asked, "Draw what that picture would look like 'all better.'" Many drew images of a rainbow and sunshine, and some children drew a series of drawings, as they wanted to "tell the whole hurricane story," as one child put it. The drawings provided a safe outlet for the children to express their feelings of sorrow and worry, while also planting the seeds of hope that things can feel better. In addition to the drawings, I also engaged children in storytelling and provided mindfulness techniques to help calm fears and anxieties.

Case Vignette: "The blue makes me feel all better"

In the following case vignette, the reader will observe how the Artistic Metaphor: Inner Resource Drawing was adapted to use with a young, grieving child in therapy. The vignette demonstrates how impactful the artistic metaphor can be, even for very young children.

Presenting problem and background: Annie, age four, was referred by her school counselor as she observed a recent change in Annie's behavior during lunchtime. Soon after lunch began, she started to cry and could not eat her meal. When questioned about why she was crying, Annie said she did not know. When the counselor spoke to her parents about the problem, they were unaware of why she was crying.

First Session

Sandra, Annie's mother, brought Annie to the first session, where they sat together solemnly on the couch. Unlike other children her age, she did not appear interested in exploring or playing with any of the toys in the room. She sat still under the wing of her mother's protective arm. The mother explained that she and her husband had questioned Annie about why she was crying, but they were not able to glean any answers about what was going on. When the mother was asked if anything had recently changed in the family, she stated, "Well, my mother died not too long ago." At that moment, the mother put her hand to her face and began to cry. At the same time, Annie started to cry too. The therapist then spoke to Annie about how very sad this was about her grandmother, and she nodded her head. The mother stated that her mother died a few weeks ago and that she thought Annie was okay with it since she never talked about it. She then mentioned that they did not let Annie attend the funeral, as they thought she was too young to understand. The therapist explored with Annie about school and the lunchtime schedule.

Therapist: "Can you please share with me about your lunchtime schedule beginning with leaving the classroom. What happens first?"

Annie: "We have to line up and walk down the hall to the lunchroom. And, then we sit down at the table."

Therapist: "Then what happens next?"

Annie: "Every day before we eat lunch, we pray for all the people that we love, and I always pray for grandma. That's when I cry because I am praying for grandma and I miss her."

Sandra (surprised): "So that is why you are crying? Because you miss grandma? I miss grandma, too."

She gave Annie a hug. It was Sandra's first understanding about why Annie might be crying at school.

This insight led to Sandra and Annie sharing more about their feelings related to grandma and her death. Next, because of Annie's young age, the Inner Resource Drawing (Mills and Crowley, 2014) was adapted in the following steps of implementation:

Step 1: Annie was asked if she would be willing to draw a picture and she indicated yes. She was handed some paper and a box of crayons and asked, "If you could draw a picture about what that sad feeling looks like, what would you draw? What would that sad feeling look like?" She looked through the group of crayons and picked out the black crayon. She then pressed the black crayon down hard on the paper as she scribbled back and forth across the page.

Step 2: Next, she was given a second sheet of paper, and asked, "If that sad feeling looked 'all better,' what would that look like?" She then picked the blue crayon and with a normal pressure on the paper she drew a box. She then took her time to color the blue within the box, being careful to stay within the lines.

Step 3: She was then asked where she felt that sad feeling inside and she pointed to her heart. The therapist then asked her to use her imagination to see what color she thought her heart looked like. She said, "black." When asked what color would help to make it feel better, she said, "blue!"

Step 4: Using her metaphor that came out of the drawings, Annie was asked to use her imagination to pretend she is coloring her heart with the blue crayon. She said that she would be willing to do this. She then closed her eyes and the therapist guided her by saying, "Okay, see that blue coloring all over your heart." Soon Annie opened her eyes and said, "Okay, I did it." The therapist asked her how she was feeling, and she said, "Good."

Step 5: The therapist then asked Annie if she could *"color in her heart the blue that made her feel all better,"* any time she felt she needed it, and she agreed to try.

Follow-up and Case Discussion

During the follow-up session, Sandra informed the therapist that Annie was doing better at school. She and her husband were now more understanding about how Annie was feeling and were able to talk to her more about her grandma. Annie said that she still prayed for grandma at lunch, but that she would use her "blue color" in her heart to help herself feel better. As Annie was doing better and the parents felt they were able to help her, closure was made at the end of the second session. This was a healthy family system, with secure attachment relationships, and although they had experienced a family crisis related to the death of the grandmother, their resilience as a cohesive system helped to quickly stabilize the situation once it was recognized. The case illustrates the power of artistic interventions to work with the inner resources from which even the youngest of clients can benefit.

THE IMPACT OF TRAUMA AND GRIEF WITH YOUNG CHILDREN

As adults, we can miss understanding that children grieve very differently than adults. Because Annie was unable to express her feelings of grief in an explicit way, her mother and father assumed that she was unaffected by the death of her grandmother. They missed recognizing her deep grief and sadness, which also paralleled her mother's unresolved feelings of grief. Davis King and Woods (2017) addressed the issue:

> "Because young children grieve differently than adults, parents and professionals often do not know how to help them, thinking they are too young to understand, or whether they even have the capacity to process grief. We now know that if you are "old enough to love, you are old enough to mourn," (Wolfelt, 2013, last para.), and preschoolers, of course, consistently demonstrate their ability to attach and love." (p. 178)

In one way or another, children will eventually be confronted with the reality of death. With that reality comes also the deep pain of grief. And the sorrow of losing a loved one *is* painful—it hurts, not only emotionally but physically. Children's grief is compounded by the messages that are given to them by the adults in their lives. As well, many children are kept separated from the grief process and may not be allowed to attend the funeral or participate in any way of saying goodbye. The exclusion of a child from the funeral process can create more problems as children try to work through their unresolved conflict and confusion. I have found that children do best when they participate in the family rituals—particularly if they are given the choice to attend a family funeral or not. Many young children decide they do want to participate. The initial impact of death is confusing not only for children, but for the parents and adults in children's lives. It's hard to know how to communicate about the death, and the euphemisms of past generations are still circulating. For example, when we tell a child that the family pet was "put to sleep," some children (depending on their age) will be waiting for them to "wake up" again. In addition to art therapy interventions that can enhance the healing process, storytelling is another impactful intervention. There are a lot of great therapeutic children's stories available to help explain death to children and help with the grief process. The book by Joyce Mills (1993) entitled *Gentle Willow* tells the story of a caring squirrel who helps his friend, Willow Tree, through the dying process and contains imbedded metaphorical messages of healing.

In the next two Chapters (5 and 6) we will explore how art assessment and intervention modalities are used with children within Family Play Therapy sessions.

Chapter 5

FAMILY IN EXPRESSIVE ARTS AND PLAY THERAPY: OVERVIEW AND ASSESSMENT

"But just as the root systems of plants often have to be divided for healthy growth to continue, the different generations within a family may have to pull apart for a while for each to find its own healthy identity."

Fred Rogers, (2005, p. 51),
Life's Journeys According to Mister Rogers

"Family play therapy" emerged as a term in the early 1990s to describe the techniques of practitioners who were schooled in both play therapy principles and traditional family therapy concepts, and then combined the two practices together (Schaefer & Carey, 2004). Only rarely were family therapists educated with sufficient therapy skills to relate to children (Green, 1994), so family play therapy evolved from the need to find more "child-friendly" ways of incorporating children into a family therapy session. The history of family play therapy is credited by Gil (2015a) to have its roots in the work of Carl Whitaker and Virginia Satir, both of whom advocated for the inclusion of young children within family sessions. In the 1960s Satir (1988) incorporated experiential activities into family sessions that included children as young as three. Whitaker and his colleague David Keith (2004) advocated for "outside-the-box" interventions they labeled play therapy and advocated for the therapist to play with the child, offering metaphorical and paradoxical interventions, writing: "In psychotherapy, the primary reality is metaphorical. This is an easy jump for children to make. . . . Part of the therapist's job is to teach the metaprocess of living with multiple meaning levels" (Keith & Whitaker, 2004, pp. 189–190).

Family play therapy interventions utilize play-oriented techniques that match the developmental level of the children in the family. Engaging the family through play thus allows for all family members to participate in the family therapy session. Family play therapy as a treatment modality can encompass a wide range of problematic life circumstances and/or conditions, including attachment problems. Therefore, family play therapists must synthesize a wide range of knowledge, including family play therapy principles and techniques; child developmental stages; family dynamics and systems theory; child and family assessment methods; sibling dynamics and birth order; family life stages; individual, family, and group process; and attachment and bonding interpersonal relationship dynamics related to the birth parents, foster parents, adoptive parents, and other caregivers. The following discussion will review some basic family therapy concepts that are essential to recognizing family dynamics within sessions.

FAMILY SYSTEMS: BACK TO BASICS

Family systems theory was borrowed from the field of cybernetics, which emerged from the scientific and commerce industries in the 1940s. Cybernetics examines how systems are interrelated and regulated in terms of feedback loops, structure, and patterns of organization. Gregory Bateson, an anthropologist and ethnologist, is credited as the major force in applying cybernetics principles to family communication processes (Goldenberg & Goldenberg, 2013). Systems operate and maintain themselves based upon a range of open or closed flow into and out of the system. In terms of families, we can view how they are organized based on a continuum range of "open" to "closed" family systems. Satir (1988) categorized family systems based upon four factors: 1) family self-esteem; 2) communication styles; 3) flexibility of family rules; and 4) outcomes. Open systems identified as having "high" self-esteem and communication styles between family members were observed as "direct, clear, specific, congruent, growth producing" (p. 135). Family rules are considered current and flexible with the freedom to change, and have varied opinions. Family outcomes are "related to reality, appropriate and constructive" (p. 135). Closed systems, on the other hand, are viewed as having "low" self-esteem, and communication is seen as "indirect, unclear, unspecific, incongruent, and growth-impeding" (p. 134). The rules are covert, out of date, and relatively fixed and unpredictable. Outcomes may be "accidental, chaotic, destructive and inappropriate" (p. 134). Overall, Satir viewed these closed and open systems as anything relating to ". . . your self-worth, your communication, together with your rules and your beliefs, are the ingredients that make up your family system" (p. 136). What is recognized is that family systems tend to maintain in fixed patterns of relating, and for better or worse, systems tend to work to maintain a homeostatic balance. Therefore, any type of family assessment or intervention, especially in expressive arts and play therapy modalities, can then intrude upon that static balance. This can sometimes be unsettling and even painful for family members to experience, as there is a strong pull to maintain the status quo. This is true even if that status quo is not serving the family to its highest potential. Change, when unfamiliar, can be seen as a threat.

When working with children, therapists must view the family system as a whole. A common perspective in the family therapy literature is that the children's problems can be symptoms of other problems and issues related to the parents or other family members in the household. Sometimes, when therapists are working with a child, it eventually becomes clear that the overwhelming anxiety that the child is presenting with is connected to the fact that his parents have decided to get a divorce (for example), and they have not told him yet. It is possible that the child has overheard that secret parental discussion, or the child may have figured it out by the many other subtle behaviors being displayed by the parents. There is an old saying in family therapy: *"If you want to know what's happening in the family, just ask the children."* It can soon become apparent that we are working from the bottom up, meaning we begin to discern that the child's symptoms are often a consequence of the family's overarching distress and problems. The "problem child" is thus viewed as the "symptom bearer," as the behaviors of one family member can be representative of behaviors related to others in the family. The patterns of relationship within the family are examined and seen as a source of information for planning interventions. In some situations, it is best to start at the "top," working with the parents first to address directly what's happening within the family. As well, the best solution may be to work with the family all together.

In other situations, the child's source of symptoms can be clearly known as initiating from some type of experience that the child has been exposed to in life, such as being bitten by a dog or having to go to the hospital for surgery. However, it is predictable that the family's existing emotional and interactive patterns of engagement may dictate how the family handles the external challenges the child is confronted with. For example, do families talk openly about problems or privately between subsystems? How are decisions finally made when family members disagree? This is where the therapist's keen assessment skills and knowledge about family therapy systems and play therapy methods combine. Sometimes it becomes a therapeutic intuitive contemplation about how to decide to work with the child individually, see the family together, or find a balanced alternating implementation of both.

One of the goals in family therapy is for each family member to gain a sense of freedom of autonomy, or what Murray Bowen (1976) labeled as *self-differentiation*. He defined a "well-differentiated" person as "one whose intellect could function separately from the emotional system" (p. 66). When therapists are working with children, this may show up as a child having a respected opinion about a situation, even if the parental system decides that the child is not mature enough for an activity—such as going to a movie theater independently with a group of friends without parental attendance.

GETTING PARENTS COMFORTABLE WITH EXPRESSIVE ARTS AND PLAY

For adults, trying to recall their childhood play is like trying to remember a song they once knew all the words to, but now can only hum the tune, because the lyrics are forgotten. Just as therapists who work with children need to get in touch with their playful, child self within, we also need to support parents to get comfortable with the idea of play. As we grow older and life becomes more serious, we can forget our innate ability to play or how we played as children. As well, engaging in an expressive art activity—drawing, painting, molding clay—can also be perplexing and awkward for parents. Unless we have pursued and honed our art skills in life, most of us have about a fourth-grade level of art aptitude. Asking a police officer father, for example, to draw a family tree genogram or play on the floor with toys, when he's not accustomed to drawing or playing, can be awkward, intimidating, or embarrassing. At the same time, we tend to de-value children's play. Donaldson (1993) wrote: "The de-meaning of play's spirit fundamentally alters the context of children's lives. Our adulteration of play transforms how we view ourselves [and] how we act with children . . . (p. 47)." Donaldson offered several messages we give to children that can work to stifle their play:

> Don't play in the house! Don't play with your food! I don't have time to play now! Don't play in those clothes! Play quietly! Don't play around! Go outside and play!

> I'm too busy/old/tired/big to play! You shouldn't play with them! Don't play in the rain!

> Don't play so roughly! Don't play with yourself! (p. 47)

These phrases about play may strike a familiar tone for the reader. Perhaps the parents we work with might find themselves in these words, either as memories spoken to them as children or phrases they have spoken to their own children. One way to help parents connect to an understanding of healing art and play modalities is through the thought-provoking, ancestral discussion found at the beginning of Chapter 1. We can assist our families to consider their ancestral and cultural inherited strengths of imagination, play, and creativity that helped them to thrive and heal. Depending on the family circumstances, the following sample question may be suitable: *"Consider for a moment how your ancient relatives might have helped themselves heal and overcome challenges in their lives."*

Moreover, as therapists who work with children, it is incumbent upon us to model a comfortable lightness of being in the presence of families. This means that, if I am encouraging parents to get up from the couch and move their bodies to music, sing a closing goodbye song, touch clay, or create a feeling family board game while sitting on the playroom floor, I need to display my own genuine self-assurance to do so. This requires a sense of vulnerability. We can help parents tap into their own childhood experiences of play, simply by asking them to tell a story about a childhood memory when they played. This can be a door for them to reconnect with their own inner capability to play. As well, we want parents to develop an appreciation for their own children's play. One way to do this is to task parents to act as curious observers of their children's play. This can occur simply by encouraging parents to quietly sit back, watch, listen, and pay attention to their children's play engagement. A helpful way to support parents to get to the SOUL of their children's play is through the acronym:

S ilence
O bserving
U nderstanding
L istening

Family Expressive Arts and Play Therapy in Sessions

The unique aspect of family play therapy is that the interventions are expressive arts and are play-oriented. As discussed in the previous section, the types of activities that we are inviting our families to participate in takes a lot of letting down of guard and humility, especially for adults. Often you are exposing family members to a new way of interacting together. You are taking them into new and unfamiliar territory, and they may feel a little timid at first. It is therefore critical that the therapist takes the lead to model an ease of engagement through the process. The therapist's own creative and playful use of self in the sessions is paramount. Family expressive and play therapy sessions, therefore, are very different than individual sessions with children. Individual sessions may be predominantly nondirective, following the lead of the child to choose the play items. They can also be directive, or both, depending on the child and the presenting situation. But in family sessions, the therapist's role is primarily directive.

A family expressive and play session may follow a certain progressive rhythm that has a beginning, middle, and end to include: 1) initial family "check-in"; 2) invitation to engage in a few different expressive and play activities, with an explanation regarding the options (this can also depend on what transpired during the check-in, as there is a rule of thumb to *follow the energy for what arises in the moment*. So there is always flexibility); 3) guiding the family through the activity (holding a safe temenos and containment for the process to happen; 4) having the family members step back from the activity when finished to observe and take in what was done—a rest and pause; 5) processing the encounter from all family perspectives; 6) summary of insights gained; 7) possible "homework" bridging from the therapy session to home and solidifying agreements thereof; and 8) closing ritual before leaving.

Advantages of Family Expressive and Play Sessions

There are several advantages to expressive family play sessions compared to seeing children individually. The following is a list of some of the benefits that can be observed.

- The therapist can observe children within the context of the family.
- The therapist can better understand family relational dynamics, such as boundaries, alliances, rivalries, distancing, triangles, and scapegoating.
- Attempts to engage children in adult conversations (more left-brain processes) can be extremely stressful, overwhelming, and very boring for children, which can lead to frustration, anger, shutdown, and disengagement. The activity of expressive arts and play is more energizing and captivating (more right-brain processes) and elicits increased cooperation.
- Therapists can act as a role models to guide parents *how* to engage in creative forms of imagination and play with their children.
- Family play sessions can serve to equalize communication between parents and children, as adults have the verbal advantage.
- Children may be better able to express their thoughts and feelings through play, painting, drawings, and stories.
- Encourages parents to think and act in "out-of-the-box" ways.
- Parents can begin to get in touch with their own "inner child."
- Play sessions can bring forth states of joy, fun, silliness, and humor; creating moments of lightness that can mitigate against more painful and challenging issues.
- It gives parents and children an opportunity to creatively examine and work through problems and brainstorm alternatives together.
- Directs the therapy process from potential parental complaint about their child's behavior to more creative expression and understanding.
- Enjoyable family play sessions can create positive reinforcement for children to want to return to the office.
- Children feel more connected to their parents as they come to see their playful and creative side.
- The expressive art and play activities can act as "buffers" from more difficult, emotionally laden content.

- Parents gain a window into their children's play and can learn to value and understand the child's thematic and symbolic world of play.
- The whole family gains a new internal-working-family model of what it looks and feels like to imagine, play, and create together.

Guiding Principles for Family Sessions

Below is a list of guidelines that parents need to understand regarding family sessions, and these may be covered within an initial appointment with parents. The guiding principles are as follows:

- The therapist's role in family play is more *directive*, however, choices may be offered, such as: "We have several options to play today, we can create a feeling board game, or engage in a drawing activity, or tell a story with puppets." Clarify that family play sessions, in most instances, are not free play.
- The therapist sets the parameters of the activity that can then be flexibly co-created with the parent's and child's vision for engagement with the activity.
- Parents are asked to take responsibility to provide redirection of their child's behavior, not the therapist. The exception may be if it is an in-office rule, such as not to open private desk drawers that belong to the therapist.
- The therapist must take care to keep sessions emotionally safe. Therefore, parents must agree that children are able to express themselves fully without fear of punishment or retaliation at home. This means that children need to feel safe that they will not get into trouble for sharing after leaving the session. Additionally, arguments are not continued after leaving the office.
- Everyone is treated and spoken to with respect.
- Parents and children need to be aware that if a family secret is revealed, then that secret becomes available as a therapeutic issue for the present session. Parents are also aware of the legal bounds of liability for reporting any concerns of abuse or harm to the child.
- If the child refuses to participate, that is okay, and they are never pressured or scorned.

The *Art* of Family Assessment: Beginning Stages of Therapy

This chapter is not intended to teach a thorough child and family bio-psycho-social-spiritual-cultural assessment. The reader is encouraged to seek out other resources to gain a full perspective of all the necessary components that go into a well-rounded assessment, such as in Nancy Boyd Webb's book, *Social Work Practice with Children*, Fourth Edition (2019). However, in relationship to child and family trauma, we need to establish a clear understanding of the presenting problem from all human ecology perspectives. This includes gaining a release to speak to other sources, such as teachers, school counselors, health care providers, past therapists, and so forth to better comprehend the problem. Satir (1988) indicated that sometimes we need to put on our metaphorical "detective hat" to discover what is happening within a family. In using the detective hat analogy, as we need to ponder: *What is really happening for this child? With this family? Why is there incongruency between behavior and what is spoken? Who are all the external supportive systems for this family? Are there times when this family works well together?* At other times the trauma the family is facing is more straightforward—they lost their home in the hurricane. The wisdom of assessment is that, in addition to gaining a grasp of the

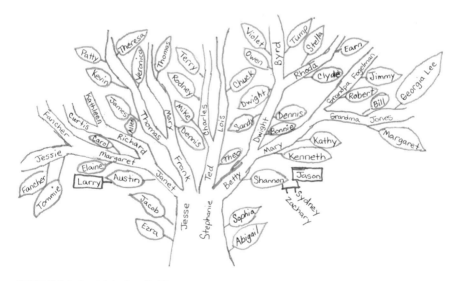

FIGURE 5.1: Sophia's Family Tree
SOURCE: USED WITH PERMISSION FROM STEPHANIE CROWLEY AND SOPHIA

family's interrelated dynamics, it is at the same time also an intervention where family change, growth, and self-awareness will happen. The following sections are some family play and expressive arts assessments that can be implemented during beginning phases of treatment.

Draw a Family Tree Genogram

When working with a child individually or with a family together, it is helpful to begin with a three-generational genogram, which has foundations in systems theory (McGoldrick, Gerson, & Petry, 2008). Therapeutic genograms are structured family system diagrams with agreed-upon symbolic representations. One of the easiest ways to do a family genogram in family play therapy sessions is to have the family members draw and then fill in an actual "tree" with branches and leaves that can represent each person. As the family may be unfamiliar with the concept of a genogram, the therapist may need to explain the reasons why a family genogram can be beneficial—if only to understand the major family support systems. As well, if the reader is unfamiliar with genograms as therapeutic tools, the McGoldrick, Gerson, & Petry (2020) book *Genograms: Assessment and Intervention* is an excellent resource for all the ins and outs of creating a genogram.

During and after the creation of the "Family Tree Art Assessment," the therapist will need to actively guide the family process. Some of the questions to consider are: *Who are all the people in this child's life who care about this child? Where do they live (local or distant)? How much access does the child have to interact with those family members? How do the parents get along, or not, with these extended relationships? Who is living and who has died whom the child was connected to? What are the emotional connections in and between relationships? What are the external systems that interface with the family (schools, church, health care providers)?* The following are suggested steps of implementation.

The Family Tree Art Assessment: Steps of Implementation

Materials and setup: Large drawing paper (18 × 24 inches is a good recommended size), colored pencils, crayons, paints, or markers of various colors, and miniature play items. Family members may be comfortable doing this activity on the playroom floor or sitting around a table. The therapist introduces the concept of a genogram to the family and explains why this will be helpful to the family play therapy process.

Step 1: Make the paper and art supplies available for the family members to select their materials for the activity.

Step 2: Family members discuss how they would like to create their "tree." For example, families usually draw a tree trunk and then draw branches for the tree. One side of the tree can be designated the mother's side of the family (right) and the other side for the father (left). The larger branches can represent the family generations, from grandparents and, if known, great-grandparents, with the smaller branches stretching to leaves representing the individual members of a family. (Note: Sometimes families sketch out the tree first in pencil and then fill in with their chosen art materials.)

Step 3: The therapist observes how the family makes decisions together, who takes the lead and who sits back, and so forth. The process of the activity is just as important as the final product.

Step 4: Once the genogram is completed, the therapist can then have the family step back and share what they learned or found helpful about the process. The therapist asks questions about the interrelated family emotional connections, such as who is close or distant from whom and how do they interface with each other. The goal is to understand the varied family member perspectives. Caring and supportive relationships are among a family's greatest strengths and sources of resilience.

Gil (2015a) suggested an additional step of having family members pick a miniature figure (often used in sandtray processes) that represents their thoughts and feelings about each family member on the genogram. This assists to deepen awareness and insight. One way I have guided the session is to invite family members to take turns selecting miniatures to represent each person on the genogram, and then to share why they chose the figure they did. This continues until everyone has had a turn. For example, in one family session, I invited each family member to take turns selecting a miniature that represented the thoughts or feelings of the different people drawn on the family tree. The child found a goose that she said reminded her of her mother because she was always "like a mother goose looking after us." For the father, she chose a blue monster with a smile on its face and said that she picked it because her "Dad may sometimes seem scary, but deep down he is a good guy." The child chose a little puppy dog for herself and stated, "I like to play." It can be helpful to revisit the family tree during a subsequent session, because the genogram can be seen anew when distance is provided.

THE FAMILY TREE ART ASSESSMENT

The need for the therapist to complete their own genogram has long been advocated to grow self-awareness and to help in identifying personal biases and countertransferences that could potentially arise in therapy sessions. With this in mind, I invite you to reserve some time in your schedule to engage in the following practice exercise: The Family Tree Art Assessment.

THE PRACTICE

The Family Tree Art Assessment

In this exercise, you are asked to adapt the steps that are listed above under the *Genogram Steps of Implementation* and then "draw" your own family tree. Try to fill in the diagram for at least three generations (more if you are able). Consider how your family's generations have impacted you and your current family system. As an added step, you can then select miniatures that represent the varied thoughts and feelings related to the family members. If you're comfortable, share with a partner your Family Tree Art Assessment and selected miniatures. Explain any insights that you gained from the process, and how those insights are relatable to you in the present. Alternatively, you can privately journal some of your insights.

COLLABORATIVE FAMILY TIMED DRAWING ASSESSMENT

The family timed collaborative drawing is adapted from the Collaborative Drawing Technique developed by Smith (1991) and is a valuable tool to assess family dynamics, as it gets family members out of their left-brain thinking and into the right-brain hemisphere processes. The family is asked to collaborate on a spontaneous drawing, which can include even the youngest of children. Indeed, one of my most successful family assessments included a three-year-old child. As well, since the activity is completed in silence, I have found that even the most reserved of adolescents find it a favorable process to engage. This assessment can be a valuable activity for information resourcing and can usually take up the whole session to complete. For this reason, the richness of doing and processing the assessment also ends up as an intervention of therapeutic change too.

Collaborative Family Timed Drawing Assessment: Steps of Implementation

Materials and setup: Large drawing paper, various colored markers, second-hand timer, and table for activity. Some families may prefer to sit together on the playroom floor.

Step 1: Family members pick one marker each. They are advised that they will be using the same marker through the whole activity. Write a key on the corner of the paper: Red=Mom, Blue=Dad, Green=Child. This will help you see immediately who drew what.

Step 2: The therapist is the "timer" for each "round," which is timed in seconds progressing as follows: 30, 20, 15, 10, 5.

Step 3: Each member takes turns, with the youngest going first, and the therapist guides the activity by saying "START" and then "STOP . . . NEXT" for the next member to begin. *Drawing Tip*: It is helpful for each family member to draw on the paper in the same directional "front" perspective. This is best accomplished by turning the drawing toward each family member when it's his or her turn to draw.

Step 4: Once completed, the image is processed as explained in the following sections.

Further instructions: The therapist answers all questions and clarifications about the activity before beginning. However, the therapist also advises that there is no talking until the activity is over. When the therapist says "STOP," the drawer must stop drawing, and the next family member quickly begins when the therapist says, "START." It is helpful to keep the pace moving swiftly so that members do not have too much time to plan out what they are drawing (thus keeping them out of left-brain processing), which can allow for spontaneous images to emerge.

Therapist questions and observations before, during, and after: All along, the therapist is taking mental notes related to family interactions and how the drawing takes shape. Did anyone break the rules and talk during the process, or draw out of turn? Did they draw a joint picture together? Or did members draw several unrelated and disconnected images? Who added on to another's drawing? Who interfered or scratched out another's image? Who used the least amount of space on the paper? Who used the most space? Did anyone write words? Who kept drawing after the therapist said STOP?

Processing the image: Once completed, the drawing is then set up at the eye level of the youngest member, so members are no longer looking down at the drawing. This helps to change perspective. At this point, the family is asked to stand back at a distance from the image and quietly take in what they see. Betensky (1987) calls the distancing process "intentional looking," and this can be a moment when clients are able to become aware of some of the unconscious, embedded messages that were "deposited, half-knowingly," in the drawing (p. 158). The therapist asks the question: "What do you see?"

Members then describe exactly what they see in the drawing—what are the scenes or objects. To focus this task, the therapist asks each member to begin the sentence with "I see . . ." For example, "I see a swing set." "I see sand and an umbrella with us sitting on beach chairs under the umbrella." The "I see" helps to move members away from potential critical judgment of the image, as well as taking note of the image symbols present. The next question statement is: "I feel . . ." This is when each person states how they feel when they observe each of the scenes or objects. For example, a mother might say, "I feel happy when looking at the beach scene of us sitting together relaxing." The therapist then expands on the questions following the statements that are provided. Additionally, some of the therapist questions and observations noted above can then be asked to expand the conversation. Even questions such as "What was your favorite part of doing this activity?" or "What was your least favorite part?" can bring up some revealing answers. One young child asked his mother if they could do this drawing again at home together.

COLLABORATIVE FAMILY TIMED DRAWING ASSESSMENT

As this activity requires skill building, it is recommended that therapists practice in role-playing enactments with an arranged group of peers or non-client family or volunteers prior to working with a client family. The task of implementing this activity requires the therapist's attention on many different levels, and ideally, if the family size is greater than three, it would do well to have a co-therapist to assist with the intervention. With the above section in mind, I invite you to plan a time to engage in the following practice exercise: Collaborative Family Timed Drawing Assessment.

THE PRACTICE

Collaborative Family Timed Drawing Assessment

Coordinate a group of peers, relatives, or even a real volunteer family to role-play a session where you will practice the Collaborative Family Timed Drawing together. You will take on the role of therapist while your volunteers, peers for example, form themselves into a mock family, taking on different family member roles: mother, father, children. Gather the materials and follow the steps as described in the paragraphs above from start to finish, where you will be guiding the "family" as you time them. When the drawing is completed, tape the drawing to a wall, and have your group step back from the drawing to observe it and then answer the questions as listed in the above instructions. Note that, even though this is a role-play activity, you will still need to be sensitive to the thoughts and feelings that arise during the processing of the drawing, because sometimes deep feelings can emerge even in a role-play. To add to your learning experience, ask your volunteers to provide you with feedback regarding what they thought was helpful and what might not have worked. Use this as an opportunity to build your skills for this activity.

WHEN FAMILY EXPRESSIVE AND PLAY THERAPY SESSIONS DO NOT GO AS PLANNED

As a final note to this chapter, I want to circle back to emphasize that family systems are extremely complex. For that reason, child practitioners in the expressive and play therapy fields who choose to work with the whole family must engage in comprehending the range of family therapy literature, education, training, assessment, and techniques of intervention. As well, even if a therapist has determined to begin by seeing the child individually, it must be remembered that the child is still connected to a whole family of interlocking emotional networks. We need to get a handle on the structural formation of the family—alignments and subsystems, how decisions are made, who holds the power in the family, how attachments are formed, how intimacy is managed, how conflicts are handled, and so forth. A solid working knowledge of family systems theory is a must. This is because it is very easy for new practitioners in the field (seasoned ones, too!) to very quickly and naively get triangulated in over their heads in daunting and complicated family dynamics—think child custody battles. Unfortunately, I've been caught off guard on more than one occasion. The following case scenario is an example of how easily a therapist can be blindsided within a family session and shows how we can draw upon our knowledge of family systems to make our best effort within the moment to accommodate.

"No one can come into MY family and tell me what to do!"
Who has the Power in the Family?

Soon after seeing a mother and her 13-year-old daughter, Susan, in therapy sessions, the play therapist, Carol, felt that she was not getting the whole picture on the young teen's problem. Susan had been referred from the school counselor because she was expressing feelings of depression and difficulty in making meaningful friendships. Both the mother and daughter mirrored each other very closely in physical appearance, dress, and personality, which was very soft-spoken, timid, and shy. Susan was an only child living with her mother and father, and Susan's maternal grandmother lived nearby. A first clue about the family's home dynamics was a comment from the mother that the father did not like the grandmother coming to the house.

Further assessment with Susan concluded that she had a low-grade, ongoing sadness that could potentially be diagnosed as dysthymic disorder, but did not meet all the diagnostic criteria. She was assessed as not suicidal. Carol evaluated that a cognitive-behavioral play therapy (Knell, 2011) approach would be helpful, as Susan's perceptions of herself were skewed, and this intervention addressed some of the irrational thinking. To help in that, Carol gave Susan some things that she could do at home to bridge some of the new ideas and behaviors into action. Her mother agreed that she would be a support at home, too. However, Carol thought she was missing something in the assessment and soon asked if the father would be willing to come to a session. She was hoping to understand his perspective on his daughter's behavior. The mother called Carol the day before the appointment and said that the father had agreed to attend, but that was all she said, nothing else. Carol was unprepared for what happened next.

At the next session, the family was sitting sullenly in the waiting room when Carol invited them into the office. Both the mother and daughter were quiet and staring down at the floor. Carol thanked the father for coming and said that she was hoping he could help her understand more about how Susan could be helped to feel better in her life. At that point, the father spoke up in a rage, and pointing and shaking his finger at Carol, he yelled, "*No one has the right to come into my home and tell me what to do!*" He was not just angry. He was furious. He went on for several minutes fuming and shaking his pointer finger directly at Carol. Carol sat quiet and attentive, consciously thinking about her body posture and giving the father direct eye contact. She maintained a calm and nondefensive stance and gave him space to vent.

When he was finished, Carol allowed a moment of silence and rest. Carol realized she needed to model respect if she was going to gain respect in return. Matching his serious urgency of the moment and with sincerity, she looked the father in the eye and said, "*You* are right, I absolutely do not have the right to come into your home and tell you what to do! And, it shows a lot about how much you even care about your daughter that you chose to take your time to come here today. Thank you for doing that." The father immediately relaxed and sat back in his chair, and the mother and daughter looked up from the floor. There was still more joining and work to do during the session, but Carol had an "in" to meet this family where they were at. After the father understood that Carol was not there to subvert his authority in the family system, Carol was then able to gain his perspective of the problem and his hopes for his daughter's happiness.

Case Reflection

In this above case scenario, Carol realized that she had initially failed to understand from the mother about the father's perspective of Susan attending therapy, prior to the session. Asking the question about the father's perspective on therapy might have better prepared Carol for the family session: "What does your husband think about Susan attending therapy?" Well-accomplished family therapist Harry Aponte advised that we need to understand the structure in the family system—especially who holds the power or *force*. Force, as defined by Aponte (1976) is the "relative influence of each member on the outcome of an activity" (p. 434). Family therapy principles help us to distinguish between a range of boundaries from flexible to rigid. In observation of how varied boundaries in the family can manifest, Aponte observed, "The father who maintains all the power in his family is another example of rigid boundaries as he refuses to allow anyone else in the family to share his executive functions" (p. 440).

Carol missed seeing Susan in the larger context of the family system. The lesson is that we can offer new ways of helping our child clients, but if those who have the power within the system are not on board or in agreement, then all the good that may transpire in therapy sessions may be circumvented by those who hold the force of outcome. So, what to do in that moment of intense barrage? Obviously, the ventilation of strong feelings by the father needed time and space, and Carol needed to be patient and listen. As well, from the wisdom of Harry Aponte, we need to learn how to respectfully *join* a family system. To do that, we need to come from a place of sincerity and authenticity. Entering the family system and building any sense of alliance means starting where the family is at. In this case scenario, the father was the head of the household, and that needed to be respected and handled with sensitivity. Such situations in therapy can be *make-it-or-break-it moments*. This means that if some alliance with the father was not gained, the child and mother might not feel safe to continue coming to appointments, and risk the reprisal of the father.

We now turn to Chapter 6, where we deepen child and family healing through middle phase to closure types of expressive and family play therapy interventions.

Chapter 6

DEEPENING FAMILY BONDS THROUGH EXPRESSIVE AND PLAY THERAPY INTERVENTIONS

"A nurturing, healing home smells as if bread were baking even when nothing is in the oven. A true home feels as if people were singing and dancing even when everyone is away.
When there is silence, a visitor can feel and hear the OM in it."

John Heider, *The Tao of Daily Living* (2000, p. 109)

This chapter builds upon Chapter 5, which laid the overall foundations for the use of expressive arts and play therapy with families. It provided some ideas for how to approach the beginning phases of assessment and family treatment strategies. This chapter moves the therapy into the middle stages of reliance, integration, and action to deepen child and family connections and healing.

FAMILY SESSION PROGRESSION: CHECK-IN, MIDDLE TIME, CLOSING

Each family session should follow a predictable rhythm of progression, which promotes a safe holding environment of containment and temenos. In this, there is a ritual of opening or check-in, a middle phase of time together, and a strategy for closing the session. One way I have opened a family session is to provide a "listening" shell, such as a conch shell or other similar shells that can be pressed to the ear and "listened" to, to hear the "ocean." These types of shells require that one must be quiet and focus intently to hear the sound.

I prefer the shells that have smooth edges. Thus, the metaphor of the shell, as it is passed around to the members of the family, reminds members to focus and listen intently to each other. The "rule" is that whoever has the shell has the "floor," and others need to listen and not interrupt until the member passes the shell or says it is okay to give feedback to what was said. Keep in mind the overriding rule that everyone has the right to pass and not say anything (refer to Chapter 5 for a review of the family guidelines). The middle phase of each session will hold the focal point of the family intervention, which is the primary focus of this chapter.

The end of the session may be briefer than the opening, depending on time left in the session. It is the responsibility of the therapist to monitor the time to leave enough room for closing. Sometimes, I have closed the session with each family member summing up their session experience or how they are feeling in the moment in one to three words. For younger children, this can be adapted to *sing* their feeling word. This works well when parents may be more spontaneous and comfortable letting their guard down. As well, each family member can make up a closing goodbye song to the tune of "Frère Jacques," also known in English as, "Are you sleeping?" The therapist can begin by modeling the song and singing a feeling: "*I am feeling, I am feeling . . . very happy, very happy. Thank you for coming, thank you for coming. See you next week.*" This song tune (or any other) can also be used as an opening ritual of reconnecting during the beginning check-in. In this way, there is a song for opening check-in and a song for closing that might be especially engaging for young children. Thus, structuring family sessions to have a clear opening check-in, middle phase, and closing provides a secure, familiar space for children and families to flourish.

A CLOSURE SONG

With the above section family closing song "Frère Jacques" in mind, I invite you to take a few minutes to engage in the following practice exercise: A Closure Song.

THE PRACTICE

A Closure Song

In this exercise, I encourage you to take a moment to adapt the "Frère Jacques" song to your own words and feelings. Beginning with the words "I am feeling" is a good fit for the tune of the song. And, if you are not familiar with this song, a quick Internet search will provide several options to listen. Likewise, you may know of some other songs that you can adapt to a goodbye closing or even as a ritual "hello" check-in song at the beginning of the session. Practice singing the song to yourself, or ask a partner to sing along with you.

Changing Family Story Scripts through Puppet Play

Puppet play has long been used with children in play therapy sessions as an intervention. Gil (1994) uses puppets as tools for conducting family assessments. In my playroom I have a puppet theater that children sit behind and then tell their stories through the curtain. Puppets provide a way for children to engage their problems and at the same time they provide a distancing from the immediate problem. I have used puppets in different ways, from introducing myself to a shy child to puppet child interviews (the puppet asks the child questions), to having children using the puppets to practice new behaviors. Sometimes I have used the puppets to help children write new life story scripts.

Structural Family Therapy is interested in paying attention to the interpersonal transactional processes among family members, and it is aimed at intervening to create healthier patterns of communication (Liebman, Minuchin, Baker, & Rosman, 1976). The therapist can initiate family *enactments*— a term Minuchin used to denote having the family re-create in the therapy room an example of an interactional transaction that might have happened at home. The interactional patterns of relating among family members tends to stay fairly predictable, regardless of the issue at hand. The majority of our daily patterns of communication—whether within our personal relationships, work environments, or other areas of contact—are mostly old and worn-out scripts often passed down through generations. Some work for us in positive ways, while others can create and re-create unhealthy life interactions that can hinder us from reaching our highest potential. Changing the scripts that no longer serve us takes a concentrated effort of self-examination. A next step in therapy might be to facilitate new scripts for how members can interact and respond to each other. When including young children in sessions, we can create enactment through the use of puppets. The following composite case study showed how I worked with a father, mother, and her two daughters to create new scripts of relating.

Presenting Problem

The mother had originally sought therapy for her two daughters to assist with improving their relationship. A few weeks later, the father, Tim, was laid off from work, resulting in severe emotional stress. This created increased family arguments and discord between the parents, the parents toward the children, and between the children themselves, whose own strained relationship was exacerbated by the emotional stress of the parents. The mother, Linda, was a stay-at-home mom with the two daughters, Mia and Lilly, ages 8 and 10 years, respectively. The mother was feeling pressure to find employment, and the children's grades in school were dropping. Tim was both depressed and angry about the layoff. Additionally, the home conflicts often carried over into the school environment, where the children would treat each other antagonistically.

The parents were at a loss about how to handle the problem, and consequently were either playing referee between the children or yelling to try to get them to change their behavior. At the same time, the parents were angry with each other, and the mother privately described her relationship with her husband as "drifting apart." The family was stuck in negative patterns of communication that caused a perpetual state of tension in the household. This was the backdrop for the following family session, which was in the reliance stage of therapy. Although Tim had attended an initial intake with Lilly, this was his first session together with the children.

I am acutely aware of the unhealthy patterning of behavior and communication that can often be resistant to change. However, I have discovered that families and individuals *can* break away from old patterns of communication, revise their roles, and enjoy life more if they can rewrite their habitual scripts. During the following session, I listened closely to each family member, and how they played out an enactment through the puppets—who said what to whom, how it was said, how it was responded to, and so on. Essentially, I was listening for their internalized and repetitive blueprints of relating, as revealed through the puppet story.

Materials and Instructions

A variety of puppets were placed together on a table for family members to choose. Since much of their stress happened in the evenings after school, I directed the family "Use your imaginations to tell a puppet story about *a* family during the week after school, from the time the kids get home from school all the way through until bedtime. (I emphasized the word "a" family versus "your" family to provide some distance from the intensity.) Although the family was advised they could decide their own roles as puppets, both girls grabbed the alligator puppet and handed it to the father and said, "You are the father." Linda chose a black-and-white cow puppet and said she would be the mother, and Lilly chose the sad-looking doggy and Mia, a smaller donkey with a sad face, and they decided to be the puppet children. Below is a transcription of one portion of the story, which shows a glimpse into how the typical family patterns of transactions normally played out.

> SIDE NOTE: Sometimes the families or children do this through the puppet theater, during which I might record the puppet show for us all to review together afterward. If possible, I highly recommend this option, as it gives the family a chance to step back and see themselves from another perspective. Due to confidentiality, the recording is done with the parents' permission on one parent's cell phone. That way the parent has the option to immediately delete the recording after it is reviewed, and it removes any concern of the recording storage. However, standard documentation of what transpired in the session is noted.

The Puppet Family Story

Cow (mother): Hi, Donkey and Doggy, how did school go today?

Donkey (Mia): I have a lot of homework.

Cow (mother): How about you, Doggy, do you have homework too?

Doggy (Lilly): Yes, can I watch some TV now?

Alligator (father): (in a firm voice) No, you need to start your homework! If you don't start it now you will be up late doing your homework. You can watch TV after you are done.

Doggy (Lilly): But I am tired, and I want to watch TV. I promise to do my homework.

Cow (mother): (to Alligator) I think it is okay if the kids watch TV now.

Alligator (father): (to Cow, in angry tone) You always do that. Anytime I try to get the kids to do something, you always try to undermine what I am saying.

(The Doggy puppet then hits the Donkey.)

Donkey (Mia): (to the Doggy) Ouch, you hit me! The Donkey hits the Doggy back.

Alligator (father): (Angry tone) Stop that! Go to your room!

The Donkey and Doggy move across the room.

Mother (out of role): The mother puts down her puppet exasperated and says, "This is what happens at home. When this happens, I try not to say anything because I know that it will only get worse. The girls are always picking on each other."

Therapist: "What happens next? How does it work out after the girls are in their rooms?"

Mother: "Usually things calm down, but we never talk about it."

Father: "Then they will have to start their homework."

Therapist: "How about we go back to the puppet story now, so we can see how the rest of the evening goes afterschool until bedtime?"

I try to pull it back into the metaphor of play as the session can easily turn to complaints about the children, thus potentially alienating them from the process. The family then continues with the puppet story, which can be viewed as a parallel of how the family typically engages after school. They continued the story to show dinnertime, after-dinner cleanup, bathtime, getting ready for bed, and the ritual for saying good night. After they were finished, I asked them to talk about the story process. The mother advised, "Well, this is pretty much how it goes after school." We then moved to the next step of the family puppet intervention.

Changing the Family Story Script

I asked if they would be willing to try something new. I then directed the conversation to a discussion on Shakespeare, and plays, and movies, and storytelling. I shared with them the line from William Shakespeare's play *As You Like*

It: "All the world's a stage, and all the men and women merely players." The parents were familiar with this quote, but not the children, and I explained to them how Shakespeare lived a long time ago and more about what he meant by those words. The children understood how story characters needed to memorize their lines by reading from a script. Using Shakespeare's metaphor, I asked the family members to see themselves as performers acting out scenes in a play, and to view their communications as memorized and rehearsed lines. I explained that in order to create change, they needed to *change their scripts.*

They were then asked to use the example of the puppets' after-school problem related to homework and TV time to rewrite their scripts of what their puppets would say to each other that would create a "happy ending." The "happy ending" motif is central to this exercise because it helps to push the interactions toward resolution. I said, "Let's write the story together on paper, and I will be the secretary writing it down, and then we can tell the puppet story again using the new agreed-upon script."

To again distance the family, I suggested we start the story by saying, "Once upon a time there was a puppet family, and this is what happened after school." I then suggested that they could start with what the Cow (mother) puppet first said, "Hi, Donkey and Doggy, how did school go today?" They endeavored to find fresh ways to negotiate compromise and proffer respect, and I wrote down their new *lines* for the puppet story and when finished, we staged a "rehearsal."

Puppet Family Story New "Script" Rehearsal "Do-Over"
Cow (mother): Hi, Donkey and Doggy, how did school go today?
Alligator (father): Hi, how did school go?
Donkey (Mia): Good, but I have a lot of homework.
Doggy (Lilly): Yes, can I watch some TV now?
Alligator (father): When do you think a good time would be to do your homework?
Donkey (Mia): Can I watch some TV first? I'm tired and need a break.
Alligator (father): That's okay, but I need to know when you think is a good time to start homework. Let's look at the clock.
Doggy (Lilly) and Donkey (Mia): (They act like they are looking at the clock . . . they check the father's watch on his wrist. Everyone laughs.) How about 4:30?

Alligator (father): That's good. We'll turn off the television at that time and start.

Cow (mother): How about a snack? I can make some popcorn.

Doggy (Lilly) and Donkey (Mia): Yes, mom, that would be so good!

During the following appointment 10 days later (the father did not attend this appointment), the mother shared that there were fewer instances of conflict and stated, "We all worked hard this week to constantly rewrite our scripts." The task also had an unexpected result: The children's attitudes toward each other in school also changed, and they began to see each other as useful allies instead of competitors. Sometimes I reframe to families that we can always try a "do-over" if an interaction does not go well. There is always time to say, "Hey, that conversation did not go well, so let's try a do-over." This helps to create a new script.

> SIDE NOTE: It was clear the parents disagreed with how the children should be disciplined and tasks managed, which was exacerbated by the father's anxiety related to his job loss. I later suggested to the parents that it might be helpful for them to seek couples counseling to deal with some of the current stressors and to discuss their different views of parenting. Although I do couples counseling, sometimes it is best to recommend a separate therapist to do the couples work. One benefit is to have another therapist who can assess the couple's relationship, and this removes the potential of getting triangulated into the parental dynamics and being seen as taking sides, which can then jeopardize the family play therapy time together.

REWRITING INTERPERSONAL SCRIPTS

With the above section in mind, I invite you to take a few minutes to engage in the following practice exercise: Rewriting Interpersonal Scripts.

THE PRACTICE

Rewriting Interpersonal Scripts

In this exercise, think of the last time you had a conversation with someone—a coworker, a husband or wife, a child, a family member—that did not go as you had hoped. Maybe you felt uncomfortable during or after the conversation. Consider that you may have habitual and patterned ways of responding to communication with others. Call to mind the uncomfortable conversation, and consider how you would rewrite your lines and how you would respond. Take some time to journal your new script. Imagine how this could be helpful during future interactions.

COLLABORATIVE FAMILY FEELING BOARD GAME

Another expressive family art and play therapy method is to work with a family to create a Collaborative Family Feeling Board Game. This activity is useful as

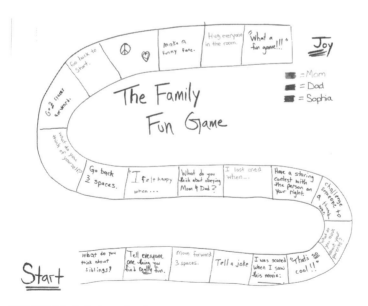

FIGURE 6.1: Collaborative Family Feeling Board Game entitled: "The Family Fun Game"

SOURCE: COURTESY OF THE CROWLEY FAMILY. USED WITH PERMISSION.

a tool to help increase family understanding and bonds, and provides a way for everyone to be heard.

Materials: Large white poster board, markers, dice, and tokens to move through the spaces of the board. Sometimes families can make their own tokens out of paper (origami figures), clay, or they can choose a miniature. In the following steps, the therapist can direct the family by having them take turns first to create the basic formation of the game.

Collaborative Family Feeling Board Game: Steps of Implementation

Step 1: Decide where the family is more comfortable creating the board game. Some families want to use the children's table, and others prefer to sit on the floor around the poster board.

Step 2: I usually ask the youngest to go first by choosing a corner where we write the word "start" and designating a different corner as "finish." At the finish, I sometimes have them write a word that represents their vision for a positive family goal or outcome for what they are working on. For example, maybe they would like to see their family "happier" or "at peace." An alternative is that they can draw a symbol that represents a quality of what they want—so a "sun" or "rainbow" may represent the happiness. Some children may like this better.

Step 3: Ask a family member to draw a path that goes from start to finish. This line is then double lined—meaning drawing a second line that parallels the first line but provides some space between them. Then have them draw lines to make spaces that the tokens will land in once the game is made. Children usually understand this, as they are used to playing board games. Sometimes I show them a store-bought board game in the office that gives them a visual reminder of what that looks like. It is important to make the spaces large enough so that family members have enough room to write or draw inside them. The large poster board allows for several spaces to be drawn so that members can fill in a few different spaces, allowing for varied idea options. I help to guide this portion of the drawing, especially with the younger children who may need more guidance.

Step 4: Each family member chooses a color to write in the spaces—use a key to designate who is green, yellow, blue, and so on (for example, mom=blue, child=red, father=green, and so forth.). Once they choose their color, I ask them to stick with it, as this helps to give a quick visual reminder who drew or wrote what in the game. However, if they need another color, of course that works, too, but I just add it to the key, such as child=red and purple.

Step 5: Have family members fill in the spaces with doing/thinking/feeling questions or comments and game-type add-ons. The game add-ons help to give some distance from the questions and can be fun for children. This is a time when members work independently to fill in the spaces and they are asked not to comment on what others are doing until the game is completed. Members also have the option of drawing a symbol to represent a thought or feeling instead of writing words.

Examples of feeling questions: "Say a time you felt sad," or "I felt sad when . . ." (the family member completes the sentence).

Examples of doing: Sometime these can be silly (we need to have fun during the game, too) such as, "Act like a monkey," or "Tell a joke," or "Give a high-five or hug to someone in the room." *Examples of thinking:* "What do you think about divorce?" or "What do you think homework?" *Examples of game add-ons:* "Go forward two spaces" or "Go back to start," or "lose a turn."

Step 6: Have family members come to a consensus for a game title.

Step 7: When the game is completed, spend some time having the family members share what they wrote inside the boxes. This way everyone can get a good sense of the game and what to expect before playing.

Step 8: Play the game with dice and answer questions for each.

Further instructions: After the game is completed, the therapist can give the family a choice: The game can be played as a family and the therapist can observe, or sometimes the therapist can play along. Both ways work well. When playing the game, if an adult gets to the end of the game first, I have the parent (or myself) go back to the start of the game. This means that the game is not over until all the children have completed the game. The game also acts as a buffer when family members are addressing some of the difficult content. If one parent is absent during the session, sometimes the game can be bridged to home, and the family can then play the game together at home, thereby including the absent parent in the therapy.

One note of caution: It is wise for the therapist to assess whether sending the board game home with an absent parent would be in the best interests of the child or children, as the therapist will not be present to hold the containment of safety. It is possible some strong feelings may be expressed that would be more appropriately facilitated during an office session. Again, this will need to be a question of the therapist's clinical judgment related to the presenting problem. And of course the absent parent can also be invited to another session to play the game.

Case Vignette: Spill Your Heart Out Game!

Presenting Problem

The mother and father were going through a bitter and painful divorce, and the children—Shelly, aged 6 years and Adele, aged 9 years—were caught in the middle. Both children were exhibiting somatic symptoms of severe migraines and bellyaches. As is the case in high-conflict divorces, parents often desire for the children to choose sides, and may tell the children information that is beyond the scope of what young children can understand, or may be considered highly inappropriate to share, such as extramarital affairs or drug use by a parent. The children were also being asked by both parents which parent they wanted to live with. The mother initially brought the children to therapy, and over time the father was able to attend some of the sessions (separate from the mother). During the beginning stages of therapy, the mother was refusing to allow her children to see the father. The separation from the father was very upsetting and angering for the children, and these emotions were directed toward the mother.

As the sessions with the mother and children became heated and argumentative and therefore unproductive, I suggested creating a collaborative family board game, which they all agreed to do. Following the outline in the steps of implementation (see above), a board game was created that the children then titled, "The Spill Your Heart Out Game." They then played the game together, which seemed to defuse and calm some of the underlying anger. The game questions and comments assisted in allowing the children and mother to better hear each other's thoughts and feelings.

The children decided they wanted their father to come to the office, because they wanted to create their own board game with their father. Note that, because the mother had been part of creating the board game, the game could not be shown to the father without the mother's release, since her thoughts and feelings were attached to the board game, and not just the children's words. So in this case, a new board game would need to be created.

Discussion: Even the most collaborative of divorces—where parents make their children's emotional health a priority and do not discuss adult matters with children—can be devastating for children (Wonders, 2019). However, high-conflict divorce cases are extremely traumatizing for children. As in many divorce cases, sometimes the children can be the more mature voices in the mix. The children presented in this case example decided that a solution to the custody battle was the need to create a known schedule for when they could see their father. During the playing of the children's customized Spill Your Heart Out Game, they were able to tell their mother their feelings and the therapy held a containment for the mother to sincerely listen to her children's needs. It was also during this session that she agreed the father could come to a therapy session with the children.

COLLABORATIVE FAMILY FEELING BOARD GAME

It is recommended that the Collaborative Family Feeling Board Game be implemented first with volunteer peers, friends, or family to practice a few times prior to using it within a family session. With the above section in mind, I invite you to engage in the following practice exercise.

THE PRACTICE

Collaborative Family Feeling Board Game

Coordinate a group of peers, relatives, or even an actual volunteer family to role-play a session where you will practice creating a Collaborative Family Feeling Board Game together. You will take on the role of therapist while your volunteers, peers for example, form themselves into a "mock" family taking on different family member roles: mother, father, children. Gather the materials and follow the steps of implementation as described in the paragraphs above. You will be guiding the "family" through each step. Ask members to work quietly, or at least not to comment on what others are writing in the spaces until the game is completed. When the game is completed, take some time to have each family member share what they did in each square. After everyone has shared, ask what they would title the game. Now play the game together. Note that, even though this is a role-play activity, you will still need to be sensitive to the thoughts and feelings that arise during the playing of the game, as sometimes deep feelings can emerge. To add to your learning experience, ask your friends to provide you with feedback about what they thought was helpful and what might not have worked. Use this as an opportunity to build your clinical skills.

CREATING A FAMILY MOTTO

Much of our work with family systems is to address the distancing and disconnection within relationships. My inspiration for "Creating a Family Motto" happened when I was visiting Deer Park Monastery in Escondido, California, and the monks and nuns were in the midst of creating a banner to carry as they participated in the San Diego Pride Parade. The banner with its motto, "Together We Are One" (refer to Figure 6.2) struck me as heartfelt way to unify a community. The Merriam-Webster dictionary defines the word "motto" as "a short expression of a guiding principle." In this, I considered how we can help

FIGURE 6.2: Creating a Group Motto: Deer Park Monastery, Escondido, CA
SOURCE: AUTHOR. USED WITH PERMISSION FROM THE MONASTICS AT DEER PARK MONASTERY.

our families to create their own family motto that could set a tone of building family bonds through a unifying guiding principle. In some situations, this could be a vision for how they would like to see hopeful change within family connections. Likewise, this is a great group therapy activity to support members to bond under a unifying principle. One family experiencing a crisis created the motto, "We've Got This!".

Creating a Family Motto: Steps of Implementation

Materials: Large poster board or large drawing paper, markers, washable paints, paint brushes, glitter, glue, and other art items available for clients to choose.

Step 1: Introduce the idea to a family or group about creating a family motto that can act as a guiding principle of need or desire. This is a time of brainstorming, and the therapist can write down the ideas suggested. This might take some time, and it is important for all members to pull together to agree on the motto.

Step 2: Next, decide how the words will be written on the poster board and in what style. Bubble art? Maybe each member can take a turn writing or painting a word.

Step 3: After the words are written, family members can then put their handprints on the poster as an affirmation of agreement. This can happen by tracing the hands with a marker or using washable paints. The hand can be painted and then placed flat on the poster board. Of course, there will need to be a way for clients to wash their hands afterward.

Step 4: Discuss with the family where they would like to place their new family motto creation. It is recommended this be in a common household area where everyone can see it often as a daily reminder.

THE PRACTICE

Creating a Family or Group Motto

Creating a Family or Group Motto can be an enjoyable and creative activity to do together with family or friends. Coordinate a group of peers, relatives, or even an actual volunteer family to role-play a session where you will practice creating this activity. Gather the recommended materials and begin by brainstorming a collective motto that all can agree on. This might take some time. Follow the rest of the steps of implementation for this activity as listed above until you have a final motto. Process with your group their experiences and ask for feedback regarding what they thought was helpful and what might not have worked. Use this as an opportunity to build your clinical skills.

FAMILY BLOCK FEELING STACKING GAME

This family game was adapted from the wooden stacking block game Jenga, and there are a variety of similar wooden stacking block games that can be bought and adapted for this activity. Once the chosen stacking set is acquired, the therapist will then need to customize a set for therapeutic use. It is recommended to begin by separating the set into two piles, one that will be kept blank and the other that will be used to write a variety of general questions. The questions can include general getting-to-know-you questions such as, "What is your mother's favorite color? What is yours?" Other questions can assess for thoughts and feelings, such as, "Name three wishes," or "What do you think about before you fall asleep?" or "Or if you could change one thing, what would it be?" The blank blocks are kept for the children and parents to write their own questions. I have used this activity often, and one of the benefits is that it can be a quick activity that does not require a lengthy process to organize and make, and can work well when there is limited time during a session.

Family Block Feeling Stacking Game, Steps of Implementation

Step 1: Have the blocks available on a table, or if the family chooses, this can be done on the playroom floor, but it will need a solid foundation for the blocks to be set upon.

Step 2: Stack the blocks by threes on top of each other, alternating diagonally to create a tower using all the blocks.

Step 3: The youngest goes first and pulls out a block from the tower. If the block has a question, the child then answers the question, or they can pass. If the block is blank, they have an option to write their own question on the block. At that point they can ask another member to answer the question.

Step 4: After the question is answered, the block is then placed on top of the tower to build it higher, and the next family member takes a turn. The fun part of the game is that, as it grows taller, the stack becomes more challenging until a block is pulled and the stack tumbles. The family decides to continue the game or to stop the game and move to a different activity.

THE PRACTICE

Creating a Family Block Feeling Stacking Game

Creating a Family Block Feeling Stacking Game can be an enjoyable and creative activity and the time and effort to create it can pay off tenfold in the playroom. A quick search on the Internet will easily find a wooden block stacking game, or some department and craft stores may have one in the toy section. Brainstorm a list of questions that you think would be helpful and important to elicit during a family session, and then write those questions on 50 percent of the blocks and keep the others blank so that family members can write their own questions. Once you are done, you are ready to play! It is recommended that you initially play with a group of willing volunteers just to get the swing of the game. To add to your learning experience, ask your volunteers to provide you with feedback about what they thought was helpful and what might not have worked. Enjoy!

Chapter 7

NATURE AS "CO-THERAPIST" IN EXPRESSIVE ARTS AND PLAY THERAPIES

*"The best remedy for those who are afraid, lonely or unhappy is
to go outside, somewhere where they can be quiet, alone with the
heavens, nature and God.
Because only then does one feel that all is as it should be and that God
wishes to see people happy, amidst the simple beauty of nature."*

Anne Frank, *The Diary of a Young Girl*

Since the inception of humankind, we have evolved closely with the earth. We depend on it to survive and nurture us, but we also have an inherent need to connect with the earth at a personal level. Wilson (1993) named our deep-seated sense of attachment with the earth the biophilia hypothesis, which speaks to our pervasive attraction, or craving for "emotional affiliation" (p. 31) with nature. Norwegian philosopher Arne Naess called this innate drive to connect with the earth our *Ecological Self,* as cited by Macy and Gahbler (2010), and they further described the Ecological Self as the "radical interrelatedness of all life forms. . . . Deep ecology broadens one's sense of identity and responsibility, freeing us to experience what Naess calls the ecological self" (p. 67). Kellert (1993) elaborated that our "human dependence on nature extends far beyond the simple issues of material and physical sustenance to encompass the human craving for aesthetic, intellectual, cognitive, and even spiritual meaning and satisfaction" (p. 20). Any time we are feeling attuned with the natural world we are connecting to our biophilic self. Montgomery and Courtney (2015) imagined that we connect to our primordial essence when feeling ". . . a gentle breeze on the skin, anticipating the taste and texture of apples as they are harvested, and enjoying the scent of a bouquet of lilacs" these primary experiences are "sensory impressions that belong to a pre-verbal, pre-narrative world—the biophilic component of human experience" (p. 20). Additionally, many indigenous philosophies culturally and spiritually have foundations in the veneration of nature as highlighted by Mills and Crowley (2014):

> The natural world is our relative, our teacher, and our healer, and that everything is sacred. In these wisdom teachings, the earth, sky, moon, sun, and stars are not viewed through a scientific lens. . . . Instead, they are experienced as our *Mother Earth, Father Sky, Grandmother Moon, Grandfather Sun,* and the *Star Nation*—as *relatives* guiding, protecting, and teaching us many lessons along life's physical and spiritual paths. (p. 3)

The lens of deep ecology provides the foundations of understanding for this chapter and the utilization of nature as "co-therapist" in work with children and families.

NATURE AND SOCIETAL CONCERNS FOR CHILDREN

There is a growing interest in nature-based interventions for children, and many practitioners are searching for *and* creating new ways to meet this growing need (Atkins & Snyder, 2018; Courtney, 2017; Courtney & Mills, 2016; Dhaese, 2011; Fisher, 2019; Goodyear-Brown, 2019; Kopytin & Rugh, 2017; Montgomery & Courtney, 2015; Swank & Shin, 2015). Some of the motivation for this push is related to practitioner and societal concerns with children's growing lack of contact with nature. This is due to a variety of factors, such as an increase in technological distractions (Courtney & Nowakowski, 2018, 2019), land restrictions, safety concerns, fear of litigation, and schools cutting back on recess. In modern society, our lives are quite removed from our earth roots, and many children may not learn about the earth from direct exposure, but rather through virtual means. Some professionals are concerned that many of the behavioral disorders observed in children—such as attention deficit disorder—are in part a consequence of this disconnect (see, for example, the Children & Nature Network, www.childrenandnature.org). A phenomenon whose name was coined by Richard Louv (2008) called "nature-deficit disorder" addresses the concerning effects related to children's decreased access to the world of nature. Louv (2008) wrote:

Our society is teaching young people to avoid direct experience in nature (p. 2). The post-modern notion that reality is only a construct—that we are what we program—suggests limitless human possibilities; but as the young spend less and less of their lives in natural surroundings, their senses narrow, physiologically and psychologically, and this reduces the richness of human experience. Reducing that deficit—healing the broken bond between our young and nature—is in our self-interest, not only because aesthetics or justice demands it, but also because our mental, physical, and spiritual health depends on it. (p. 3)

Research has shown that childhood exposure to nature can have a positive effect on mental health even into adulthood (Engemann et al., 2019). The premise of including nature in expressive arts and play therapy sessions comes about because, not only is nature healing and restorative, but because we are also providing additional opportunities for children to experience direct contact with nature. In a safe and holding environment, they can relate to the natural objects and materials utilized in session in a whole new way. Thus, nature acts as co-therapist to the healing process.

THE PROFOUND EFFECT OF TOUCHING NATURE

Pause for a moment and look down at your hands and fingertips. Now marvel at this: Our fingertips our extremely sensitive with 16,000 touch sensors—more than any other part of the body (Elbrecht, 2013). Our skin receptors are the largest sensory organ of the body that are connected to our central nervous system that send messages of kinesthetic experience to the thalamus and sensory cortex. Beginning in the womb, touch is our primary means of discovering ourselves, others and the world around us. Aristotle believed that the sensory organ of touch must be related to the *heart* and understood that touch was so crucial to living that "its absence spells doom to man and all animals" (Weber, 1991, p. 18). The anthropologist Ashley Montagu (1986), sometimes referred to as the father of modern touch inquiry, believed that touch is the intermediary between all other senses. He wrote, "Touch is the parent of our eyes, ears, nose, and mouth" (p. 1).

Although nature is a multi-sensory experience, especially when outdoors (we smell the fresh air and hear a waterfall) in an office setting, touch is our primary sense of experience. When children see the nature objects in the office, it is not enough to look at them, they instinctively reach out to touch as shown in the following anonymous parent quote: "When a child was shown a special object but was not allowed to touch it, she cried out, 'Let me see it with my hands!' Feeling is important as seeing" (cited in Thomson, 1994, p. 172). Oaklander (1988) advised that the ability to discriminate varied tactile sensations is a crucial cognitive function because we are connecting to our primordial urge to know our world through engaged contact. The varied tactile sensations of touching nature can have a profound effect of comfort for children (adults too!). In his book *Sacred Path Cards: The Discovery of Self Through Native Teachings,* Sams (1990) discussed how holding a stone can help calm and securely ground us to the earth. He wrote,

> When nervous habits run us ragged, we are not feeling connected to Earth Mother. To calm the body, mind, or spirit, we need only to hold a Stone Person and breathe until the nervousness passes. This earthing influence is a way of anchoring the body to the Earth Mother and feeling the security of her nurturing influence." (p. 288)

Thus, the experience of touching of nature can act as a healing partner within the therapy process which leads us to the next section about how nature items can be utilized within therapy sessions.

BRIDGING NATURE'S "TOYS" IN EXPRESSIVE ARTS AND PLAY THERAPY SESSIONS

Many practitioners are exploring ways to balance their playrooms with natural materials, as well as providing more nature-based therapeutic interventions within the playroom and in outdoor settings. Practitioners view that nature can act as *co-therapist* within the healing process (Courtney, 2017; Courtney & Mills, 2016; Berger & McLeod, 2006).

Courtney & Mills (2016) gave an example of how nature might be utilized as co-therapist:

> Handing a shell to a child diagnosed with ADHD and asking her or him to *listen carefully* to the sound of the ocean can immediately assist in

calming and focusing the child. A story can be expanded by telling the child, "A baby sea animal once lived in this shell. This was its home, and any time he was feeling scared, worried, or upset, all the baby sea animal had to do was to crawl back into the shell where he felt all *safe, calm*, and *relaxed inside*. (p. 16)

The following are suggested nature items and ways that nature can be incorporated into therapy sessions:

- Stones, variety of gemstones (gemstones in the matrix are great),
- Variety of shells (At least one for "listening," such as a conch)
- Varied types of sand for the sand tray (for example, Jurassic Sands: https://www.jurassicsand.com)
- Leaves, bark, acorns, pinecones, tree branches
- Windchimes, singing bowls
- Botanicals, plants, flowers, natural clay, feathers.
- Natural cloth materials such as cotton and silk
- Food based items for sensory experiences such as rice, beans, macaroni, nuts (chestnuts), and seeds
- Outdoor sessions may include nature mindfulness walks (beach, trails, parks), nature scavenger hunts, and labyrinth walks.
- An office with windows for natural light, when available, is recommended. *Side note:* My best office had a large window with a view of a huge oak tree abounding with life—butterflies, hawks, blue jays, cardinals, squirrels, lizards, and even a raccoon family! The children loved it.
- Choosing natural play items instead of plastic is another way to add more nature in the room. For example, I opted for and designed a wooden (yes, sustainable) dollhouse versus a plastic dollhouse (as described in my article, "The Perfect Dollhouse" [Courtney, 2008]). An unexpected outcome was that more children wanted to play in the wood dollhouse than the plastic.

Courtney and Mills (2016) viewed that these types of nature elements can be used therapeutically as the "metaphorical miniatures containing valuable life lessons for achieving transformational healing" (p. 19). That said, some precautions regarding nature items need to be noted. Swank & Shin (2015) cautioned that some children may not be able to be in outdoor settings due to allergies, diagnoses with obsessive-compulsive tendencies related to germs, or impulsivity that requires the containment of an office for safety. Other precautions: Be conscious about the type of qualities that you attribute to nature items, as objects can easily disappear. A child can become distressed if they think they lost, for example, their "lucky" calming stone. Therefore, always state a suggestive buffer such as, "If you cannot find your stone, don't worry, I have plenty of other stones here for you." Or, "Don't worry, any stone will do." For young children, the stone needs to be large enough so there is no concern of a choking hazard. And, parents and teachers need to be agreeable if you give an object to a child to keep in his or her pocket to touch for calming. Some shells or stones can be broken if dropped and sharp edges could possibly cut a child's hand. Remember stones can also be used as a weapon. Additionally, children need to be educated about respecting nature, especially if they are collecting nature items. Many parks have policies against collecting to maintain the park's natural state. Also, if we are working with clients in outdoor settings, a separate informed consent will need to be created that addresses issues related to confidentiality and safety.

THE THERAPEUTIC ELEMENTS OF NATURE

Nature provides an abundance of metaphors that can be therapeutically utilized. For example, horticultural therapists Linden and Grut (2002) used the metaphor of the garden to address issues of loss, renewal, growth, and change. They advised that, "Metaphor is at the heart of the work of the Natural Growth Project, and parallels are drawn between the cycle of the natural world, with its successes and failures . . ." (Linden & Grut, 2002, p. 42). The multi-sensory experience of having a variety of natural objects in the playroom for children to visually explore, touch, listen to, and smell broadens the opportunity for healing. Courtney (2017, p. 112) noted several ways that nature can be utilized in therapy sessions.

- Provides a way to have contact with the earth within the therapy office
- Nature items can be a source of comfort through touch and holding
- Helps to build a therapeutic alliance
- Builds therapeutic safety & protection

- Can be utilized to reframe problems and self-perception.
- Planting of seed-thoughts.
- Acts as a transitional object between the office and home.
- Exemplifies points of therapy.
- A springboard to address emotions.
- Nature crosses cultural barriers.
- Stimulates the imagination and an avenue for storytelling.

RECONNECTING WITH NATURE

With the above section in mind, I invite you to take a few minutes to engage in the following practice exercise: Reconnecting with Nature.

THE PRACTICE

Reconnecting with Nature

Let's take a journey back in time. Find a comfortable place to sit away from distractions. Begin to get in touch with your breathing. Starting with the exhale, breathe out through your mouth, then take in a breath through your nose, and blow your breath out through your mouth again. On the exhale, imagine that you are blowing out of your body any tension or stress that you may be holding, while on the inhale, feel the nurturance of the oxygen entering your body. Sense the calming and relaxing feeling that each breath brings you. In this relaxed state, allow yourself to search for a memory when you had a *pleasant* experience engaging with nature items. This could be contact with leaves, sand, clay, stones, pine cones, bark, acorns, or shells. Maybe you remember a favorite rock where you would go and sit. Maybe you were collecting shells at the beach or making a sandcastle. Skipping stones on a lake. Here are some questions for reflection:

- Where did you have contact with your nature items? Beach? Woods? Mountains? Riverbed?
- What was the feel of these nature items like?
- Do you remember if they had a smell to them?
- What emotions did the nature items spark in you?
- What were the colors and shapes of your nature items?

- What did they feel like in your hands? Under your feet?
- Did you find a favorite nature item you kept? Do you remember finding one you gave away? Did someone give you a special nature item?

NATURE-BASED INTERVENTIONS

The following sections of this chapter will present nature-based expressive arts and play therapy for child and family interventions.

Healing with Stones

Stones have been used over the centuries for medicine, symbolism, storytelling, gift giving, superstition, alchemy, protection, religion, birthstones, trade, talismans, and divination. Stones are life-giving because they carry the minerals of life which break down into the soil, which is absorbed into the plants and eaten by animals, which humans then consume. Their life cycle has a beginning, middle, and end, and then a beginning again as the same minerals get recycled over time—nothing ever dies, it just gets transformed. As part of that life cycle, some rocks can go through a complete internal transformation of structure. But this only happens under one condition: The rock must be exposed to extreme *heat* and *pressure*. When this geological shift occurs the mineral substance in a rock is replaced by a totally different mineral substance of another. The rock can even look and feel different. Rocks that have gone through this mineral exchange are called metamorphic rocks. In Greek, "meta" and "morph" means "change of form." The original rock, prior to the transformation, is called the "parent" rock. Some examples of metamorphic rock are: limestone to marble; granite to gneiss; sandstone to quartzite; shale to slate, or shale to schist. Many children learn about the differences between rocks in school and have heard of sedimentary, igneous, and metamorphic rocks. I usually have different stone species in my office that I utilize to describe to children how the rocks change form. For example, I show the child the coal and jet stones from my collection. I then share how these stones have changed from one form to another, but under one condition—they had to go through a tremendous amount of heat and pressure to make that change. The underlying metaphorical message speaks to the neuroplasticity of the brain, and how the life challenges we encounter force us to undergo tremendous change. It is similar to another oft-quoted metaphor attributed to a Native American saying, "The soul would have no rainbow, if the eyes had no tears."

A NATURE HEALING SPACE OF TEMENOS FOLLOWING A MASS SHOOTING

In 2018, the devastating shooting at Marjory Stoneman Douglas High School in Parkland, Florida left 17 dead and hundreds in need of therapeutic services. I was invited to be included as one of 20 healers—including massage therapists, Reiki healers, EMDR therapists, and acupuncturists—offering solace to the teens, families, and school staff impacted by the massacre. While we all offered our respective expertise, what was unique was the place of meeting—outdoors on a small family farm nestled within the Parkland town limits. The farm had horses and goats for petting, as well as gorgeous, soft Silkie chickens that were accustomed to touch, so children and families were able to hold them for comfort. The most important part of this healing nature space: It was media-free. A safe place where families could come and *just be*.

Each practitioner had a space set up to confidentially and privately meet with the families. I provided stones, shells, and art materials for the families to engage with however they chose. They painted stones with symbols and words of comfort; some shared and others worked quietly. It was a humbling experience to be a witness to this most extraordinary unfolding of healing in this amazing nature setting. I had an overwhelming feeling that their healing of trauma was not just from the availability of practitioners who were there to support, but from the sacred healing power of the natural environment—the temenos of which the therapy was held.

I KNOW MY YESES AND NOS

The following intervention is based upon the idea that children and parents need help in developing an inner clarity about their ability to state *Yes* or *No*. Although this is a simple exercise, it is also very profound. Many children and teenagers may find it difficult to assert themselves with peers and may say "yes" to an activity they don't want to do. It is hard for them to say that they are not willing to participate. This can lead to some hard life lessons for children. Parents also need to understand the importance of a clear "Yes" and "No" in their job as parents. A child may ask for something and the parent may decide it is not in the child's best interest. The parent may initially say no, only to have the child push the parent to where the parent may, in frustration, change their original decision and say yes to the child's request. Of course, we understand the problem of inconsistent messaging to a child. It is within the parent's word that a child learns to trust their parent. A child may learn that when my mother said no, that if they complain or push enough, that "no" would probably change to a "yes."

This does not mean that there is not a flexibility of mind. We all need that balance of spontaneity. However, overall, a parent must consider carefully before giving an answer: "Is this request from my child really something I believe in as a 'No,' or is my 'No' really something I can consider a 'Yes'"? The best advice to parents is that being consistent in their parenting will pay off in the child's teen years when the child has more independence from the parents. Parents' guidance will help their children make decisions in the moment. As practitioners, we can support this process within therapy sessions to help children and parents understand their power as decision makers and how to best make those decisions. Satir (1985) advocated that we all need to take responsibility for our decisions. To uphold this idea, she created a medallion with the word "Yes" on one side and "No" on the other. She asked clients to hold the medallion when trying to decide "yes, no, or maybe later." She emphasized that clear statements of action directly impacted trust within relationships. Satir emphasized:

> Let yourself become aware that you are a decision maker. You are the one who acts on the resources you have—and no one, but no one else, can be responsible for what you choose. See that you can make decisions about opening and closing at your own request. (p. 15)

Conscious choice decision making is an important discussion, and for children, I might approach this activity through storytelling. In the book *The Alchemist* by Paulo Coelho (1994), a young shepherd boy sets off in search of his treasure. Along his journey, he learns about the Alchemist who is the keeper of the Philosopher's stone, and decides he wants to meet him. Using my storyteller animated voice, I tell the story of the following encounter when the boy finally meets the Alchemist:

> The old man opened his cape, and the boy was struck by what he saw. The old man wore a breastplate of heavy gold, covered with precious stones. "Take these," said the old man, holding a white stone and a black stone that had been embedded at the center of the breastplate. "They are Urim and Thummim. The black signifies 'Yes' and the white 'No.' When you are unable to read the omens, they will help you to do so. It's in the Bible. The priests carried them in their golden breastplates. (p. 30)

After the story, I discuss in more detail the importance of making clear yes and no decisions. Then I engage children in the following "StoryCraft" or "EarthCraft"—as coined by Joyce Mills—which denotes when a story is told and then bridged to an art or craft activity (Courtney & Mills, 2016). StoryCrafts ground the metaphorical therapeutic elements of the story into tangible form.

I Know My Yeses and Nos: Steps of Implementation

Materials: Smooth stones or shells, paint markers or paints, and paintbrushes, cloth, scissors, and yarn.

Step 1: Have the child pick two stones. [After we have discussed the importance of decision making, I might tell the Alchemist story to the child.]

Step 2: Have the child think of a symbol that he decides represents a "yes" and a symbol that represents "no."

Step 3: Using the paint markers, have the child paint the symbol on the stone.

Step 4: Invite the child to share his symbols and insights related to the activity. This is also a great activity as a Family Play Therapy activity.

Step 5: To support containment in the process, the stones will need a holder. For this exercise, I recommend cutting a round cloth and placing the stones in the middle of the cloth. The edges of the cloth are pulled up around the stones and then use yarn or string to tie it together.

HEART-STONES: A SYMBOL OF LOVE AND LOVING PRESENCE

The symbol of a heart shape to represent *Love* is universal the world over. It immediately crosses cultural boundaries and is recognized to mean love and heart. It's disarming. Giving heart-stones to clients in therapy deepens the nurturing holding environment and temenos of safety and protection. It can also act as a transitional object to exemplify points of therapy and can be given during a closure session. For years, I have collected heart-stones— even a *shell* at the beach can work itself into a heart shaped form. (We call our beach stones found on the east coast of Florida "sandstones.") Here's the most surprising part: To find heart-shaped stones, shells, bark, sea glass, et cetera in nature is not rare, you just need to develop a keen eye to spot them. I found the heart-stone in Figure 7.1 while hiking along a trail in the woods of northern New Jersey.

About Developing A Loving Presence in Therapy

References in the professional literature related to love in connection to working with clients is sparse. Brody (1997ab) believed that practitioners needed to develop a sense of a loving presence toward children that promoted the healing process. The renowned psychoanalyst, Erich Fromm discussed the necessary ingredients of loving in his book, *The Art of Loving* (Fromm, 1956/1970). He postulated that loving is an *art*, and since it is an art, it must be *practiced* in order to get good at it. He recognized the factors involved in practice as discipline, concentration, and patience, and that the *art of loving* requires humility, objectivity, reason, faith, and the ability to develop a self-love. This point of self-love is key.

We all want love and to feel that we are lovable. To be loved and really seen by another who is practiced in unconditionally loving is a gift. But how do we learn the art of self-love? Fromm's answer? First, *we need to learn how to be alone with ourselves and to focus our attention within.* He called this learning how to concentrate. He wrote, "Indeed, to be able to concentrate means to be able to be alone with oneself—and this ability is precisely a condition for the ability to love" (p. 94). He noted the paradox between the ability to be alone and love: "Paradoxically, the ability to be alone is the condition for the ability to love" (p. 94). So, the ability for the practitioner to develop a loving presence with clients (sometimes framed as loving-kindness, caring, compassion, empathetic resonance) stems forth from our ability for self-love as the first step.

This brings us back to the topic of heart-stones in therapy, which can act as a tangible and symbolic expression of love. Josephine Lea Iselin, author of the book, *Heart Stones*, wrote this inspiring quote: "The heart stone is a lovely vessel. When you take it home and set it on your windowsill or dresser its presence buoys you up. When you give it to a friend or lover, you give what you have

FIGURE 7.1: Heart-Stone found on trail in Butler, New Jersey
SOURCE: COURTESY THE AUTHOR'S COLLECTION

filled it with: strength, love, and confidence" (p. 1). When I give heart-stones to clients—children and adults alike—it stands as a metaphorical representation of love, nurturance, caring, hope, truth, and consciousness within the therapy context. On occasion, I have had calls from clients years later that tell me they still have the heart-stone I had given them.

A Heart-Stone of Deep Meaning

During one session, I gave a heart-stone I had found on the beach to a child client, Belinda (age 11) who was struggling with body-image and feeling disconnected from her peers at school. When I showed and handed her the heart-stone, her affect and body posture immediately shifted from sitting hunched over and looking downtrodden in the chair to instantly sitting up with a surprised expression and then smiling. "Wow, a heart-stone!" she said, looking up at me, delighted. "Where did you get this? I have got to show this to my mom." When her mother came in from the waiting room, she held the stone in her hand, and then shared that she had in her possession a special stone from one of their family travels. I said with delight, "Oh, I would love to see that stone."

At the next week's session, the mother came to the office entering with both hands cupped together as if holding something very delicate. Belinda sat close to her mother on the couch and appeared excited to be part of this intimate unveiling. The mother explained that the stone she was going to show me was found with her daughter at the beach on one of their family travels. She then lifted one hand to reveal a perfectly shaped rose quartz heart-stone that was certainly a treasure to behold. The mother beamed with delight when sharing the stone. I put my hand to my heart and held the mother's hand, and together with Belinda we shared a moment of hope and connection.

Celestite, the "Helping Stone"

Stones and gemstones can be utilized in different ways and often the properties and functions of the stones can provide metaphoric opportunities for change. For example, the mineral composition of the gemstone celestite is highly flammable and for this reason is has been used to make flares. Because of this, I tell my child clients that this beautiful light blue cluster stone is a "helping stone" that has saved people's lives. The following case illustrates the use of this stone in therapy.

Ryan, age six, was afraid to sleep in his own bedroom after experiencing a terrifying dream related to a recent family car accident. The parents had made every attempt to address the problem before bringing him to therapy. As the therapy progressed, he fell in love with the large geode celestite in my office and asked if he could take it home. Children know that the play therapy items "live" in my office, as it's their home. But on this occasion the request seemed deeper than the usual request of just wanting a pretty stone. It was decided. The stone would go home with him for a guest visit to be returned when he was ready. Like most crystals, celestite is very fragile, and a geode dropped can easily crumble into tiny pieces. So together, we carefully wrapped the stone in a baby blanket from my office. Like a proud papa, he cradled the stone close while leaving the office. I did not know what plans he had for the stone, but it felt significant toward healing. At the next session, he advised that he was sleeping each night with the stone. After about three weeks, he returned with the stone still wrapped in the same baby blanket. He gazed at the stone in his arms, gave it a tight hug, and then gentle placed it back on my shelf. To my amazement he shared that he was now sleeping back in his own room.

> SIDE NOTE: If you lend a stone, remember that once a stone (anything for that matter) leaves the therapy office, at that moment you must let it go. You cannot hold the child accountable if the stone or item does not return. Items can get lost, broken, or even stolen. Parents may not return to scheduled appointments as planned for many different reasons. You therefore need to accept the reality that once something has left it might not come back. If you are concerned about losing your favorite healing tool that may be difficult to replace, then do not make the decision to let it leave. Discuss with the child's parents options for how they can obtain a similar stone or item for their child. Birthdays and holidays are great times to buy desired stone presents for children. As well, I have a collection of polished gemstones that I give children to keep.

RESOURCING SEA GLASS

I enjoy scouring the beach for stones, but some of my most prized treasures are found in the polished glass from the sea. More commonly known as sea glass,

FIGURE 7.2: Sea Glass Runes
SOURCE: COURTESY THE AUTHOR'S COLLECTION

and made from silica, it is a pure source of sand. Sea glass intrigues, as it is essentially discarded beach trash that breaks up into sharp-edged pieces. Over time, the ocean tumbles the sharp edges until it becomes a grainy-smooth texture, which has a soothing feel when touched. One way I have adapted sea glass is to turn them into a set of runes. Runes were found to be an ancient form of communication by Northern European Germanic tribes and were essentially an alphabet (Blum, 1987). I use a Dremel tool to etch the rune symbols into the sea glass (see Figure 7.2 for examples from my collection). Children enjoy picking up the sea glass runes in my office and are curious about the symbols etched into the glass, which represent varied life experiences such as creativity, loyalty, disappointment, or secrets (Blum, 1987). I then utilized the chosen symbols as springboards for talking points.

SIDE NOTE: Children can be supported to create their own set of runes using symbols they choose to make up their own messages for picking. However, I do not recommend sea glass for this activity (see note of caution that follows), but rather to use polished stones or shells where they can paint symbols.

One of my prized beach discoveries was a piece of smooth light green sea glass that looked like it had been broken from the top of a soda bottle. It was unusual because it was formed in a curvy amorphic shape like it had been melted by fire and then for years polished smooth by the sea. It had a grainy, velvety feel to the touch—a rare art sculpture from the sea and central to the therapy in the following case vignette.

Case Vignette: A Sea Glass of Rare Beauty

The mother in my waiting room had the look of an exhausted and harried mother at her wits' end. Her quick anxious words explained that her teenage daughter was still in the car, refusing to come into the office. The look on her face implored me for help. I often think that my job as a therapist is to show up differently in a child's life than other adults. Thinking quickly, I asked on a whim, "Does she like stones? Sea glass?" The mother hesitated, but then answered, "Actually, she collects sea glass." "Great," I said, and I grabbed the prized amorphic piece of green sea glass from my office and dashed out the door. It is not the first time I have done "parking-lot therapy," and it is always a challenge. It's one of those make-it-or-break-it moments.

I knocked on the car window and she begrudgingly rolled it down. She glared at me with intense, hurt eyes. "Sandra, your Mom told me you were down here in the car, and it's okay with me if you don't want to come up to the office, but I thought you might be interested in something I have in my office. Your mom told me you liked sea glass and I have a really unique piece that I would like to show you. Would you like to see it?" (All risk-taking in therapy is really an experiment, and sometimes it works, and other times it fails. This time the response was positive.) She looked down at the sea glass I was holding in my hand, "Where did you get that from?" she asked, intrigued. "It was a surprise find walking on the beach—a real one of a kind gem," I said as I handed the sea glass to her through the car window. She eyed it intently, turning it over and around, and then, wrapping her fist around it she cracked a smile and gave it tight squeeze. Handing it back, she softened a little and said, "I like it. It's different." Finding the common ground through the sea glass acted as a transitional bridge to what became a long-standing relationship. When therapy ended, I wrapped up the special amorphic sea glass and gave it to her in a box as a gift. She was touched by this gesture and told me that she knew exactly where she would be keeping it. The sea glass belonged to her now.

SIDE NOTE: I never give sea glass to young children because even smooth glass can break, revealing sharp edges. One must also consider the presenting mental health issues of our clients—even adults—as we need to rule out the possibility of self-harm. As in all ethical respects, the rule of "do no harm" is paramount.

THE HEALING POWER OF CLAY

Clay is a developmental stage of sand and stone. Depending where clay is found throughout the world and the properties present at its formation, clay will vary in texture, color, and mineral content. Clay is a great therapeutic tool, for unlike stone, it can be shaped and molded to the will of the creator, and clay can be easily undone and reorganized if the shape is not to a child's liking. It is hard to make a "mistake" with clay, to borrow the observation of Violet Oaklander (1988). Most children enjoy working in clay and I prefer natural clay, if possible, over those with manmade synthetic ingredients. Clay is a powerful therapeutic medium that can act as a bridge by which the child's inner, unconscious world is brought forth into conscious awareness. Since natural clay is primordial, it can take a client deep very quickly and can be a powerful (advanced) tool of healing trauma (Elbrecht, 2013). Oaklander (1988) wrote that clay seems to "penetrate the protective armor, the barriers in a child" (p. 67). Souter-Anderson (2010) advised that physical contact with the medium of clay is a "sensate experience . . . that appears to stir feelings and make contact with emotions, whilst simultaneously engaging with the world of imagination, thus incorporating a metaphorical contact" (p. 51). For these reasons, practitioners are cautioned how clay is implemented within sessions and are urged to seek supervision and peer consultation as needed.

I have used clay successfully with children diagnosed with ADHD, anxiety disorders, and problems of encopresis. In one of the therapeutic directives I utilize, I ask the child or adolescent to create in clay a symbolic representation of their worry, problem, or identified affect. Once the clay figure is completed, I use an adapted Gestalt therapy method (Perls, 1969) of dialoguing with the figure stemming from what is commonly known as the "empty chair" technique (see Courtney, 2017 for a clay gestalt case example). Additionally, in the following, Oaklander (1988) suggests a wealth of clay directives that can also include a gestalt encounter:

> Visualize your world, your life. Show this in clay. Make a real [or imaginary] animal, bird, fish. Make something from another planet. Make something you'd like to be. Make something from a dream. Make a story, a scene with your clay. Make your family as people or objects or animals or symbols. Make your problem. Make your ideal family. . . . Make an image of yourself as a baby. Have a group make a cooperative panorama together. (p. 75)

ENTER BOTANICALS

Incorporating botanicals, such as flowers, into sessions can have a healing effect as they awaken our senses related to fragrance, color, touch, and texture. Horticultural therapist Elizabeth Diehl (2009) discussed how certain scents can stimulate our bodily organs to release neurochemicals that help reduce pain, induce sleep, and lower beta brainwaves, electrodermal activity, and cortisol levels. Botanicals include vines, leaves, fruit, flowering branches, and seed pods, which may be used in botanical arrangements or be incorporated into an art intervention.) My colleague and I created a therapeutic process of working with botanicals published in the *Journal of Therapeutic Horticulture*. We discussed the personal affiliations of botanicals in the following:

> Botanical products do not have a *flat* affect, but are evocative in ways that may be personal, ancestral, experiential, or archetypal in different layers of conscious and unconscious awareness. The meanings associated with living things are always going to be specific to the life experience of the clients, the landscape in which they grew up, any family interest in the out-of-doors, the foods that were common in their home or community, and the way they celebrated the holidays. The botanical's living magic enters a spectrum of experience through color, symmetry, scale, texture, scent, and shape whose attributes, interacting in light, merge with an individual's own history. (Montgomery and Courtney, 2015, p. 20)

FIGURE 7.3: Abigail, age 4, shares her hopes and dreams through her Wishing Hawaiian Lei
SOURCE: USED WITH PERMISSION FROM STEPHANIE CROWLEY AND ABIGAIL

WISHING UPON A HAWAIIAN LEI NECKLACE

In the following intervention, we are working with children from a strength-based perspective to elicit their hopes and dreams for themselves and others. We are also paying attention to the types of wishes and dreams that they hope for, as this can provide a window to children's inner worries and concerns. This intervention can also be adapted to group therapy with older children and adolescents.

Materials: Sewing thread/string, large blunt-tipped embroidery needle; flowers (carnations, roses, plumeria—any flower with a firm face).

Wishing Upon a Hawaiian Lei Necklace, Steps of Implementation

Step 1: Implementing any type of botanical session requires planning ahead to arrange for the flower's presence in sessions. This requires a discussion with the caregivers. There are different ways to acquire flowers to use during sessions: Sometimes I have brought flowers collected from my garden; or families may obtain flowers from their home gardens, supermarkets, farmers' markets, plant nurseries, or even flowers donated from a wedding or funeral.

Step 2: The stems are removed, and each flower is placed on the string by pushing the blunted needle through the middle of the flower. Depending on the age of the child the therapist may need to assist with this activity. Have the client make a wish or name a dream or hope for themselves and/or others as they string each flower. Tie off the string when finished, and the child can decide whether to wear the flower lei. Note, this could also be a bracelet or a flower crown for the head.

Step 3: As with all cut flowers, the child must be prepared that the flower dreaming-necklace will fade in a day or two, and it can be discussed how the child would like to finish with their flower lei. One way I have done this is by sharing that many Hawaiian's decide to return their flowers back to nature by removing the string and scattering the flowers or by placing the flowers on a tree. This can bring up a discussion about the cycle of life, which may be beneficial when children are in therapy due to loss and grieving. We recognized this limited timeframe, "When cut and cared for, flowers will live for a period of time in water but ultimately decay. Their day passes just as human time passes . . . the transient nature of life—takes place within the *biophilia* frame of reference" (Montgomery & Courtney, 2015, p. 20).

THE PRACTICE

Wishing Upon a Hawaiian Lei Necklace

In this exercise you will adapt the steps of the Wishing Hawaiian Lei Necklaces. Plan ahead what flowers you want, and have ready the string and a blunted needle. Follow the process of naming each flower as a designated wish or dream and, if comfortable, share your process of creation with a partner who may also do the same.

Chapter 8

MINDFULNESS, JOURNALING, DREAMS, LABYRINTH, & YOGA

"You cannot transmit wisdom and insight to another person.
The seed is already there. A good teacher touches the seed,
allowing it to wake up, to sprout and to grow."

Thich Nhat Hanh, *Planting Seeds:*
Practicing Mindfulness with Children, 2011 (p.15)

t is said that carved into the forecourt of the Oracle at Delphi in ancient Greece were the words *Know Thyself.* Of course, we more commonly attribute those two philosophical words to Socrates, but what does that mean, to know thyself, from a therapeutic stance? One way that I conceptualize this question, and what this chapter addresses, is that any time we guide our clients through therapeutic interventions that assist them to turn their focus inward—to promote inner self-awareness, inner connection, and insight—we are then amplifying ways of *knowing self.* Individual self-examination can help us grow our social engagement abilities and self-appreciation while also learning methods of self-regulation through calming, relaxing, and focusing of attention.

DISCOVERING THE MIND–BODY CONNECTION

In my early college years, I began an exploration of inner-focusing approaches of mind, body, and spirit—yoga, meditation, body therapies, and even healthy nutrition—that I still practice today. In one such self-discovery encounter, I participated in an EEG biofeedback (also known as Neurofeedback) dissertation research project a doctoral student was conducting at Florida State University. This research project produced a paradigm shift in my understanding about the interconnectedness between our internal thinking processes, our bodily sensations, and our emotional states. I was one of six participants who had no prior knowledge of biofeedback who were accepted into the study. Back in the early 1980s there was no internet on which to search ahead, so we were all entering with little understanding of how bio-feedback worked and what to expect. I am sharing the part of my experience in the research that is relevant to the content of this chapter. The following was my initial pre-test research evaluation:

> During my initial meeting with the researcher, I sat in a chair and was hooked up to electrodes, which were placed at various positions on my forehead and scalp. The other ends of the electrodes were connected to the biofeedback instrument that provided audible frequency sounds that the researcher noted based upon a series of common introductory questions such as: "What is your name? Where did you grow up? What are you studying in college?" I could listen to the range of tones, ris-ing and lowering as I answered the questions. I was then asked to try to relax my body and mind as much as I could. Since I already had a daily meditation practice, I used my knowledge to ground, focus, and let go. The now familiar frequency sounds rested at a soft quiet tone as I allowed myself to deepen my relaxed state. As I rested in this state, I quickly became aware that even the slightest thought that passed through my mind immediately generated an increase in the sound tones that registered my brain activity. Then without notice, the researcher tapped a bar that produced a startlingly loud noise. Imme-diately my body and mind reacted with a jolt, and the sound frequency of my brain wave activity simultaneously spiked to a sustaining, loud, high-pitched note. I remained quiet and neurocepted (we did not have that word then) that there was no danger; I immediately began to con-sciously try to calm myself. I could hear the frequency sound respond to my efforts as it began spiraling down from louder to quieter to then back to my original resting baseline. Note, I was not asked to do this task, I instinctively did what came natural to me in the moment.

At the end of the session, I was apprised of the unexpected "experiment" of the loud jolting noise. The researcher informed me that she had counted how many seconds it took from the time my hypervigilant state spiked, represented by the high frequency tone, to the time I returned to the baseline, soft frequency tone. She said that the speed of my return to baseline was rated in the above average category, a speedy return.

Over the course of the five-month research project, I learned more about the immediate causes and effects related to my cognitive, emotional, somatic, and sensory states when I was calm and relaxed versus when I was worried, discomforted, and stressed. Some practitioners are even developing ways to use neurofeedback to intervene with trauma (see van der Kolk, 2014, Chapter 19). By participating in this research project, I gained some valuable insights early on in my career: First, the connection between mind and body is real! Second, we *can* learn to develop an awareness of our own internal states at a physical, emotional, and cognitive level. Third, we can grow an understanding about how those states impact our daily, overall well-being. And finally, we *can* learn ways to regulate these states that can bring about change. This chapter supports these insights and will present ways of top-down and bottom-up self-regulation options for children and families through mindfulness practice, journaling exercises, dream exploration, yoga postures, and labyrinth journey-walks.

MINDFULNESS

The attention to mindfulness practice has grown exponentially within the past ten years, and child practitioners are integrating mindfulness into their practice with children (Badenoch, 2018ab; Burdick, 2014; Kestly, 2016; Siegel & Payne Bryson, 2015; Ogden & Fisher, 2015; Rappaport, 2015). Note that some practitioners may use the term *mindfulness* interchangeably with the words *imagery* or *visualization* (Epstein, 1989). Van der Kolk (2014) noted that mindfulness practice is a top-down regulation that strengthens our capacity to monitor our body's sensations. Mindfulness practice stems from the Buddhist traditions, and many in the Western world credit Thich Nhat Hanh, a Zen Buddhist master, as the "father of mindfulness" (Fitzpatrick, 2019). Born in Vietnam, he was part of the Vietnam War peace movements and in 1967 was nominated by Martin Luther King, Jr. for the Nobel Peace Prize. The Dalai Lama is also central to the mindfulness practice movement, and both Buddhist traditions stress the importance of mindfulness and compassion and being fully present in the here and now.

In teaching children mindfulness practices to develop self-regulation skills, it is imperative that practitioners first practice mindfulness themselves. Nhat Hanh (2011) advised, "To successfully share mindfulness with children, you must first practice it yourself. Your presence, your calm, and your peace are the biggest gifts you can offer to young people" (p. 41). Developing our own inner state of openness, receptivity, and mindful presence is a first step toward co-regulation and resonance within the therapeutic relationship (Siegel, 2012). Kestly (2016) described mindfulness as ". . . an intention to cultivate self-awareness without criticism. It allows us to live in what Siegel called an open plane of possibility (Siegel, 2010b). Mindfulness matters because it allows us to cultivate the relational connections that heal" (p. 22). Our own state of self-regulation and self-awareness begins by cultivating our own sense of compassion for ourselves. One of the first ways that Nhat Hanh (2011) recommended beginning mindfulness focus is to first become aware of your breath in the present moment. Prem Rawat (2016), known worldwide for his promotion of inner peace, described the preciousness of breath as "Breath brings you life. Each breath, as it comes, is a gift. Pay attention to it as it comes into you. When you can feel your own breath ushering in life, it brings a comfort and fulfillment." (p. 29)

A MINDFUL, PEACEFUL BODY OF RADIANT LIGHT

With the above discussion in mind regarding the need for a practitioner to first experience mindfulness practice, I invite you to engage in the following practice exercise: A Mindful, Peaceful Body of Radiant Light.

THE PRACTICE

A Mindful Peaceful Body of Radiant Light

You might ask a partner to read the following exercise to you as you listen and follow along, or you can record the exercise and then practice as you listen and guide yourself to practice. Read this very slowly, pausing between sentences. There is no rush. You can do this seated or lying down.

Move your body into a comfortable posture. Focus your attention on your breathing. You have a little cradle inside of you that rocks you. Just feel that rhythm of your breathing as you breathe in . . . and out . . . in . . . and out. Like the sun in the solar system, imagine that you have a beautiful, radiating sun in your solar plexus. Now imagine that sun beginning to radiate out in all directions, bringing a feeling of peace, relaxation, and calm to every cell as it moves throughout your body. The rays of light move up to your chest, to your neck and shoulders. The rays of light move down your arms to your hands and then to your fingers. The rays bring a feeling of calmness to every cell that they touch. Now see the rays of light travel up to your head, face, eyes, nose, cheeks, ears, and hair. Feel the relaxation as the light touches each part of your body. Now see the rays of light move down to your stomach, hips, your back, thigh, knees, calves, ankles, feet, and toes. Put the palms of your hands together, and see if you can feel the energy between your hands. Now put your hands on your heart, and see if you can feel the pulsing of your beautiful heart. Just listen to your heart and body. Send compassion to yourself. Maybe it has a color to it. Now, send compassion to each part of your body, including your muscles, bones, blood, and organs. Feel the radiant peace as it fills your body with gratitude. Slowly bring your awareness back to your breath and your surroundings as you orient back to your present surroundings.

JOURNALING INTERVENTIONS

Journaling is a powerful form of personal healing for children and people of all ages. One of the most rewarding takeaways of being a therapist has been opening the door for hundreds of children and adolescents to discover journaling as a healing process that they can then utilize as a safe helping tool throughout their lifetime. I believe, across the board, that it should be introduced as an option to children of all ages—even young children can draw a picture about how they are feeling in a journal. One of the most famous journals was the diary written by Anne Frank (Frank, 1952/1993), the young teenager who wrote so honestly about her experience in hiding during World War II and, sadly, died in a concentration camp. In the book's introduction, Eleanor Roosevelt wrote this pearl about Anne's diary,

> "Sustained by her warmth and her wit, her intelligence and the rich resources of her inner life, Anne wrote and thought much of the time about things which very sensitive and talented adolescents without the threat of death will write—her relations with her parents, her developing self-awareness, the problems of growing up." (p. xiv)

Anne named her diary "Kitty," and she described it as a dear friend and a place of refuge and comfort during a very dark period. Another compelling account related to journaling comes from the experiences of the American teacher Erin Gruwell, who encouraged student journaling as a novel approach to teaching. Many of her students had severe early childhood trauma experiences, and their journaling became a transformative healing tool. Their stories were documented in the book *The Freedom Writers Diary* (The Freedom Writers & Gruwell, 2009) and movie called *Freedom Writers,* starring actress Hillary Swank as Erin Gruwell.

In her book *The Creative Journal*, Lucia Capacchione (2002) wrote that journaling is serious self-reflection that requires "time, solitude and courage" and is a way to reveal the "Self to oneself" (p. 1). Therapeutic journals are more than just writing words, they are places for drawing, doodling, timelines, graphs, collages, coloring, painting, scribbling, symbolic images, portraits, poetry, letters, dream exploration, and experiential journaling exercises. I have been very touched by children who have shared their journals with me. Benjamin's grandmother died after a long battle with cancer when he was nine years old. To deal with his deep grief he wrote a poem for his grandmother which he later shared with me. Poetry always speaks from the heart. And this poem from Benjamin lays bare the profound inner wisdom that children innately possess, and it stands as an example of how poetry journaling can be supported as a therapeutic tool. With permission from Benjamin, I share it with you.

Goodbye
BY BENJAMIN MYERS (WRITTEN AT AGE 9)
I stutter, Goodbye
To my sympathetic one
Who nuzzled me, And squashed me, Adored me,
Heaps
But it's over. Done.
And she's departed, To heaven.
She was an angel, To me.
She was a star, To me.
I'm thinking of moments harshly,
I'm looking at pictures,

I really treasured her, Lots.
I'm depressed that it's terminated
A salty dripple Oozed down.
I weep
Tears stream down, Like a newborn.
It is such dread. I can't picture
With the blurs on my face.
Tears trickle down like a river.
"Goodbye" I muffled quietly.
Goodbye, Goodbye.
But I am blissful as the sun.
That is shining luminously,
Because my grandma is with me forever,
In the sky.
Goodbye, Goodbye

To learn more about poetry as a therapeutic tool visit the National Association for Poetry Therapy, which promotes healing through written language, symbol, and story, at http://poetrytherapy.org.

Creating a Safe Journaling "Write" of Passage

Over the decades our societal norms have changed, and we have lost much of the ancestral wisdom that guided our rites of passage through the developmental stages of childhood and beyond. Perhaps when parents make the decision to give their children a cell phone, that could be considered a contemporary rite of passage. They, along with their peers, have now entered the world of nonstop access to the internet and social media at the touch of a finger. We seem to have lost the art of penning our most intimate thoughts into a diary to the dashing off of a quick text with an emoji. How, I wonder, would Anne Frank have managed her horrific years of hiding if she did not have the solace of her journal, Kitty? I suggest that providing children with opportunities to journal can help to deepen their understanding of self—a "write" of passage, so to speak. With that in mind, we must consider that journaling is a very private act and therefore requires a need to feel safe to write. The following guidelines are offered to promote privacy and a sense of safety in the journaling experience.

Journaling Guidelines

1. Book journals that are used for therapeutic purposes need to be line-free, meaning it is best to find journals that have blank pages, as we need open space to move around. The best journals, I've discovered, are the simple ones, hand-made by children from folded copy paper and staples, with a front cover of custom drawings and a journal title. For a journal must *call* to its owner and a personalized front cover helps to do the trick.

2. When working with children, discussing with parents the issues of journal-privacy is paramount. The point of a journal is for children, teenagers—any of us—to feel safe pouring out our deepest darkest pains, feelings, and thoughts. If we choose to share this with others, that is our prerogative. However, there have been times when parents (siblings too!) have read the child's journal without permission. This creates a deep level of distrust. Therefore, a discussion around the use and privacy of a journal is a priority. In one case, a teenager admitted that she had purposefully left her journal out on the kitchen table because she really did want her mother to read it, even though the original presenting issue was her anger toward her mother for reading her journal without asking. Thus, the dynamics are complex, and it is best to sort this out in the beginning.

3. We get only 50 percent of the benefit of journaling when writing down our thoughts and feelings. The other 50 percent comes when we re-read what we have written in the journal.

4. Clients are advised to approach the content of their journals nonjudgmentally, with kindness and compassion. A critical viewpoint will defeat the purpose of the journaling exercises, and discussing this with children, especially adolescents, is recommended.

5. Therapists can help clients to think of the best time and place to journal.

Journaling Points of Entry: Raw Writing

Many children's writing has been stifled by the educational system insisting they write essays with perfect sentences and paragraphs, which can shut down one's creativity. It is discouraging to get back an English paper with a low grade after wholeheartedly struggling for hours to conceptualize and create.

Astonishingly, some school systems have students submit their papers through an electronic grading system, wherein no real humans are reading or grading it! Many children have unpleasant associations with the idea of writing—even when writing just for themselves. Because of this, children may be reluctant or even cringe at the thought of starting a journal. I have found success with the following interventions, which can act as a benign point of entry to foster a positive journaling experience. For clients new to the journaling experience, the question "Where to begin?" arises. I have found that the exercise of a short timed "Raw Writing" is the easiest point of entry, producing the least resistance, into the journaling process when working with older children, adolescents, and adults. This is first implemented within a session with the therapist holding the containment of the exercise.

Raw Writing: Steps of Implementation

Step 1: Introduce the exercise by letting clients know the exercise is a timed, open-ended, three-minute period of "raw writing" that can focus on whatever they would like to write about. It can be framed as "Think about what is up for you at this point in time." Or "What matters to you most?"

Step 2: Once the client is told to begin writing, they are to keep their pen moving constantly to allow for the free flow of consciousness without screening their thoughts. Advise clients that if they run out of things to write about, then they are to write just that—"I can't think of anything, I can't think of anything"—until they think of something else to write.

Step 3: Processing the experience. Clients may choose to read what they wrote to the therapist, or sometimes, the client may ask the therapist to read the writing out loud. Additionally, if the client is not comfortable with either of these, then the general overall experience of the journaling exercise can be discussed: "What was it like for you to do to this process?" "How were you feeling while writing?" "Did you find this process helpful?" and so forth. In all cases, clients are encouraged to re-read what they wrote at a later time— remember the 50/50 benefit rule? I encourage clients to practice Raw Writing at least once a day, and I work with them to help them figure out when the best time to do this might be—before bedtime? First thing in the morning? After school? This helps to ground the process into action as it is bridged into a daily schedule at home.

RAW WRITING

With the above journaling discussion above in mind, I invite you to engage in the following practice exercise: Raw Writing.

THE PRACTICE

Raw Writing

Following the steps listed in the steps of implementation above, decide on the best place and time to practice this Raw Writing exercise. Set a timer for three minutes, and begin writing without lifting your pen or pencil. Once you are finished, re-read what you wrote, saying the words out loud. This provides a new way for you to understand your feelings and thoughts—from a different perspective. Additionally, set the writing aside for a few days to gain some distance, and then go back and re-read it again. Take note of any new insights that emerge. What we journal today will speak to us differently over time.

DOMINANT HAND VERSUS NONDOMINANT HAND INNER-SELF DIALOGUING

Another powerful journaling technique draws upon both the right and left hemisphere functions, which helps us gain access to unconscious processes, providing valuable insight into the client's thoughts and behaviors. Again, this process is better for older children and adolescents. In this exercise, the client may have a specific conflict that they are working on wherein this process can help to shed some light.

DOMINANT HAND VERSUS NONDOMINANT HAND INNER-SELF DIALOGUING: STEPS OF IMPLEMENTATION

Step 1: The client's dominant writing hand is designated the part of self that will be either asking questions or making feeling and thinking statements to the "inner-self." The inner-self (IS) will be designated as the nondominant hand that answers the questions back to the dominant hand (ME).

Step 2: Beginning with the dominant hand, have the client think of a question or make a statement to the inner-self. This begins the dialogue. To answer, the pen or pencil is shifted to the nondominant hand and the client is then encouraged to use imaginative thinking to intuit an answer. This imaginative part of playing with consciousness can bring forth the creative force. Encourage the client to understand that there is no right or wrong answer, as this is meant to be a creative and playful spontaneous activity. The back and forth process may look like the following made-up conversation:

ME: I am worried that my dog is getting older.
IS: *He knows that you care about him.*
ME: I worry about him dying.
IS: *I know that you do everything you can to take care of him.*
ME: Thank you for listening.
IS: *I'm here. You are a good Mommy!*
ME: Aww . . . I needed to hear that.

Step 3: The therapist supports the back and forth process until the client decides that the subject matter has been exhausted. This can be assessed by asking the client, "Is there anything else that emerges for you in this dialogue? Do you want to keep going? Or would you like to stop now?"

Step 4: When finished, the client can choose to read the dialogue out loud (this is preferred) and then process experiences and insights. Sometimes the client asks to have the process read to them. The therapist may also ask the client if they are open to any insights offered by the therapist.

DREAMS AS A HEALING TOOL FOR CHILDREN AND ADOLESCENTS

Dream exploration with children and adolescents is an often overlooked healing tool. Over the years I have worked to encourage children and adolescents to share their dreams. Dreams can be a window into unconscious processes and can bring great insight when examined. It was through the study of dreams that early psychoanalysts came to understand how the conscious and unconscious worlds worked together to process the experiences of daily life.

The world-renowned psychologist Carl Jung masterfully gave us much insight into the world of dreams, and he believed that the symbols revealed to us in dreams were the language of the unconscious. Since much of waking life is absorbed at a subliminal level, Jung believed dreams to be symbolic messages sent to us from the unconscious that, when examined, can provide practical guidance, advice, and insight into daily living. Jung (1964) wrote, "As a general rule, the unconscious aspect of any event is revealed to us in dreams, where it appears not as a rational thought but as a symbolic image" (p. 5). Dreams may arise from the daily bombardment of minor to major emotional upsets that we may not fully process at a conscious level, and Jung (1964) described these as the "tender spots of the psyche, [that] react most quickly to an external stimulus or disturbance" (p. 11).

Some dreams may symbolize turning points in our life (as shown in the dream example below, The Lion and the Bear). Many teenagers are fascinated by the idea of dream exploration, making them less resistant to engaging in therapy. I therefore encourage them to keep a dream journal and to immediately upon awaking write down any dreams and bring them to sessions. Some people may not readily remember their dreams. Just the simple act of consciously deciding that one wants to remember dreams begins a magical process of awakening the bridge between the dream world and conscious memory. The following section presents two different ways for children and adolescents to explore dreams.

Symbolic Dream Exploration: Steps of Implementation

Symbolic dream exploration works well with older children and adolescents and focuses on a client's personal meanings and feelings generated by the symbols revealed within the dreams. Dreams can seem enigmatic for anyone, whether they be advanced in dream analysis or just a beginner. However, the following process can help guide older children to gain insight into their unconscious processes, and sometimes they are surprised at a sudden aha moment when the meaning of the dream becomes crystal clear. The following steps are recommended for exploration of dream symbolism and can be completed during a therapy session together.

Step 1: Clients begin by writing out their dream in present tense and first person (using "I") in whatever way their dream is remembered. The dream is to be written in simple, short sentences. Ask clients to include how they felt about the dream after they woke up or when they remembered their dream (fear, panic, puzzled, content, etc.).

Step 2: After the dream is written down, clients are asked to give the dream a title. Next, clients are asked to read the dream out loud as the therapist listens. When finished they are asked to describe their overall thoughts and feelings they associate with the dream. Have them add as much sensory detail as possible, colors of a room, sounds or smells, who else was peripheral to the dream, et cetera.

Step 3: Next, draw a line down the middle of a blank piece of paper, and at the top of the first column write "Dream Sentence" and for the other column put "Feelings, Thoughts, Associations."

Step 4: Have the client write the complete story, sentence by sentence, in the first column. (This may take more than one piece of paper.) Once the whole story is written out, clients are asked to go back and circle one or two words from each sentence that pops out or speaks to them. It is helpful to use a colored pencil or marker to circle the words.

Step 5: This step produces some distancing from the dream itself. The therapist guides the client to the first word circled and asks the client to describe what emotions they feel when they think of the word. These emotions are written down in the second column, across from the corresponding sentence. Next, the client is asked if the word sparks any associations in the past, present, or future. These are also jotted down across from the corresponding sentence. This process is repeated until all the circled words are evaluated.

Step 6: Once this process is completed, the therapist reviews with the client all of the feelings and associations that emerged from the circled words. These are then discussed within the context of the presented dream for further exploration. It is always best for the client to discover the insights of a dream for themselves. However, the therapist may have some insight to offer the client that could be helpful. Clients are always asked if they are open to feedback from the therapist before the therapist offers any thoughts.

To demonstrate the Symbolic Dream Exploration technique in action, I am sharing a brief personal dream I had a few years back, during a period that I recognized as a point of professional transition.

My Dream: *The Lion and the Bear*

It is nighttime and I am asleep in my bed. The warm blankets are pulled up to my chest. I wake up when a friendly lion enters the room and pounces on my chest. At the same time, a bear leaps out of my bedroom window. I immediately wake up and contemplate my dream and feel happy and content.

TABLE 8.1: PROCESSING THE LION AND THE BEAR DREAM As described in the Steps of Symbolic Dream Exploration Implementation	
Dream Sentence	**Feelings, Thoughts, Associations**
It is nighttime and I am asleep in my bed.	Feeling of contentment when I can have a good night's rest.
The warm blanket are pulled up to my chest.	I like to feel warm and enjoy the feel of cozy blankets.
I wake up when a friendly lion enters the room and pounces on my chest.	I associate a lion with a meaning of strength, determination, and leadership. The lion is friendly, and I feel brave—no fear.
At the same time a bear leaps out of my bedroom window.	I associate a bear with a sense of hibernation—of pulling back and time of contemplation.
	I feel a sense of contentment, confidence and direction from the dream experience.

Another way to deepen the process above is to ask the client to pick out some of the underlined parts and then to then have a separate dialogue with those parts. For example, I could use my imagination to pretend a conversation with the lion and bear.

Me to Lion: Do you have a message for me?
Lion to Me: It's time for you to be a leader and to take on a leadership role to guide others.

Me to Lion: Do you think I am ready for that?

Lion to Me: More than ready, that's why I am here.

Me to Bear: You are leaving?

Bear to Me: Yes, it's time now.

Me to Bear: Thank you for being with me.

Post-Dream Contemplation

This dream came to me a few years ago when I was completing my Ph.D., which consisted of intensive research and studies that required a lot of private time and contemplation and not a lot of time out in the world—which I think of as being akin to a hibernating bear. I think of a lion as strength, determination, and leadership. The dream confirmed for me that it was time to take on more of a leadership role in my career—which felt like a courageous step. It also showed me that I would feel a sense of comfort and warmth in my new leadership role.

My Dream Cartoon Story

The *My Dream Cartoon Story* intervention works well with children ages 3 to 11 years, as it imparts a storytelling cartoon process to the dream. This technique is especially helpful when children have nightmares or recurring dreams. The dream art process works like a cartoon strip: In this each frame is drawn to tell the dream story from start to finish. Using my dream again as an example, we begin with a basic storyboard, and then the child draws the images to go along with the scenes.

Step 1: Have children begin with a storyboard.

Step 2: On paper, create frames where children will then draw their images as decided in the storyboard. If possible, also have them add thinking and talking bubbles in the frames to show their characters communicating.

The next step is optional but can be helpful if a child is having nightmares or problematic recurring dreams.

Step 3: Ask children to use their imagination to add a frame to their dream story that creates a scene for how they would want their dream to end to make it have a "happy ending."

TABLE 8.2: Dream Scene Storyboard	
Title	*"The Lion and the Bear"*
Frame 1	Drawing of myself sleeping peacefully in bed at night with the warm covers pulled up to my chest. Draw window next to the bed.
Frame 2	Draw a friendly Lion pouncing playfully and happily on my chest. I am not afraid and I am shown as calm and content.
Frame 3	Draw a Bear leaping out of the window. The Lion is still with me. Draw myself looking content and happy.

Brief Example of the My Dream Cartoon Story *in Action*

Jon, age 9, shared a dream in which he was stuck on an island surrounded by sharks that were circling the island, and he was not able to get off. This terrified him. He drew each scene, using four cartoon frames to show himself stuck on an island with sharks circling. When he was finished, I empowered him to use his imagination to decide how he would like for his dream to end that would create a happy ending. He closed his eyes and thought for a moment. When he opened his eyes, he said with exuberance, "I know, a policeman could come out on a boat and pick me up and take me back to shore." I said, "Great, would you like to draw that in the last frame?" Feeling empowered to take control of his dream destiny, he quickly went to work and drew his final vision for the revised version of his dream with a police boat at the island rescuing him and bringing him back to shore. This final step is powerful, as it draws upon the child's own inner strengths and resiliency for change.

A DREAM EXPLORATION

With the above discussion in mind, I invite you to engage in the following practice exercise: A Dream Exploration.

THE PRACTICE

A Dream Exploration

Choose one of the dream explorations above (*My Dream Cartoon Story* or the *Symbolic Dream Exploration*), and follow the steps to implement that process. Once you have completed your dream exploration, and if appropriate or comfortable, find a partner and share your dream process. (Note, if you have not remembered a dream recently, you can consciously tell yourself that you want to remember a dream. You might be astonished that you remember one. Give it a try!)

YOGA AND OUR MOVEMENT SENSES

In my first year of college, I volunteered in a nursing home and ran groups for the elderly residents. The most popular class was Yoga for Wheelchairs—which always packed the room full of elderly male and female residents closely parked next to each other in a wheelchair-horseshoe form. During one session, when we were stretching forward in the "downward dog" yoga position—albeit adapted—one woman, who had been quiet and withdrawn, suddenly began an almost uncontrollable giggle. At once, all heads turned toward the giggling resident—with staff jaws dropped in curiosity and residents staring in astonishment. And, if there is anything we know about laughter—it's contagious. Soon the smiles broke wide, and then, you guessed it—everyone started chuckling along. But not at her. They were enjoying the moment of joy *with* her. It was like a light had turned on, creating a cathartic emotional release. At that moment, I witnessed how kinesthetic movement directly affects emotional release and resilience.

We forget that we have more than five senses. The vestibular and proprioceptive senses are referred to as the sixth and seventh senses, respectively. The vestibular sense is all about balance, equilibrium, and coordination. It's the sense that helps us learn how to ride a bike, swim freestyle, comb hair, pluck eye brows, cut with scissors, and zip a zipper. Inverting our head is one way to stimulate our vestibular sense—think downward dog! Our proprioceptive sense interprets stimulation at receptors in our joints and muscles every time we move our body and it helps us make our way, spatially, in the world. McGilchrist (2009) states that most of our proprioceptive awareness is localized in the right hemisphere and is linked directly to the "physiological changes in the body when we experience emotion." He elaborates, "The right hemisphere's superiority in the emotional realm is explicitly linked to this close physiological relationship with the body" (p. 69). Both senses perform together like paired dance partners, wherein vestibular stimulation supports our bodily functions toward coordinated balance and independence, and our proprioceptive sense assists to organize our body's spatial and emotional regulation.

Children need to move! Of course, we all do—even nursing home residents in wheelchairs. Impassioned discussions regarding children, technology, and screen time engagement are stirring much debate among practitioners (Aiken, 2016; Courtney & Nowakowski, 2018, 2019; Stone, 2019). And recently a special issue of *Play Therapy Magazine*, entitled "Technology in the Playroom" (Stauffer, 2018), was devoted to the topic. An overarching question is how do we balance the need for children to engage in ample sensory movement with the reality of increasingly screen-based, technological, and sedentary lifestyles? Neiman (2015) poignantly highlighted the unintentional consequences of how replacing old-school game playing with playing the same game on an app can, in fact, rob a child of important benefits of multisensory physical activity and proprioceptive experience:

> For example, a child was shaking a cup with dice for the Yahtzee game. Trying to be helpful, the principal asked the child if he would like the app for the game on his iPad. My goal was for the child to move his arm and hand as he shook the container. I wanted him to feel the smooth texture, temperature of the dice and to hear the sound the dice made as they hit the table. I was using the sensation from shaking the jar for proprioceptive input. By simply using the app, these goals would be lost in the experience; all the sensory motor experiential learning removed. (Neiman, 2015, p. 1)

Yoga and the Traumatized Child

Yoga, with Indian origins dating back thousands of years, was introduced to the west in the late 19th century, and today yoga classes can easily be found in almost every city across the U.S. and in many countries worldwide. Yoga

FIGURE 8.1: A mother assists her two children in a downward dog yoga pose.
SOURCE: COURTESY OF CARMEN JIMENEZ PRIDE, PHOTO BY NATALIE PRIDE

employs bottom-up regulation, and van der Kolk (2014) conducted ground-breaking research on the effects of yoga on traumatized clients, showing profound changes in mind and body awareness to support healing from trauma. Traumatized clients need to learn to feel safe in their bodies, and van der Kolk (2014) asserted that yoga practices are one way to make that happen. Trauma is stored in the body as emotional memory as " . . . muscle tension or feelings of disintegration in the affected body areas: head, back, and limbs of accident victims, vagina and rectum in victims of sexual abuse" (van der Kolk, 2014, p. 265). Janet Adler, a pioneer in the field of dance therapy called Authentic Movement, described the importance of developing a healthy "inner witness" (Adler, 2002). For infants and very young children, that inner witness is not yet developed, and therefore it is only through the body that trauma can be known and healed. She writes, "The body knows, remembers trauma at a cellular level, but without a present and strong inner witness when the trauma is occurring, what the body knows cannot be remembered" (p. 40). The therapist can act as a safe "outer witness" that supports a container for the child to develop their inner witness into their sensory and emotional experience.

In body psychotherapies, practitioners are interested in discovering how the connections between embodied learning, thoughts, and emotions are intricately linked. (See also Chapter 10 for more discussion about body therapies.) We are observing how clients move, sit, stand, walk, posture, breathe, and hold their shoulders and chest. Ogden and Fisher (2015) advanced the acceptance of the idea that body posture plays a vital role in how we think and feel about ourselves. Body posture is correlated to the spine's alignment and the surrounding muscles, and Ogden and Fisher imparted that various experiences that are traumatic for children can directly impact the body's posturing, as described below:

> Traumatic and suboptimal attachment environments promote postural adaptations suited to unsafe, rejecting, or critical conditions. If caregivers reprimand a child for crying and showing negative emotions, the child will learn to hold back emotions and tears, sometimes aided by tension and a rigidly upright spine. In other settings, a child's safety or well-being is better assured by patterns of compliance, submission, or "invisibility." The spine and core of the body then might collapse, slump, or droop. Fixed postures, such as a chronically slumped spine or "military" posture, can be viewed as positions from which only select emotions and behaviors can be possible. (Ogden & Fisher, 2015, p. 347)

During my first yoga class at age 19, my instructor informed us that the ancient yoga masters believed that the secret to youth was a flexible spine and that most of the asanas (aka, body postures) revolved around connecting to different parts of the spine. Ogden and Fisher (2015) advocated that when clients are supported to "lengthen their spines," that this can shift their inner core perceptions of themselves, and that it is difficult for clients to feel "depressed or ashamed if their spines are vertically aligned and their shoulders are dropped back into a squared but relaxed stance" (p. 348). Yoga positions can help to beneficially adjust core spine posture. Some child therapists who have discovered the benefits of yoga on their own somatic and sensory integration have sought additional training opportunities to bring yoga practices into child expressive and play therapies (Neiman, 2015). Play therapist and social worker Carmen

Jimenez-Pride (2018) is founder of FreedOM Yoga, Inc. She developed a set of visual cards depicting several yoga postures that make up the *Sun Salutation*, which is comprised of a series of body positions that are completed in succession. Jimenez-Pride uses these cards with traumatized children to bring "present moment awareness, connecting the mind and body to assist with emotional regulation and cultivating a relationship of trust and love towards the body" (personal communication, April 4, 2019).

I have utilized yoga poses to help traumatized children, to gently heighten their awareness of the connection between their mind and body, and to support the development of self-regulation skills. The children also gain the ability to develop what some call a "bodily-sense of self" by tuning into their body organs and skeletal and muscular systems. As an example, a withdrawn, bullied child who presents with a slumped core can be empowered by holding the *Warrior* pose, which helps them ground, breathe, and discover their inner, core strengths through focusing and feeling their body, spine, muscles, and organs aligning and growing stronger. Somatic therapies can bring up forgotten and implicit memories held within the body, especially with traumatized children, thus it is vital to introduce body work very slowly, attuning closely to the child and following their lead. Therefore, the child should hold a yoga posture for only a few seconds, and after each pose, practitioners should check in with the child to hear about any sensations, thoughts, and feelings that arose for the child. The child may then decide to stop, or they may decide to engage in the same pose again or try a new one. Unlike traditional yoga classes where an instructor may adjust a student's form while holding a position, when using yoga poses as a therapeutic tool, the therapist never corrects the child's form. The goal is for clients to tune into their bodies with a simple, relaxed breath, to develop an inner witness for whatever emerges in the moment. The point is that the child is always in the "driver's seat" during a yoga and body work session, and the therapist only guides with attuned awareness. Also, as for any new therapeutic technique, practitioners need to have specialized training and supervision in yoga or any other type of somatic therapy before bringing it into practice with clients.

DANCING WITH MYSELF

In our world of increasing technology, it is becoming harder for our clients— or ourselves—to take timeout breaks from our phones, computers, answering messages on Facebook, and so forth. In this, we forget to move our bodies— we forget our core alignment as we become more habituated to passive and inactive activities. And good for all you readers who do have a regular movement practice—aerobics, yoga classes, hiking, gym workouts, or walks on the beach. Upon meeting a new friend, I inquired about her profession. "Oh, I teach the elderly how not to fall," she answered. "How do you do that? I asked. "By teaching them how to move," she answered. Now very intrigued, I followed up, "And, how do you do that?" She smiled, "By teaching them Tai Chi." Hmm . . . now that's a brilliant idea! One of the quickest ways to move is to dance, which is another somatic therapy that we can bring into expressive and play therapy sessions with children and adolescents (Golly, Riccelli, & Smith, 2017; Lefeber, 2014). With this discussion in mind, I invite you to engage in the following practice exercise: Dancing with Myself.

THE PRACTICE

Dancing with Myself

When was the last time you danced? Consider the circumstances: Were you with others? A wedding? A lounge? A party? How did you dance? By yourself? With a partner? What was the music? In this exercise, I encourage you to dance in private—alone, just for yourself. You will need to put on your favorite music— preferably something you can sing along to. Most music speaks to the heart and not the intellect, and music therapists know well the myriad healing and neurological benefits of sound, which augment health and happiness (Lane, 1994; Miles, 2005). In Ayurvedic medicine, the voice is used to bring vibration to the organs and bones of the body to move energy and blockages. That said, this exercise involves music, dance, *and* your singing voice. Choose familiar music that lifts your spirits and prompts you to sing along while stimulating positive memory in your muscles to perk-up. Plan ahead the best time for your alone dancing, or get up and move now. Here are the guidelines: Cue the music, begin to move your body, and allow your voice to be heard. Sing loud. Sing off key. Dance silly. Dance jumpy. Be free. Sway. Dance in circles. Close your eyes or keep them open. And, most important, be kind and nonjudgmental toward your singing and dance adventure. Get in touch with your inner witness and when you are done, journal your experience! You can even have a designated dance and movement journal. Don't stop there. Experiment with different types of music, songs, and dance.

Another option is to do the dance process above by beginning with a "hand dance." (Hand dancing is a great place to start for children that may be more reluctant toward whole body movement.) Allow your hands to speak and dance a story—think of Hawaiian Hula dancers and how they can tell a story through their hands. Note that some clients are so frozen in their trauma that just gently supporting rhythmic movement beginning with the fingers is a huge step forward.

Learn more about the therapeutic benefits of music and dance at the American Music Therapy Association [https://www.musictherapy.org] and the American Dance Therapy Association [https://adta.org].

A MINDFUL LABYRINTH JOURNEY

The labyrinth as a therapeutic healing tool is an emergent practice. Traced back over 4000 years, the labyrinth's origins remain unknown (Lonegren, 2015). It's important to understand that labyrinths are different from mazes, which have dead ends and different path choices. The unicursal labyrinth design (meaning a single path) is thought to be a metaphor for life's journey. From a another perspective, it is also believed to represent an inward spiraling to the center of the brain where humans are thought to meet their inner Self. One of the most famous labyrinths is at the Chartres Cathedral in France. Built in the 11th century, during a period when Christian pilgrimage to the holy land was desirable, the labyrinth served, in part, as a way to simulate that holy journey.

Several years ago, I was gifted with an amazing labyrinth on my home property by John Heider, a friend who values the profound healing benefits of labyrinths (Heider 1985, 2000). "You must walk the labyrinth three times in and out," he said in a personal communication, "in order to get the full benefit." It was then, when I had daily access to a labyrinth at my own home, that I discovered the healing path of conscious walking. When visiting the Deer Park Monastery in Escondido, California, I participated in a mindful group walk led by the monastics. During the silent walk we were instructed to pay attention to our breathing as we paced step by step and breath by breath—much like what happens in facilitated labyrinth walks.

Labyrinths for healing are used in many different settings, including substance abuse treatment facilities and even in prison settings (Curry, 2000). While teaching Social Work and Spirituality, a graduate level course, I arranged a labyrinth facilitation for the students. The students were guided in a three-part process that included the journey walk in, time in the center of the labyrinth, and the walk out (see steps of implementation on the next page). When finished, they processed their experience in two ways: first by immediately journaling their experiences, and then through group discussion. The group sharing process revealed deep emotions and insights from their experiences, with reactions ranging from feeling joyful release to tearful exchanges to sparks of insight. Curry (2000) highlighted some common labyrinth experiences, "As people tread through the turns and counterturns of the labyrinth, the world begins to drop away. Walking, breathing, begin—things that we never think about in the day-to-day whirl of life—become conscious and

FIGURE 8.2: Author in mindful contemplation walking the labyrinth at the Ghost Ranch, Abiquiu, New Mexico

SOURCE: PHOTO BY ROBERT D. NOLAN

deliberate" (p. 6). Labyrinth facilitations can be particularly helpful in group settings and for family work. Some labyrinths can be reserved for private facilitations. This brings up an important ethical issue: when facilitating anything outdoors, clients will need a separate informed consent that addresses any type of nature-based outdoor facilitation, as confidentiality in outdoor settings is difficult to control.

Walking A Mindful Labyrinth Journey: Steps of Implementation

Step 1: Intention—What is the purpose for the walk? What issues is the client working on? What are the obstacles to growth? What does the client hope to gain from the walk?

Step 2: Contemplation—The mindful walk into the center. Pay attention to each step and breath and each twist and turn of the labyrinth. Also, notice without judgment, the various thoughts and feelings that arise on the path to the center. Instruct clients to pay attention to the movements of their body. Do they feel stiff, loose, free, closed or open? What feelings emerge?

Step 3: Release—Arriving in the center, allow the clients a moment to center, ground, rest, and release. The center time can include a process of letting go of undesired patterns and calling in a new path of opportunity. It is also about renewal.

Step 4: Re-visioning—Instructions for the walk out of the labyrinth are the same as for the walk in—pay attention to each step and breath and each thought and feeling that arises. During this time, clients are asked to contemplate their life dreams, goals, and desires for their next step in life.

Step 5: Ground the experience by thinking about new patterns of action and what was learned from the experience. Group or family sharing sharing can happen during this time, or clients may journal their experience.

THE PRACTICE

Walking A Mindful Labyrinth Journey

Find a labyrinth in your area. Many cities and towns have at least one labyrinth. One of my favorite pastimes when traveling is to check if the area has a labyrinth, and if it does, I make every effort to go to it. Try to locate your nearest labyrinth, and then follow the instructions listed under the Walking A Mindful Labyrinth Journey: Steps of Implementation. If you are unable to locate a labyrinth, no worry, this exercise can be adapted to a hiking trail, a walk on the beach, a stroll through a local park, even a walk down the sidewalk and back. Think about whether you want to walk alone or with a partner, family, or group. Just know that your experience with other people will be very different than if you do this by yourself. When you have completed your mindful labyrinth journey (in whatever way you were able to make it happen), answer the following questions:

- What was your overall experience of the journey?
- What was your initial intention for the journey?
- What thoughts and feelings emerged for you?
- What did you learn about yourself?
- Did anything happen that surprised you?
- How do you understand your intention for the walk now?
- If you journeyed with other people, did you learn anything from walking with others?
- What steps will you take to put your insights into action?

IMPORTANT CONSIDERATIONS FOR RESPECTFUL ENGAGEMENT

Essential to the topics covered in this chapter, we need to keep in mind that families come from diverse cultural and religious backgrounds. Various family systems may not resonate with some of the practices presented in this chapter such as yoga or mindfulness, which may be perceived as spiritual paths from other cultures. For example, since mindfulness has foundation in Buddhist traditions, some parents from different cultures or religious backgrounds may be uncomfortable allowing their children to engage in mindfulness practices. However, Brother Minh Hoa, an ordained Buddhist Monk residing at Plum Village in France, says that based on the Buddhist traditions of Thich Nhat Hanh's organization, "Buddhism is not a religion, but rather a *practice*" (Brother Minh Hoa, personal communication, April 2, 2019). We may learn, during an initial assessment, a family's preferences. We need to understand and approach these preferences with respect.

Chapter 9

FOSTERING ATTACHMENT AND BONDING THROUGH FIRSTPLAY KINESTHETIC STORYTELLING

"The bodily felt awareness furnishes the drive toward relating.
Through his felt body the child becomes aware of himself.
This bodily felt awareness carries the consciousness of the self."
Viola Brody, PhD, Founder Developmental Play Therapy

*F*our-year-old Johnathan—with his hands waving excitedly in the air— *runs toward me down the long office hallway saying, "I brought my hands with me today!" Delighted, I respond, "I see them. Here they are. Should we count them to make sure they are all there?" I intently search for his cues of engagement with the question. He is smiling and nodding his head in affirmative, "Yes." As he gives me his right hand I say, "Okay, let's say hello to this hand. Here we go," and I begin to count: "One, two, three, five, six!" I pause in anticipation of his response. He knows the silly game, as we have done this before, and he knows I am pretending to count wrong to playfully connect. "I have five fingers!" he said giggling. "Oh, my," I said laughing, "Miss Janet has forgotten how to count. Let me try again. One, two, three, four, five! Five, you have five fingers on this hand. Shall we count and say hello to the other hand now?" But the other hand was already lifting and giving itself to me and I comment, "Do you see that? Did you see how this hand wanted to say hello, too?" He is laughing, and he lets me count his other fingers.*

BACKGROUND AND TOUCH

The above child interaction was inspired by my training with Viola Brody, PhD, founder of Developmental Play Therapy (DPT), a touch-based, therapist-implemented play therapy intervention and foundation for FirstPlay Therapy. Some background: In 1993, I attended a training with Brody and was intrigued by the uniqueness of DPT, with its emphasis on healing children with varied attachment problems through caring and attuned touch. After several years of receiving extensive training and supervision in DPT, I chose to complete my dissertation in DPT, and Brody was on my dissertation committee. Since Brody's death in 2003, other practitioners (see, for example, Schwartzenberger, 2020) and I have carried the teachings of DPT to a new generation of play therapists. Although the participants in the trainings understood DPT as a powerful healing modality, they often raised one concerning issue: TOUCH! They were apprehensive about the liability issues concerning practitioners touching children.

To put touch in a therapeutic context, we need to understand that back in the 1950s, when Brody developed her approach, the topic of touching children was not a major issue of concern among professionals. However, the heartbreaking revelation of children being abused by adults in positions of authority came to the forefront in the 1980s, and concerns of professional liability regarding the touching of children heightened (Carlson, 2006; Courtney & Nolan, 2017; Field, 2014); the need to address ethical considerations regarding touch and children became paramount. It was clear that the field needed to review the use of touch with children anew. In my efforts to effectively address professional considerations of touch, I have examined this topic through several means, including: doctoral research in DPT, in which I examined practitioner's experiences of touch (Courtney & Gray, 2011, 2014); co-editing a book, *Touch in Child Counseling and Play Therapy: An Ethical and Clinical Guide* (Courtney & Nolan, 2017); conducting survey research examining child practitioners' attitudes and experiences of touch in play therapy and child counseling sessions (Courtney & Siu, 2018); providing professional trainings on the ethics of touch; and acting as Chair of the Practice and Ethics Committee through the Association for Play Therapy, in which I assisted to coordinate the organization's updated version of the "Paper On Touch" (Association for Play Therapy, 2019).

The outcome of all my deliberations about touch in the treatment of children? First, we know that touch is vital to human growth and development, without it, we may perish—even if other basic needs, such as nourishment and hygiene, are met. We need to be touched in caring and nurturing ways. It is not optional. I also discovered that touching children is an "ethics-related lightning rod," as Reamer (2017) puts it, and many therapists are highly concerned about liability related to touch (Courtney & Siu, 2018). My contemplations on the topic led to a paradigm shift in my thinking, and I decided to adapt the foundations of DPT to a new model called FirstPlay Therapy. In this model, practitioners work directly with the parents and available caregivers to guide, facilitate, and supervise *them* to provide the touch-based play interventions. With this change, the concerns of liability are diminished. FirstPlay Therapy is designed for two different developmental levels: for ages birth to two years is FirstPlay Infant Story-Massage, which is discussed in Chapter 10, and for ages two and above is FirstPlay Kinesthetic Storytelling, which is the focus of this chapter.

SOMATIC PSYCHOTHERAPIES: A GROWING PARADIGM SHIFT

Schore (2012) wrote that the current embracing of mind and body modalities is a fundamental change away from the "Cartesian mind/body split" (p. 8) that has "plagued" psychology, pediatrics, and other fields for decades. Dr. van der Kolk (2014) described his shift in thinking about the psychological field's neglect of the body, "I discovered that my professional training, with its focus on understanding and insight, had largely ignored the relevance of the living, breathing, body, the foundation of our selves" (p. 89). It was the work of Wilhelm Reich (Reich, 1977/60) that laid the groundwork for somatic interventions and his work is often credited for the theoretical foundation of the mind-body connection in the field of body psychotherapies. In body psychotherapies, the connection between the body, mind, and spirit are viewed as one, as revealed in the following statement from the United States of America Body Psychotherapist website:

> Body-oriented or body-centered psychotherapy is an expansive, emerging, multi-faceted field that affirms the inseparability of mind, body, and spirit. It draws from somatic psychology which sees the mind revealed not only in relational styles, dreams, and cognitions, but in neurophysiology,

posture, gestures, movement, bodily tensions and more. It explores the therapeutic possibilities of somatic roads to the unconscious and healing while honoring the wisdom of general psychology and psychotherapy through expanding and contributing to it. (https://usabp.org/)

That said, expressive and play therapists are exploring and developing ways to assist children through trauma experiences through somatic therapies (Courtney, 2012; Courtney & Nolan, 2017; Courtney, Velasquez, Toth, 2017; Norton, Ferriegel, & Norton, 2011; Levine & Kline, 2007; Richardson, 2016; Scharlepp & Radey, 2017). Because FirstPlay Therapy is a touch-based, nurturing intervention with its focus on the mind–body relational attachment between parents (or caregivers) and children, it naturally falls under the umbrella of somatic or body therapies.

FIGURE 9.1: FirstPlay Therapy Kinesthetic Storytelling Foundations

FIRSTPLAY KINESTHETIC STORYTELLING® FOUNDATIONS

FirstPlay Kinesthetic Storytelling is an attachment, touch-based, storytelling intervention that synthesizes several different theoretical foundations, including developmental play therapy, filial play therapy, attachment theory (Bowlby, 1988; Schore, 2012), peer massage in school programs (Palmer & Barlow, 2017), mindfulness practices, and the body of research on touch (Field, 2014; see Table 9.1). Ericksonian-based storytelling principles (StoryPlay) (Mills & Crowley, 2014) is another foundational underpinning of FirstPlay Therapy, as the touch-based techniques are imbedded within a strategically crafted metaphorical healing story. Practitioners then demonstrate the therapeutic story techniques to parents on a teddy bear or pillow while the parent simultaneously uses the same techniques to draw the story on the child's back. For this reason, children may know this approach not as Kinesthetic Storytelling®, but as a fun and relatable name known as "BACK Stories." The word BACK is meant as an acronym that supports the underlying benefits to children related to FirstPlay Kinesthetic Storytelling® and stands for "B": Be focused, "A": Attachment, "C": Connection, and "K": Kindness. The following sections provide a review of the underlying theories followed by a composite case study.

DEVELOPMENTAL PLAY THERAPY

There is no doubt that Viola Brody, Ph.D., founder of Developmental Play Therapy (DPT) and one of the pioneers in play therapy, was a woman ahead of her time. Brody (1997ab) advocated early on that children *needed* caring touch for healthy emotional and psychological growth and development—a fact that modern research now reveals to be true (Field, 2014; Linden, 2015). "Touch is our first communication" she advocated, hence the title of her book, *The Dialogue of Touch* (Brody, 1997b). Brody strongly emphasized that through the joyful relationship of respectful and caring touch by an attuned adult, children gain a sense of a "felt self," or a bodily sense of awareness, which helps them develop a "centering place within"—an "I" as she called it. Brody emphasized that children's development of an inner core-self needed to happen *first,* before a child could be ready for higher states of emotional and cognitive development. Children who experience caring touch are then able to develop empathetic attachment relationships with others and also to better self-regulate their emotional states. She also distinguished the difference between children's emotional developmental age versus their chronological age. Brody advocated that children could best receive therapeutic touch through the healing relationship of an attuned therapist who was trained in the specific utilization of what she called "developmental games." This developmental pre-symbolic play, or what I call *first-play* activities, can be exemplified by those early playful touch games that one might observe joyfully happening between a mother and young child, such as patty-cake or peek-a-boo. Brody believed that the touch component involved in these developmental games was intrinsically healing and that children who missed those crucial first-play stages of development (because of abuse or neglect, for example) can be helped by a therapist trained in DPT to "go back and pick up what they missed" (Brody, 1995).

The influence of Brody's work is far reaching, and TheraPlay cofounders Jernberg and Booth acknowledged the impact of Des Lauriers's and Brody's "model of healthy parent-infant interaction" to the development of TheraPlay: "Recognizing the work of Austin Des Lauriers and Viola Brody, an intuitively natural approach that could be understood . . . we adapted their methods [to TheraPlay] to help children. . . . And it worked!" (Jernberg & Booth, 2001, p. 31). They further elaborated that TheraPlay utilized Brody's therapeutic attention to the healing significance of the "nurturing relationship between therapist and child including touch, rocking and singing, and physical holding" (p. xxvi). They stated the nurturing component was "one of the most important aspects of TheraPlay" that provided an "affirmative and hopeful emphasis on the child's health, potential, and strength" (p. xxvi). Booth (2018) commented that she viewed Brody's therapy as an "intuitive and spiritual approach" with a "clear sense of the importance of touch to provide wonderful healing experiences for children" (p. 26). On another front, Becky Bailey, founder of Conscious Discipline, which is a widely acclaimed program in schools, acknowledged the influence of her Developmental Play Therapy training with Brody in her book *I Love You Rituals* (Bailey, 2000).

THE NEUROBIOLOGY OF TOUCH

Since we are facilitating caring touch between parents and children, and some-times corrective experiences of touch, it is valuable to understand the current neurobiology research, as practitioners will educate parents about the interpersonal, emotional, and social benefits of touch as related to the FirstPlay interventions. Historically, touch has been the least researched of all the senses (Field, 2014). Over the past 30 years neuroscience research has led to a deeper understanding of how the neural pathways in our body and brain are connected to memory, touch sensations, emotions, and trauma (Field, 2014; Linden, 2015; Porges, 2018; Schore, 2012; van der Kolk, 2014). In this, we have also gained new insights into how touch is related to empathy and interpersonal relationships. Sensory mirror neurons are activated when we watch another person being touched (Ramachandran, 2008), and these neurons are connected to a network of resonance circuits (Badenoch, 2008). Because mirror neurons make it possible for us to develop empathy for another, Ramachandran (2011) has fondly labeled these cells "Gandhi neurons" (p. 124). Additionally, emerging research has found that light caring touch, of a certain gentle stroke velocity, triggers afferent C fibers that play a part in the development of the social and emotional part of the brain (McGlone, Wessberg, & Olausson, 2014). This type of touch is the same type of nurturing touch that a parent may give to a child.

Additionally, neurotransmitters such as oxytocin, serotonin, and dopamine are released when we are provided with certain types of nurturing and caring touch experiences (Schore, 2012). The release of oxytocin, sometimes called the "love" or calming and connectivity hormone (Field, 2014), lowers the stress hormone cortisol, which can help children become calm. Uvnäs-Moberg (2003) wrote, "Pleasant touch and warmth activate the calm and connection system, bringing on a feeling of well-being" (p. 108). Contrarily, high levels of cortisol are released when children are abused and subjected to physical harm through slaps, smacks, hitting, and beatings—including corporal punishment—when a child is unable to fight back or flee, and can lead to diseased neural networks (Durrant & Ensom, 2012). Research on the effects of physical abuse revealed long-term negative effects on children, including higher levels of depression; anxiety; drug and alcohol abuse; aggression toward parents, siblings, peers, and, later, spouses; and higher incidences of antisocial behavior, among other problems (Durrant & Ensom, 2012).

ERICKSONIAN-BASED STORYTELLING THROUGH STORYPLAY

Joyce Mills, PhD, developed a resiliency-focused play therapy model called StoryPlay. In this model she adapted Milton Erickson's work to create therapeutic stories for children. It was thus through my training in StoryPlay (Mills & Crowley, 2014) and in Ericksonian hypnotherapy with Steve Lankton (Lankton & Lankton, 1989) that the roots of Ericksonian metaphorical principles of healing are adapted to the creation of FirstPlay Stories that also include a kinesthetic, or touch-based, element (Courtney, 2013a). The right hemisphere is activated in processing metaphorical types of storytelling, and clients can extract meanings that are relevant to them that can support new responses and ways of relating. Lankton and Lankton (1989) advised that ". . . therapeutic metaphors do not engender the kind of resistance to considering new ideas that direct suggestions often can. They are considered as gentle and permissive, not a confrontive or demanding way to consider change" (pp. 1–2).

Brody (1997b) highlighted the link between imaginative storytelling, or what she called *fantasy*, as related to attachment, memory, and touch. She advocated that fantasy is essential to successful attachment, as fantasy assists to continue a relationship with an attached figure when the other person is not there. In other words, she is speaking to the internal memory schemas that we carry within us based upon our attachment relationships. In essence, storytelling that happens between a parent and child supports the memory building in the attachment relationship. In FirstPlay, it is through the avenue of caring, respectful touch in combination with storytelling that generates our ability to *feel memory*.

FILIAL PLAY THERAPY

In filial play therapy, trained practitioners guide, facilitate, and supervise parents to provide attentive and attuned parent training in client centered play therapy techniques. Filial play therapy was founded by Louise and Bernard Guerney in the 1960s, and they advocated for parents being the "change agent." FirstPlay has adapted this direct parent training principle to then guide, facilitate, model, and supervise parents in FirstPlay Kinesthetic Storytelling. (Note, the same is applied to the FirstPlay Infant Story-Massage model). Louise Guerney wrote, "The advantage to assigning a therapeutic role to the parents is that they become temporarily removed from the entanglements of the family dynamics. They learn new ways of relating to the child. They execute new concepts and perceptions of family relationships . . . parents become part of the solution instead of part of the problem" (p. x). Practitioners model the story techniques on a large teddy bear or pillow while the parent simultaneously draws the story techniques on the child's back.

MINDFULNESS PRACTICE

Children can sense the mood of their parents—especially when parents are anxious, upset, and stressed. It is therefore imperative that parents learn strategies to help themselves focus, calm, and self-regulate, and in FirstPlay, this is the first step in teaching parent–child attunement. In this, we try to help parents become more present in the moment. Thich Nhat Hanh advocated that mindfulness is simply recognizing everything that is happening in the present moment—having an awareness of breath, of sitting, of talking, and so forth in the moment (Nhat Hanh, 2011). Badenoch (2008) advised that there is a growing body of research that supports the assertion that sustained attention "produces not only momentary functional changes in neural connections, but enduring structural changes as well (p. 133)." In FirstPlay, prior to beginning the activities or telling the kinesthetic story, parents are guided to find a peaceful place within themselves by learning a brief method to "calm and relax" using a *Rainbow Hug* imagery (Courtney, 2015). At the same time, they are supported to take a moment, center in, and connect with their child. Likewise, the child is also supported to quiet and calm themself. Prem Rawat (2016), known worldwide for his global peace initiatives, advised, "The first step [to rid conflict] is for individuals to nurture and practice peace within their own hearts" (p. 13).

FIRSTPLAY KINESTHETIC STORYTELLING PARENT MANUAL

The FirstPlay Kinesthetic Storytelling Parent Manual assists practitioners in facilitating parents in therapy sessions and is divided into four modules: Module I includes introductory, "Getting Started" activities that are designed to meet the needs of the younger child and to familiarize children with the interactive parent–child experiences. Module II provides "Ready Made" FirstPlay stories and activities that have already been created. Module III provides "Creating Stories From Scratch" and outlines a simple step-by-step way for practitioners to create therapeutic interactive stories with the parent and child from scratch, utilizing a "FirstPlay Storytelling Child Interview Grid." Module IV is where "Children Become the Storytellers" and practitioners work directly with children to formulate their own stories that they write, draw, and tell. The case presented in this chapter demonstrates Modules I and II in action.

FIGURE 9.2: Stephanie Crowley tells a FirstPlay® "BACK Story" to 3-year-old, Sophia while she imitates her felt experience of touch on a teddy bear.
SOURCE: USED WITH PERMISSION FROM STEPHANIE CROWLEY AND SOPHIA

FirstPlay Kinesthetic Storytelling Guiding Principles as Provided to Parents and Caregivers

As provided in the parent manual, practitioners review with parents the following guiding principles for the first-play therapy sessions.

- Above all, enjoy your time with your child.
- YOU are the expert on your child! Your FirstPlay practitioner will listen to you for what you know is best for yourself and your FirstPlay time with your child.
- Relax and have fun! As you relax—it also helps your child relax.
- The stories are a springboard for fun and imagination. This is more important than telling the story as written or to know all of the hand movements.
- Develop a daily special FirstPlay time together—even if just for 10 minutes—a little positive attention to your child goes a long way.
- Always ask permission from your child prior to an activity or a story. You can do this by simply saying, "Hey, would you like for me to tell you a 'BACK Story'?"
- Avoid areas that are bruised or with rash.
- Tune into your child's verbal and physical responses.
- Follow the child's lead regarding when they have had enough of the activities.
- The child is respected as the guide to a parent regarding the type of touch—such as a little firmer or lighter touch, or slower or faster movements.
- If you are able to tell only a small portion of the story—especially for little ones with short attention spans—then that is enough for the moment.
- Be careful of fingernails or jewelry that may scratch during the telling of the story.

Case Vignette: Busting the Myths of Attachment Relationships in Foster Parenting

Background

The following case composite presentation is formulated to address common issues related to foster parenting and how FirstPlay Kinesthetic Storytelling can intervene to support attachment and bonding in cases of developmental relational trauma. In this scenario, Kerry and Mike have cared for Samantha, who was placed with them when she was 18 months old. At the time of referral, she was three and a half years old. They were seeking counseling because they were recently informed by their foster care social worker that they could adopt Samantha. Prior to that time, there was a possibility that Samantha might be placed back with her biological mother.

Initial Intake Session with Foster Parents

"We were told in our foster care group training not to get too close to the foster children that were placed with us," Kerry said frowning, looking up after speaking to search for my reaction. I was listening attentively as she shared her journey of being a foster mother to Samantha. Mike sat silently on the couch while Kerry continued to explain: "We were told the reason we should not get too close to the children placed with us was because they might be going back to their biological parents and that it would jeopardize the attachment relationship with the biological parents if the child became too attached to us."

> SIDE NOTE: As Kerry made this statement about not getting too close to a child, my mind pulled up files of other foster parents who had told me the same thing in their foster parenting classes. And, I was always puzzled by this statement of advice. Several years ago, I had provided training for new foster parents, but this recommendation was not part of the curriculum. Also, I have never found this recommendation supported in the literature or within research studies. In fact, the attachment literature supports that attachment happens when two factors are present: 1) how consistent the caregivers are in providing care to alleviate a child's distress, and 2) the joyful interactions within the parent–child relationship. Children who are provided with caring and joyful caregiver experiences gain an internal working model, perhaps for the first time, of what a loving and secure attachment relationship looks and feels like that can then be transferred to other relationships. I deem the advice to foster parents to not get to close to a child they are caring for because of concerns about attachment (especially for a very young child) as an earnest, but misguided, professional myth.

Kerry continued, "So we followed the advice, not to hug her too much, or let her get up on our bed, and now we are told that we can adopt her, and we want to adopt her, but . . ." Kerry's lips started to quiver and appeared on the verge of tears. Mike reached out and touched her hand to offer support and Kerry's voice cracked as she began to cry, "But she acts like she does not like us. She won't listen and she does not like for me to hold her, and when I try, she screams and pushes me away." Her words of deep pain poured out as if she had held them in for the past two years since Samantha came to live with them. I allowed a gentle space for Kerry to share more. Mike also felt rejected by Samantha and stated, "I think she would rather be with Kerry, so I just gave up trying."

I explored in more detail with Kerry and Mike their two-year journey with Samantha, including holidays, her connection to other relatives, and times when the relationship felt more connected. I learned that Kerry's mother lived in the area and frequently had contact with Samantha and babysat her when Kerry and Mike needed her to. They attended church weekly, and they shared that they had a lot of support from the congregation and that Samantha attended Sunday School each week. I felt an overwhelming heartfelt compassion for this family. Like some foster parents, they were unable to conceive, despite fertility treatment attempts, and decided to become foster parents with the hope they might be able to adopt a child through that avenue. I spoke with them about the FirstPlay model and how it can support the building of attachment in relationships through attachment-based kinesthetic storytelling and other activities. They understood that most of the interventions did not involve the use of toys, but were interactive experiences to grow the parent–child attachment relationship though joyful singing and playful developmental games. They agreed they would be open to engaging in this intervention and agreed to attend the next session without Samantha so that they could learn some of the activities before meeting together with Samantha.

Impressions

Although the past two years had placed a strain on their relationship, Kerry and Mike appeared supportive of each other and held a shared vision to work on building the attachment relationship with Samantha. They cared deeply for Samantha and were willing to invest in the therapy process to make the necessary changes and to prepare to transition to adoptive parents.

Treatment Plan

1. Meet with parents for a second appointment to review and teach FirstPlay activities to Kerry and Mike prior to an appointment with Samantha.

2. See Samantha conjointly with Kerry and Mike for weekly sessions to model, guide, and supervise nurturing and joyful FirstPlay activities between Samantha and her parents within play therapy sessions. Introduce beginning level FirstPlay activities and, in later stages of therapy, Kinesthetic storytelling to Samantha and parents.

3. Assess the attachment relationship between parents and Samantha.

4. Build a relationship of safety and trust with Samantha and support her attachment relationship with Kerry and Mike.

5. Help guide the parents to establish safe boundaries, set limits, and create a daily schedule for Samantha.

6. Process with parents feelings of guilt and pain regarding Samantha's placement with them.

7. Bridge FirstPlay activities to the home environment for prescribed daily times of implementation for each parent. FirstPlay included nurturing, calming, joyful, exciting activities.

8. Include Kerry's mother in the therapy sessions so she can participate in the developmental games when she is with Samantha.

9. Give Kerry and Mike outside reading recommendations so they can learn more about attachment and foster parenting and understand their situation in relation to the attachment literature and in relation to other foster parents with similar experiences.

10. Coordinate with the foster care social worker as needed to support the family as they transitioned from foster parents to adoptive parents.

Second Appointment With Foster Parents

Mike and Kerry came to the next appointment and advised that they had gotten the books I recommended, and the information was helping them to better understand Samantha. This session was intended to familiarize Mike and Kerry with some of the FirstPlay activities, which we would first practice together and they would then practice with Samantha during the next session. I also discussed with them the importance of touch to the attachment relationship.

> **SIDE NOTE:** I have found that introducing the interventions to parents first, without the child present, makes it easier for parents to better understand what will be happening in the session with their child. It also gives them an opportunity to have their questions answered and to practice the techniques. Sometimes when a parent comes to the office individually, I participate directly in the interventions with the parent, and when both parents attend, I guide them to practice the activities directly with each other.

I shared with Mike and Kerry several first-play interventions that we would later practice with Samantha, including the following:

- "Guess What I'm Drawing"
- "Follow What I'm Drawing"
- "The Itsy Bitsy Love Bug"
- "Patty-Cake"
- "Row, Row, Row Your Boat"
- "Twinkle, Twinkle, Little Star"
- "Making Pizza Pie"
- "The Magic Rainbow Hug"

The process of implementation is as follows: a) calm, relax, and connect, b) ask permission, c) practice the activity, d) attune to child's responses and state what is observed, and e) follow the child's cues, lead, and needs. Since this would be a new experience for Samantha, I recommended that we start with the introductory activities, as a gentle beginning. As a first step, I guided Mike through the calm, relax, and connect "Rainbow Hug" imagery as he placed his flat palm on Kerry's back to connect with her. He then asked permission from Kerry to do the activity, "Can I do this FirstPlay activity with you?" And Kerry said, "Yes." This helps to set the tone of respect. Kerry and Mike then took turns role-playing—pretending to be Samantha—as I guided them through the steps of implementation. This process also helped them to develop more compassion for Samantha and to understand the world through her eyes. For example, for the "Guess What I'm Drawing" exercise, Kerry sat in front of Mike with her back to Mike and pretended to be Samantha. He then drew a heart on her back and then paused and waited for her to

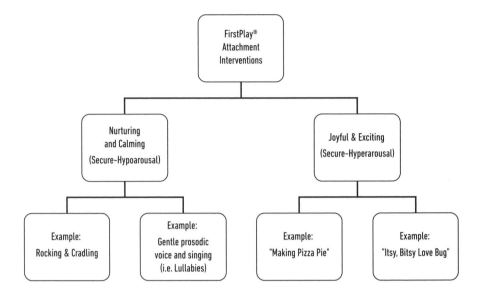

FIGURE 9.3: FirstPlay Interventions Are Developed for Two Attachment Elements of: 1) Calm-Nurturing & 2) Joy-Filled Exciting Experiences

"guess" the shape. After a few shapes we processed together what their experiences were, and then they reversed roles. We then went through and practiced all the activities together, and I helped them understand more about the importance of attunement and the importance of "seeing" each other unconditionally. When we were finished, they understood better why we needed to have a separate appointment to review and process all the activities. I explained that during the first session with Samantha, I would be allowing Samantha to explore the room and get familiar with me before the activities were introduced.

First Appointment with Samantha and Parents:
Creating Temenos and a Safe Holding Space
Upon entering the room, I greeted Samantha with a hello, squatting down to meet her at eye level. She did not make eye contact with me, and when she spied the toys in the containers on the shelf, she quickly darted over and pulled them off the shelf and picked through the toy figures. I moved to the shelf and sat next to her. Mike and Kerry sat on the couch and watched the interaction. She was an attractive child with blonde hair and green eyes, and I was struck

by how much she looked like the foster mother who had the same features. I said, "This room has a lot of toys that you can explore and play with." I wanted to give her permission to explore and feel comfortable within the room. She did not look at me and kept opening containers and looking around the room. There was very little interaction with the parents.

She found the puppets and dumped them on the floor. I asked, "If you were going to pick a puppet for your Mom and Dad, which ones would you like to pick for them." I was trying to see if I could observe any interactive engagement between the foster parents and Samantha. She picked the shark for the father and the bird for the mother and handed the puppets to them. She chose the Bear puppet. I then guided, "Hmm, I wonder . . . if these puppets were going to play together, what would they play?" Samantha thought for a moment and then silently pushed her puppet into their puppets. The father said to her puppet, "Now that's not the way to play!" Samantha then dropped her puppet and turned away to look at some of the other toys. Kerry and Mike looked at me imploringly, as if not sure what to do or how to handle the interaction. I could sense the deep pain and sadness of disconnection between the parents and Samantha. At the same time, I appreciated the vulnerability of these foster parents as they sought help and their openness to guidance to finding new ways to heal and build the attachment relationship.

After allowing more time for Samantha to explore the playroom, and as planned with the parents, I explained to Samantha that I had been working with Mom and Dad to share with them some fun activities that she might like. I then asked her if she would be interested in learning a fun game called "Guess What I Am Drawing," in which Mom would draw on her back.

Therapist: "Mom will draw a shape on your back and then you can try to guess the shape," I explained.

Samantha: "Okay," she said, interested, with her head down as she sat between her mother and father on the couch.

Therapist: "The first thing we will do is blow a long breath out," I said modeling the breath while everyone followed along. Next, Kerry practiced making a connection by placing her hand on Samantha's back, as we had practiced in the previous session.

Kerry: "Would you like for Mommy to draw on your back?" Kerry asked. (Samantha nodded her head, yes.) Kerry drew a heart shape on her back.

Samantha: "What?" she said and quickly turned around and looked at her mother, puzzled.

Kerry: "Can you guess what I just drew on your back?"

Samantha: "Do that again!" She said as she put her finger to her mouth, giggling.

Kerry: "Okay, here I go again. Guess now."

Samantha: "A circle?" she said with a puzzled face.

Kerry: "Guess again," she said smiling, making eye contact, and then drawing the heart again.

Samantha: "Uh, what is it? I don't know," she said turning to Kerry. It seemed that Samantha was ready for Kerry to tell her the shape.

I suggested that Kerry draw the shape on the palm of Samantha's hand, and she could then see it. Samantha held out her palm and looked down at her hand as Kerry drew the heart again.

Kerry: "Okay, I am going to draw slow so you can watch me," Kerry said slowly as she watched for Samantha's reaction and cues of engagement. We had discussed and practiced this attunement in the session prior.

Samantha: "A heart?" she said questioning looking up at Kerry.

Kerry: "Yes, it's a heart, because I love you," Samantha smiled and leaned into Kerry's arms and they hugged. Kerry continued, "That's right, I love you, Samantha and we are so happy you are with us."

Samantha started to giggle and enjoyed this new type of attention from her mother. They agreed to practice this at home during the week.

SIDE NOTE: Processing kinesthetic experiences on the back is a more abstract process of internally connecting somatosensory experiences of touch to cognitive thought processes. It is like switching from right-brain to left-brain processing.

Session Impressions

From an attachment theory perspective, Kerry was assessed as the *primary* attachment (who Samantha would turn to *first* to lower distress) figure to Samantha, while Mike was assessed as a *secondary* attachment figure. In many situations, the father may also be judged as a primary attachment figure, with both parents offering two different types of attachment experiences (Bowlby, 1997). Although Samantha's chronological age was three and a half years, her emotional developmental age was much younger—more like a two year old. To our delight, she took very quickly to receiving the nurturing touch; she even appeared starved for this type of attention. This need for caring touch and attention could very well be the result of the foster parents' restricted behavioral interactions over a two-year period in which they meant to follow the recommendations offered in the foster care training classes to not get too close to the child, so as not to interfere with the biological parent attachment relationship.

Summary of Subsequent Sessions and Home Activities

Over the next several weeks, the attachment-based activities were slowly introduced in sessions with the bridging of the activities to home. The activities were introduced from the simpler "Getting Started" activities to ones that required slightly longer periods of engagement such as "The Itsy Bitsy Love Bug" (adapted from the *Isty Bitsy Spider* and sung to the same tune). Since Kerry was home during the day, she planned for three FirstPlay sessions of 15–20 minutes, in which she would engage with Samantha in the developmental games as practiced in the office, followed by times when she would cradle and rock Samantha in a rocking chair. This produced balance within the window of tolerance (see the Window of Tolerance Chart, Figure 2.1) ranging between exciting, secure-hyperarousal first-play activities, followed by relaxing and calming secure-hypoarousal moments (i.e., lullabies). Mike's time for playful connection was in the evening hours after work, and Kerry's mother also engaged in the activities with Samantha. Samantha started to come to the sessions ready for relational engagement.

During one session with Kerry (Mike was working), I guided Kerry in singing the FirstPlay activity for "Twinkle, Twinkle, Little Star . . . What a lovely girl you are . . ." As she sang this song to Samantha and did some simple hand movements, Samantha regressed to a much younger stage of development. She turned over on her back on the playroom carpet and, like a young infant, she began to speak in a regressed, baby-talk voice. (This can sometimes happen within this type of nurturing therapy intervention). In this intimate moment I sat back so Samantha could only see Kerry, and for the first time, Kerry began to interact with Samantha at a whole new level of care, talking to her in a sweet, tender, prosodic voice about how much she cared for and loved her.

SIDE NOTE: The goal of the FirstPlay activities is not to intentionally regress the child, but it can occur naturally as part of the therapy. It is a very intimate moment and speaks to the neuroplasticity of the brain. It is known that children who missed those crucial FirstPlay stages (e.g., through neglect) can return to an earlier stage of development and "pick up what they need and bring it forward to the present" (Brody, 1997b, p. 9). Additionally, Porges (2018) discussed how these types of interactions, including the prosodic voice, recruit the autonomic nervous system to support a co-regulation between parent and child that occurs within the cues of safety that supports the social engagement system (as discussed in Chapter 2). When these regressed interactions happen and are honored and respected within the relationship, after the session is completed, paradoxically, the child can appear to look and act older—closer to the child's true chronological age.

To Kerry's amazement, at the end of the session with Samantha, she looked and acted older. Kerry had never before experienced Samantha in this intimate way, and it deepened their relationship connection. After this session, Kerry shared that they were having more periods of cradling where she rocked and sang to Samantha.

Six Week Session with Mike and Kerry

After six weeks of therapy, I met with Mike and Kerry without Samantha present to discuss how they and Samantha were progressing. What I heard during this appointment was a very different description of Samantha compared to our first session. Kerry stated that Samantha was now coming to her for affection (hugs and cradling time), which she had rejected in the past. She was listening more when it was time to clean up toys. Meals were less of a "battle" and she was going to sleep better at night and had fewer tantrums during the day. What was most touching, and left me standing in awe of this work, was when Mike took a turn to share as follows:

"I feel like for the first time I have a relationship with Samantha, and the other day when I came home from work and walked in the door, Samantha came running to the door, happy and excited because I was home saying, 'Daddy's home, Daddy's home!' She was happy to see me."He stated, "She never did that before. Now she is happy to see me." He realized the major shift in their relationship and how he felt much more bonded to Samantha and felt her desire to be with him.

Final Case Discussion

At this moment, I realized that something very profound had happened. We, as mental health practitioners, can talk about the attachment relationship and speak about the various ways that attachments can be built, healed, and changed; but to witness the "theory" playing out in real time was extremely heartwarming and affirming. What I felt during the beginning sessions with Mike and Kerry was a sense of desperation and hopelessness and that they had "tried everything" they knew to help Samantha. I realize that it is the place of the practitioner, my responsibility, to hold the beacon of hope out to families that things can get better, and life can feel happier as a family. What can sometimes happen, especially when little change is observed from session to session, is that the practitioner can drop into the family's depth of doubt, not seeing a way out of the bleakness. There have been occasions when I have experienced a heaviness of wallowing through the family's burdens. It is important to recognize when this happens and to take steps to see the family from a new perspective, such as by seeking peer consultation or supervision.

However, in this case, Mike and Kerry became co-creators and partners in the therapy process, which led to the final outcome of change. Meaning, it was Mike's and Kerry's determination to put in the time and effort daily and their *trust* in the process of implementing new behaviors to meet Samantha's needs that ultimately made the difference. They were empowered to be the "change agents" in Samantha's therapy. As well, Samantha had to learn to trust Mike and Kerry to meet not just her physical needs but also her emotional needs, which were not met in her early infancy development due to abuse and neglect.

As Samantha matured and could sustain and receive longer stretches of attention and focus, I gradually introduced the next level modules of Kinesthetic Storytelling® interventions, such as the short version of the "Magic Rainbow Hug" (Courtney, 2013) (see Resources, page 207). Within a few months, the adoption process was finalized, and we celebrated Samantha's adoption in the office.

A FIRSTPLAY STORYTELLING CHILD ACTIVITY: MAKING PIZZA PIE

With the chapter foundations for FirstPlay Kinesthetic Storytelling in mind, I invite you to engage in the following practice exercise: Making Pizza Pie.

THE PRACTICE

Making Pizza Pie

Find a partner to engage in the Making Pizza Pie activity. Before beginning the activity, formally ask your partner if it is okay for you to draw on his or her back during this activity. Do this as an intentional asking of permission, even if your partner has already agreed to the activity. Additionally, ask them to tell you if they want you to stop at any time or if they need you to adjust the pressure of the touch. This is important to the process and sets a tone of respect. Next, follow the steps below.

Step 1: With your partner, first decide the ingredients to go on pizza (try for a least three ingredients—the more the better).

Step 2: Next, pretend to pour flour and water on your partner's back, and then "knead" the dough [use fingertips to massage the back (be careful of fingernails), and adjust the pressure according to your partner's input].

Step 3: Roll out dough [use flat palms to spread out dough].

Step 4: Gently chop up the ingredients (cheese, pepperoni, vegetables, etc. to go on the pizza). Use the side of hand to gently "chop" the ingredients. Name each ingredient and say what you are doing and check in with your partner at the same time to elicit feedback, such as: *"I am going to chop up the broccoli now. Here we go. Do you think I have cut up the broccoli enough or should I do more?"*

Step 5: Pretend to put the pizza in the oven. Optional: If appropriate, during this time you can wrap your arms around your partner and rock back and forth making a soft "shhhh" sound as the pizza is "cooking." [Check in and ask your partner, "Is the pizza ready yet? Is it ready?" Follow the lead of your partner for readiness or not.]

Step 6: Pretend to take the pizza out of oven. Draw a circle on your partner's back, and then slice the pizza into triangles with the side of your hand.

Step 7: Pretend to eat—"Yum, yum . . ."

When you are finished, switch roles so you can experience Making Pizza Pie, too.

Children enjoy the Making Pizza Pie activity and I have successfully used this intervention to enhance the attachment relationship with many children and families.

Chapter 10

HEALING TRAUMA THROUGH FIRSTPLAY INFANT STORY-MASSAGE: AN EMBODIED INFANT MENTAL HEALTH AND PLAY THERAPY INTERVENTION

"The body is our sensation, our felt emotion.
The body is our experience of ourselves,
our temple in which the light of our spirit burns."
Janet Adler, *Offering from the Conscious Body,* 2002

This chapter introduces an infant mental health and play therapy model, FirstPlay Infant Story-Massage, and discusses the importance of touch to healthy development. Included in this chapter is a group case study of young mothers residing with their infants in a substance abuse treatment shelter. The infants were known to be exposed during pregnancy to drugs taken by the mothers—who also had traumatic childhood histories. A brief review of the opioid crisis and neonatal withdrawal is also addressed. The group case study demonstrates how the mothers were guided in FirstPlay to provide corrective experiences of touch and to attach and bond with their babies.

FIRSTPLAY® INFANT STORY-MASSAGE

As brain research has skyrocketed over the past three decades, so has our understanding of the importance of infant mental health. As a result, the field of infant mental health is rapidly expanding, and new models of therapy for this population are emerging. Play therapists are responding by creating and adapting known play therapy models to meet the specific needs of the birth-to-three population. These adaptations have become a subset under the play therapy umbrella that is called *Infant Play Therapy*. Many of these models of intervention are provided in my book entitled *Infant Play Therapy: Foundations, Models, Programs and Practice* (Courtney, 2020). FirstPlay Infant Story-Massage, falls under this emerging category.

As discussed in Chapter 9, FirstPlay Therapy is offered for two different developmental stages: for infants, from birth to 36 months (the focus of this chapter) and for children aged three years and above (Baldwin, 2019; Courtney & Nowakowski, 2019; Courtney, Velasquez, & Toth 2017). The foundations between the two models are much the same but have some differences. The main supporting theories of both models include Developmental Play Therapy, Filial Play Therapy, mindfulness practice, and research into touch. The differences are that FirstPlay Kinesthetic Storytelling focuses more on Ericksonian-based storytelling (Lankton, 2004; Lankton & Lankton, 1989; Mills & Crowley, 2014; Mills, 2015) and borrows from the peer massage in schools programs (Palmer & Barlow, 2017)). Whereas, in FirstPlay Infant Story-Massage, a manualized model, we borrow from the infant mental health and infant massage literature and research to develop an attachment-based developmental play therapy infant model.

In FirstPlay Infant Story-Massage, parents are taught to provide gentle touch techniques to their baby through a therapeutic story as guided and modeled by the practitioner, who demonstrates the activities on a baby doll (Courtney & Nowakowski, 2019; Courtney, Velasquez, & Toth 2017). The focus of the therapy is nurturing the inner resiliency of parents toward positive growth and change (Kain & Terrell, 2018). In this, parents are supported to be the "change agent" as practitioners facilitate them to attune to their baby's nonverbal language and cues of engagement.

FIRSTPLAY ATTACHMENT TOUCH AND BODY

Infants are somatosensory beings who learn about their world through their bodies and through the body contact of others. It is through touch that infants learn about themselves and the world around them, and touch is the first sense to develop in the womb. How and in what ways babies are touched are paramount in the attachment process (Courtney & Nolan, 2017). Touch and attachment go hand-in-hand—literally! While touch is the first sense to develop in utero, movement is an infant's first language—this is the only means by which the developing baby can communicate with his mother. And, communicate they do. Mothers are very much attuned to the amount of movement they can feel during pregnancy, from leg stretches and kicks to flips. And mothers communicate back to their infants through touching their hands to their belly and through their voices. Touch, movement, and vocalizations (including crying) remain the predominant ways that infants and their parents continue the dialogue after birth.

Infant massage techniques (Field, 2011; McClure, 2000; Schneider & Patterson, 2010) have also been adapted to the FirstPlay model to promote infant mental health and parent–child attachment. Giving caring, tactile skin stimulation to infants has been a longstanding phenomenon in the world for centuries. Field (2014), a leading researcher in touch, noted that infant massage is practiced as part of an infant's daily routine in many parts of the world, including Nigeria, Uganda, India, Bali, Fiji, New Guinea, New Zealand (the Maori), Venezuela, and Russia. Frederick Leboyer (1976), a French obstetrician well known for his gentle birthing techniques, wrote one of the first books on the subject entitled *Loving Hands: The Traditional Indian Art of Baby Massage*. However, it is Vimala McClure (2000) who is most often credited as bringing infant massage to the awareness of the American public.

Perry (2006a) lists "therapeutic massage" as a developmentally appropriate intervention for ages birth to two years, because infants need "rhythmic movement" and "patterned sensory input (auditory, tactile, motor)," "simple narrative," and "attuned, responsive caregiving and emotional and physical warmth" (p. 41). Additionally, the emotional development of the right-lateralized "human social brain" is, in part, supported by the "tactile-gestural nonverbal communication functions" between parent and infant (Schore, 2012, p. 257). Field (2003) advocates that providing nurturing touch to infants benefits both the baby and the caregiver giving the massage. (Refer to Chapter 9 for further discussion about touch). Research has revealed the qualitatively and quantitatively positive benefits of infant massage and parent–infant touch interactions (McClure, 2000; Feldman, 2011; Field, 2011; Ferber, et al., 2002; Linden, 2015; O'Brien & Lynch, 2011; Stack & Jean, 2011; Underdown & Barlow, 2011; refer also to the Touch Research Institute at the University of Miami (http://pediatrics.med.miami.edu/touch-research) and the Center on

the Developing Child at Harvard University) (https://developingchild.harvard
.edu/). The benefits of infant massage include:

- increasing parent–child attachment and bonding by creating nurturing and joyful intimacy;
- helping infants experience the sensation of relaxation;
- promoting a deeper and more sound sleep;
- increasing oxygen and nutrient flow to the cells;
- improving digestion and bowel elimination;
- initiating the process of teaching babies about caring positive touch and respectful personal boundaries;
- reducing stress and distress and improving emotional regulation;
- decreasing heart rate and blood pressure; and
- stimulating the release of oxytocin, which is important for calming and connectivity.

GROUP CASE PRESENTATION

Intervening With Mother and Infant Dyads in Substance Abuse Treatment: Embodying Corrective Experiences of Touch Through FirstPlay Infant Story-Massage Groups

The following sections are provided as a foundation for understanding and a backdrop for the case study presented later in this chapter.

Background: The Opioid Crisis, Neonatal Withdrawal,
and the Trauma Impact on the Infant

According to the Centers for Disease Control and Prevention, the rate of women with Opioid Use Disorder giving birth quadrupled between 1999 and 2014 (Centers for Disease Control and Prevention, 2019). Opioid Use Disorder is defined as a problematic pattern of opioid use that leads to problematic impairment and/or severe emotional distress (American Psychiatric Association, 2013). Neonatal Abstinence Syndrome (NAS) is defined by a group of symptoms found in infants who were exposed to opiate drugs while in the mother's womb. Neonatal Drug Withdrawal is the term used for the symptoms of infant drug withdrawal (Hudak & Tan, 2012). NAS and Neonatal Drug Withdrawal symptoms are similar and are characterized by frequent high-pitched crying, difficulty sleeping, tremors, poor feeding and nursing, emesis [vomiting], abdominal cramping, loose stools, fever, respiratory distress, stiff and rigid bodies, muscular pain, and emotional suffering (Hudak & Tan, 2012). Tragically, according to McQueen & Murphy-Oikonen (2016), there is no standard of care treatment for NAS following birth, and infants are given pharmacotherapy, consisting of opioid replacement either by oral morphine or methadone solution to ease symptoms, which may include seizures.

Children born to substance-abusing parents are at higher risk of being abused and neglected compared to children whose parents are identified as substance abuse-free. Schore (2012) discussed that social experiences and variations in maternal care can either create greater risk for infants or support greater resiliency in later life. Specifically, "relational trauma in infancy alters the developmental trajectory of the brain" as the child grows (p. 9). Children exposed to trauma experiences in utero or postbirth or are abused or neglected are rated as more susceptible to post-traumatic stress disorder, borderline personality, schizophrenia, and major depression (Schore, 2012; Thomson, 2004). No doubt, NAS is a traumatizing experience for infants that is encoded within their implicit memory. Osofsky, Stepka, and King (2017) write that they have used their experience and research into infant mental health to "help dispel the myth that infants and toddlers are not affected by trauma" (p. 5).

Although awareness and concern regarding the opioid crisis is growing, there is also push back, which appears to downplay the effects of drug exposure—in utero and after birth—on infants. Some call the attention to the opioid crisis "misguided panic" (Sharfstein, 2015) and equate this attention to what some considered an overreaction in the 1980s and 1990s regarding the exposure of babies to cocaine in utero (Okie, 2009). But we are understanding more and more about how developmental trauma is encoded in the body in the sympathetic and parasympathetic branches (Heller & LaPierre, 2012; Ogden, 2018b; Ogden & Fisher, 2015; Porges, 2018; van der Kolk, 2014). Although over time infants may physically and developmentally recover from drug exposure at birth, as Sharfstein and others contend, we must understand the emotional and psychological impact of trauma on the developing infant (Badenoch, 2018a; Ogden & Fisher, 2015; Schore, 2012).

To build secure attachments, the "social engagement system," mediated through the parasympathetic branch of the vagus nerve (Porges, 2018), requires an attuned caregiver who can interact with the infant through face-to-face contact and through the infants signaling behaviors, such as crying, smiles, cooing, and so forth. Through the attachment process, infants also acquire the behaviors of contact with others such as, reaching out, grasping, eye contact, holding on, letting go, pulling toward, and pushing away (Ogden, 2018a). When an infant is born positive for drug exposure and is experiencing neonatal drug withdrawal, this natural engagement system is compromised. NAS is a terrifying and painful experience for infants. A nurse working in the neonatal intensive care unit (NICU) disclosed, "We always knew the babies that were going through drug withdrawal by their high-pitched crying, stiff trembling bodies, and seizures. It was so heartbreaking for us caring for these babies to watch." In my work in foster care (late 1980s and early 1990s), practitioners were taught by NICU nurses how to securely swaddle drug exposed (mostly cocaine at the time) infants in blankets to give them a sense of security.

Gilligan (2012) coined the term *neuromuscular lock* as the physical state resulting from the body's reactive responses to trauma related to the "4Fs," meaning: flight, fight, freeze, and fold (refer to the discussion in Chapter 2). As these states of trauma embed, or "lock," within the body, they can literally block us in the healing process and from feeling higher states of joy or what he calls the "creative life force." As traumatized infants neurocept their environment as hostile and dangerous, their protective defenses are triggered. And since infants are not able to fight or flee, they "freeze," which shows up as immobilization and dissociation, or they "fold," which manifests as collapsing, numbing, depression, apathy, or lethargy.

SIDE NOTE: Gilligan's concept of "neuromuscular lock" may be akin to Reich's concept of "character armor" or "muscular armor," where an individual develops a rigid body that creates an emotional deadness that blocks connection and emotional release (Reich, 1960, p. 10). Reich believed that body armoring can begin within the newborn infant, and he took a special interest in the welfare of infants by founding the Wilhelm Reich Infant Trust Fund, which he dedicated to the care and security of infants everywhere.

Emerging Field of Epigenetics

Within the emerging field of epigenetics, we understand more about the role of nurture versus nature and the impact of trauma on the developing brain. The Center on the Developing Child at Harvard University highlighted the effects of adverse experiences, including fetal drug exposure, in the following:

> . . . adverse fetal and early childhood experiences can—and do—lead to physical and chemical changes in the brain that can last a lifetime . . . malnutrition, exposure to chemical toxins or drugs, and toxic stress birth or in early childhood are not "forgotten," but rather are built into the architecture of the developing brain through the epigenome. The "biological memories" associated with these epigenetic changes can affect multiple organ systems and increase the risk not only for poor physical and mental health outcomes but also for impairments in future learning capacity and behavior. (Center on the Developing Child at Harvard University, 2019)

Paula Thomson (2004) also described the impact of trauma in utero in the following:

> The development of the human brain is a species-typical unfolding determined by the interplay between our genetic heritability and the expression of this heritability during both activity-independent and experience-dependent processes (p. 9) . . . These species-typical genetic markers driving early embryonic and fetal development are exquisitely vulnerable to alterations from environmental factors occurring within the cell and around the organism . . . The neurotoxicity model suggests that the developing brain is vulnerable to damage caused by excess chemical release from neurotransmitters/neuromodulators and neuropeptides/neurohormones in response to chronic or repeated unpredictable stress. When the developing embryo and fetus experience prolonged periods of stress, the stress response becomes toxic for its vulnerable and immature brain (p. 10) . . . Early trauma, whether experienced pre- or postnatally, is encoded and processed at the subcortical and unconscious level. These spinal cord, brain stem and deep limbic structures are active very early in gestation . . . (p. 11).

How to Help?

A National Public Radio segment on *All Things Considered* (NPR, 2018) highlighted succinctly through the program title that, "Babies Born Dependent On Opioids Need Touch, Not Tech." In this story, they interviewed a physician in Kansas who is spearheading changes in how infants who are born testing positive to opioids are cared for. To be certain that infants are receiving adequate touch experiences, she advocates allowing infants to be with their mothers after birth, versus being separated from their mothers in NICU. Research has shown that infants exposed to nurturing touch through gentle massage can reduce withdrawal symptoms in infants prenatally exposed to drugs. Infants who experience this kind of touch have increased immune system responses, cry less, exhibit a more calm temperament, and excrete lower amounts of catecholamine stress hormones in their urine (Wheeden, et al., 1993). Field (2014) reported that cocaine-exposed preterm infants in a neonatal unit who were provided with massage three times a day for 10 days exhibited 28% more weight gain per day, fewer postnatal complications, and less stress behaviors than those in the control group.

Because infants cannot verbally tell us their internal experience, we must pay close attention to the behavioral responses of the infant: their cries, grimaces, flinches, pulling back of limbs, or lethargic behavior, and so forth. Once an infant has tested positive for opioids or other substances at birth, the parents and infants may enter into a state or county system of dependency, where the baby may either be removed from the parent and placed with a relative or foster family, or reside with the mother in residential center in which the parent is mandated for treatment. In any of these situations, it is up to the available caregivers (mother, foster parent, grandparent, aunt, etc.) to help the infant not just with their basic physical needs, but also with their emotional needs. We understand untreated early trauma can compromise the development of the right side of the brain, as discussed in detail Chapter 2. Research and literature supports the positive outcomes of early intervention with infants assessed as at-risk (Osofsky, 2009; Osofsky, Stepka & King, 2017). FirstPlay Therapy was developed as a preventative and therapeutic intervention. The following group case example shows the impact of FirstPlay Infant Story-Massage over five sessions with a group of mothers and their infants, residing in a substance abuse treatment facility.

BACKGROUND OF MOTHERS ATTENDING THE FIRSTPLAY GROUP

A FirstPlay Infant Story-Massage group was held weekly at a women's residential substance abuse shelter for five sessions, running approximately 60 to 90 minutes in length. The infants attended the group sessions with their mothers, as the program policies mandated that mothers be with their infants. Mothers were discouraged from allowing other group members to hold their infant, except the day care workers in cases of mothers who were employed. All the mothers were known have abused opioids, such as oxycodone and heroin, and for some there had been polysubstance abuse, including alcohol, cocaine, or ecstasy, during pregnancy. All the infants were born drug-positive, as many of the women used substances up until delivery. Many of the mothers had experienced severe trauma in their childhoods and were either homeless prior to entering the program, with some turning to prostitution in desperation to support their drug addiction, or they were in unhealthy, physically and emotionally abusive relationships. Many of the mothers were court ordered to undergo treatment, as the treatment center offered a viable option for the infants to be placed in foster care. Some of the mothers had other children who had been placed in foster care and subsequently given up for adoption because the mother had failed to meet the reunification requirements. The racial backgrounds of the mothers included Hispanic, Caucasian, African American, and Haitian.

The mothers knew that the group was part of a research study to examine the outcomes of the FirstPlay infant model when working with mothers and infants in a residential treatment facility. They each signed a release and informed consent form to participate in the five-week study. The weekly curriculum and process are outlined next.

Goals of the FirstPlay Infant–Parent Group

a. To educate the mothers about the importance of nurturing touch, attachment, and bonding.

b. To guide mothers to be "change agents" and to attune (e.g., read their infant's cues) and respect (e.g., ask permission to touch) their infants and to create cues of safety through prosodic intonations.

c. To teach and facilitate FirstPlay activities (music, touch, and attachment).

d. To teach and guide FirstPlay Infant Story-Massage techniques.

e. To approach the parents from a resiliency and strength-based perspective.

Five-Week FirstPlay Mother–Infant Group

Week One

This week the FirstPlay model was introduced with a psychoeducational discussion, handouts, and a video related to the importance of attachment and bonding, as well as a group sharing about the mothers' birth experiences and their questions and concerns about their babies. Because the group members also agreed to participate in this group as a qualitative research study, the mothers were asked to draw a mother and child, and these drawings were created and collected on the first and the last day of the of five session group. This art directive was adapted from the work of Gillespie (1994), and was part of my dissertation that included the analysis of drawings (Courtney & Gray, 2011). The drawings were made by practitioners who were asked to draw a picture of a therapist and child. The directive was open-ended to allow group members to decide what this meant for them. However, participants were asked to draw whole bodies and not use symbolic representations.

Week Two

During this week, group members examined their own experiences of attachment. They watched a video related to infant mental health, developing secure attachments, and bonding. Then the group members examined their own experiences of primary, secondary, and tertiary attachments through a Circles of Attachment activity. The mothers also participated in a mindfulness imagery in which they were guided to imagine being cradled and cared for in a nurturing way. They were then invited to engage in an expressive arts intervention where they could create a clay representation of their mindfulness experience. The mothers were then invited to share their experiences and clay representations if they were ready.

Week Three

Group members were introduced to the *FirstPlay Infant Story-Massage Parent Manual* (Courtney, 2015) and the importance of nurturing touch. The manual was divided into two parts: one for the story-massage activities and the other for the FirstPlay developmental activities. Several FirstPlay activities were demonstrated during this session and the story-massage activities were planned for the next session. Through discussion and introduction of the activities, it was discovered that although the mothers were familiar with the developmental nursery games presented, they had not been engaging in these or any other activities.

I demonstrated the FirstPlay activity *Twinkle, Twinkle, Little Star* on a baby doll while the mothers sang and practiced with their own infants. However, the words, "how I wonder what you are" were replaced by, "what a lovely baby you are . . ." In this activity, the parents are taught to gently dance their fingers up the baby's legs and stomach. The introduction of music stimulates feelings of safety, Porges (2018) informs, thus the mother can impact infant emotional states by how the song is sung, increasing arousal with lively singing or inducing calmness with soft singing.

> **SIDE NOTE:** Research on music and the brain demonstrates that music stimulates emotional and hormonal states by activating the limbic system, including the "hypothalamus, hippocampus, amygdala, and parts of the thalamus that wrap around the brain stem" (Miles, 2005, p. 4).

Next, they practiced *Patty-cake, Patty-cake Baker's Man.* In this activity, the mothers were guided to gently tap the baby's feet together (not hands) while saying rhythmically the words to Patty-cake. *This Little Piggy* was adapted on the spot by asking the mothers to think of their own words of food that their babies might like (e.g., bananas) as shown in the following adaptation:

This Little Piggy *FirstPlay Directions*
This little piggy went to the market. *(Wiggle the big toe.)*
This little piggy stayed home. *(Wiggle the second toe.)*
This little piggy had _____ *(Fill in blank with yummy food; wiggle the third toe.)*
This little piggy had some. *(Wiggle the fourth toe.)*
This little went wee, wee, wee, *(Wiggle the fifth toe.)*
All the way home. *(Run fingers up the body to "dance" on chest.)*

FIGURE 10.1: *This Little Pig Went to Market*
by Lilly Martin Spencer, 1857.
SOURCE: NEW BRITAIN MUSEUM OF AMERICAN ART (DSC09337): PUBLIC DOMAIN

SIDE NOTE: For centuries, joyful developmental games, played by parents
with their infants and children, have been an essential part of our human
evolution, and the use of *This Little Pig Went to Market* was first noted
in the early 1700s. The endearing image in Figure 10.1 shows a mother
engaging in this playful activity with her infant.

All mothers participated in the activities and were encouraged to practice the
activities with their infants daily.

Week Four

All mothers were present with their infants, aged two to six months. The mothers were familiar with what to expect for the demonstration, as the "FirstPlay Parent Manual" information had been reviewed with them the week before, including contraindications for infant massage, reading a baby's cues for readiness and engagement, and a touch awareness checklist (e.g., fingernails can scratch a baby). They were advised that they could participate in whatever way they chose. Therefore, some mothers chose to have their babies sitting in their laps and others had their infant on the floor on a pillow with a blanket. The mothers in the group were guided and supervised in the FirstPlay Story-Massage activity called *The Baby Tree Hug*, which I modeled on a baby doll while the mothers simultaneously practiced with their infants. During the FirstPlay demonstration, attunement and attachment was facilitated in the following ways: a) using calming, relaxing, and connecting imagery; b) demonstrating the *right kind* of touch (e.g., not too light or too much pressure); c) speaking to the baby; d) speaking for the baby; e) seeing and being seen; e) using prosodic voice; f) modeling engagement; and g) lowering the mother's performance anxiety through easy and simple guidance.

In *The Baby Tree Hug*, we pretend the baby's body is a beautiful tree:

- **Larger Branches:** Hips to ankles
- **Main Root or Taproot:** Feet—Bottoms and tops
- **Smaller Side Roots:** Toes
- **Tree Limbs: Arms**—Shoulders to wrist
- **Leaves:** Hands
- **Fruits or Flowers or Nuts:** Fingers
- **Stems:** Wrist
- **Front Trunk:** Mid-body—Stomach and chest
- **Hollow of the Tree Trunk:** Stomach
- **Back Trunk:** Back, spine, and top of shoulders
- **Sun:** Head (the "sun" shines down on the tree)
- **Sun's Rays of Light:** Hair
- **Moon:** Ears
- **Smiling, Happy Face:** Face

Process of FirstPlay Implementation

The mothers were provided with a *FirstPlay Infant Story-Massage Parent Manual,* and therefore could follow along in the books during the demonstration. The group was facilitated in a calming, relaxing, and connecting Rainbow Hug imagery in which the mothers were guided to relax, focus, and be present with their infants. They were guided to gently place one hand on their heart and the other on their baby's chest to feel a sense of connection while they imagined a beautiful rainbow giving them both a warm and caring hug. The mothers were next taught and guided to ask for permission to touch from their infants before they began the story activities. This sets a tone of respect for the infant, and at the same time, parents are taught to assess the cues of their infants for readiness to engage. Some soft relaxing lullaby music was played in the background, which added to the sense of a nurturing holding environment.

FIGURE 10.2: Stephanie Crowley demonstrates an attuned heart connection with 5-month-old, Ezra, prior to beginning a FirstPlay session.
SOURCE: USED WITH PERMISSION FROM STEPHANIE CROWLEY

Selected Mother–Infant Process Recording

To illustrate a mother–infant dyad experience, I will focus on a selected process recording related to one mother (Tina) and her infant, Jordan. Tina sat next to me in the circle and appeared to be an attentive and eager learner throughout the process. She put one hand on her heart and one hand on her baby's heart and made eye contact with Jordan during the Rainbow Hug connecting imagery. The facilitation continued with reading a part of the story, followed by a demonstration of the story-massage techniques on the baby doll while Tina (and the other mothers) followed along.

FirstPlay Therapist to group: Okay, so I will read part of the story, and then I will demonstrate the techniques on the baby doll, and then you can follow along. First, you can all decide what kind of tree you would like to pretend your baby will be.

Tina: [who decides on an apple tree] Should I take off Jordan's clothes? [Tina had been holding Jordan in her arms, and she put him down on the pillow and blanket. Jordan was quiet and alert—the best time for the First-Play Story-Massage.]

FirstPlay Therapist: That is certainly fine. It is your decision, and some people like that, as we know that skin-to-skin contact is import. Just leave his diaper on. (All FirstPlay® facilitations are completed with the diaper on).

Tina: I would like to do that. *[Tina removes his clothes.]*

FirstPlay Therapist: The apple tree has long strong branches. The first branch begins here at the very top and ends all the way at the bottom. [After reading the story, the massage technique is guided.] This is called the *Branch Leg Glide*: With one hand supporting the baby's foot and leg, use the other hand to glide down the leg beginning at the top of the thigh to the ankle. Massage both the inside and the outside of the legs.

Tina: [When Tina touched Jordan's leg, he immediately began to coo and talk and move his body limbs and make eye contact with her. Tina was staring down at him and amazed to see Jordan's response. Jordan's response caught the attention of all the other mothers in the room, who made positive comments to Tina about his reactions.] Look at him. He really likes this. I've never seen him like this.

FirstPlay Therapist: Yes, I see how much he is enjoying your touch. Go ahead and tell him directly how happy you are to see his reaction. You can speak to him directly about what you are seeing. You can ask if he would like for you to do that again. [Use of a prosodic voice was modeled to show how she might ask that question to Jordan. Part of attunement is to help support the parent to learn to talk directly to their infant and also to learn to *listen* and state back what they observe. Tina was prompted to ask Jordan if he would like that again, modeling how mothers might begin a dialogue.]

Tina: [nodding her head in understanding and looking at Jordan] I see you really liked that. Would you like that again?

FirstPlay Therapist: [In a soft voice, so as to not disturb the interaction] Let's watch and see how he responds to your question, then comment to him about what you see.

Tina: [watching Jordan, who started wiggling his body and smiling back at Tina] You are smiling at me and moving your body all around.

FirstPlay Therapist: And, I see that you are smiling at him and he is smiling at you.

Tina: [Looks at the therapist, smiling and nodding her head as if discovering something new about Jordan and also something new about herself.] [*The Baby Tree Hug* story-massage was facilitated for the rest of the session.]

The group was reminded that the next session was the last.

Week Five: Closure of the Group and Discussion

Participants were again asked to draw a picture of a mother and baby and also to write a final, closing evaluation. The mothers were then given the pre-course drawings and asked to compare the two and comment on what they saw, while observing the drawings from a loving and caring perspective, and to share any insight or understanding they had gained about themselves based on their evaluation of their drawings.

Members were invited to share their pre- and post-drawings, and group members gave consent for sharing insights into their drawings with each other. The group members answered a final group evaluation. In the evaluations, all of the mothers wrote that they wanted to learn more FirstPlay developmental games and more story-massage techniques. Due to the fact that the curriculum consisted of psychoeducation about the importance of attachment and bonding and the participants' examination of their own attachment experiences, many participants indicated that they now understood more about the importance of touch to bonding, attachment, and brain development. As an act of closure for the group sessions, photos of the mothers with their babies were taken and given to the mothers.

A FIRSTPLAY ACTIVITY (ADAPTED FOR AN OLDER CHILD) *TWINKLE, TWINKLE, LITTLE STAR*

With the chapter foundations for FirstPlay Infant Story-Massage in mind, I invite you to engage in the following practice exercise: *Twinkle, Twinkle, Little Star.*

THE PRACTICE

A FirstPlay Activity: *Twinkle, Twinkle, Little Star*
This activity requires that you let your inner child out to play. Find a partner to engage in the singing FirstPlay activity of *Twinkle, Twinkle, Little Star.* (If you are unfamiliar with this song, you can easily find it through a quick internet search and listen to it online.) Before beginning the activity, formally ask your partner if it is okay to engage in this activity together. This asking of permission demonstrates respect. Try the activity in different ways, from singing the song and activity in a more animated enjoyment of play to a softer, slower, and calmer way of singing and using the movements. Discuss with your partner the differences between these styles in the activity.

Twinkle, Twinkle, Little Star

(Facing your partner, hold your hands up in the air and with your partner playfully tap your fingers together in a light downward motion)

What a lovely _____ *(fill in the blank, "friend, husband, child, etc.)* **you are.** *(Hands on shoulders, looking in partner's eyes.)*

Up above the world so high, *(Flat palms together up in air—gentle rock.)*

Like a diamond in the sky, *(Circle flat palms together downwards.)*

Twinkle, twinkle, little Star. *(Again, hold hands up in the air and playfully tap fingers downward together.)*

What a lovely _____ *(fill in the blank, "friend, husband, child, etc.)* **you are.** *(Lean in and give your partner a hug and/or pat on the back.)*

CONCLUSION

Infants are often perceived as being unaffected by traumatic experiences because they do not retain a conscious memory of the trauma. This societal myth of infancy has caused much harm as we have overlooked the crucial needs of this population. As discussed in Chapter 2, neuroscience literature overwhelmingly concludes that infant and childhood developmental trauma alters the brain and results in enduring problems related to executive functioning skills and emotional, behavioral, cognitive, social, and physical challenges. What is clear is that early intervention and prevention with infants and families that are culturally sensitive can make a positive difference in a child's life trajectory. The field of infant mental health is rapidly expanding, and new models of therapy for this population are emerging. Working with parents and their infants through FirstPlay Therapy interventions draws upon the parent's inner strengths to promote bonding and attachment, as it offers a therapeutic manualized model of providing respectful touch through joyful play experiences.

Resources

WEBSITES

- Association for Play Therapy (APT): www.a4pt.org
- American Art Therapy Association (AATA): https://arttherapy.org
- American Dance Therapy Association (ADTA): https://adta.org
- American Horticulture Therapy Association: https://www.ahta.org/
- American Society of Group Psychotherapy and Psychodrama (ASGPP): asgpp.org/index.php
- American Music Therapy Association (AMTA): www.musictherapy.org
- Animal Assisted Play Therapy: risevanfleet.com/aapt
- International Expressive Arts Therapy Association (IEATA): www.ieata.org
- International Association for the Study of Affective Touch (IASAT): iasat.org
- National Association for Poetry Therapy (NAPT): poetrytherapy.org
- National Coalition of Creative Arts Therapies Associations (NCCATA): www.nccata.org
- Play Therapy International: www.playtherapy.org
- United States Association for Body Psychotherapy: www.usabp.org

THE MAGIC RAINBOW HUG

The Magic Rainbow Hug (Short version)

There once was a little _____ *(girl; boy; cat; dog; favorite animal of child, etc.)*; and she/he *(use the same gender as the child)* was outside playing.

Draw an outline: *Person or animal on the back of the child.*

It was a beautiful day and the sun that warms and lights the whole world was shining bright in the sky. The rays of the sun shone out in all different directions—some go up, some go down and some go to the sides.

Sun: *With a fist, make a circle on the middle of the back; then draw "rays" out in all directions.*

The little *(say character)* was having fun laughing, running, skipping, and jumping around.

Running: *Move your fingers around on the back as if the child or animal was playing.*

But then the little *(say character)* looked up in the sky and saw some dark clouds rolling in.

Clouds: *With two fingers make an outline of three clouds on the upper back.*

So, the little _____ *(say character)* looked to the side and saw a beautiful safe place to go. It was a _____ *(castle; house; tent; name whatever the child would like)* and they ran into the safe place and they were all <u>safe</u> and <u>protected</u> inside.

Shelter: *Draw an outline of the shelter with your finger and then run your fingers across the back into the shelter. Emphasize the words safe and protected.*

They watched from a window as the wind began to blow. It blew faster . . . and faster . . .

    and faster . . .

Wind: *Move your hand from side to side, first with the flat palm and then with the back of your hand.*

. . . until it began to rain.

Rain: *With both hands begin at the shoulders and stroke downward with your finger pads . . .*

Then it rained stronger and stronger until it turned to hail.

Hail: *Use your fingertips and playfully bounce up and down at different spots on the back.*

Then the lightning came.

Lightning: *Take your fists and make long zigzag motions starting at the top of the shoulder and moving back and forth across the spine to the bottom of the back.*

Then it began to thunder.

Thunder: *Take your fists and lightly pound across the shoulder top and down the sides of the back taking care not to hit the spine. Adjust your touch to the needs of the child.*

*Most children—and adults like this part. *At this point I try to have the child use sound on the exhale like an Ahhhhhh . . . Make the sounds with them, too.*

Then the leaves started to swirl. They begin on the ground and move, up, Up, and UP to the sky. And, it happened again—they blew up, Up, UP to the sky. Swirling and twirling all around. And, once again, up, Up, UP—swirling and twirling.

Swirling Leaves: *Start at the base of the spine and use your fist to make circular swirling motions moving up the spine to the top. Repeat three times.*

Then all of a sudden, a strong wind comes and blows all . . . those . . . dark . . . clouds . . . away.

Clouds Blowing Away: *Take your hands and sweep across the child's back from right to left. Have the child take a deep breath and pretend they are blowing all of the dark clouds away.*

Then the sun came out again and shone bright again in the sky.

Sun: *With a fist, make a circle on the middle back; then draw "rays" out in all directions.*

Then the little _____ *(name character)* ran out to play. Next, *(he/she)* looked up into the sky and saw a beautiful rainbow suddenly appear. The rainbow had the colors of green, blue, yellow, purple, red, and more . . .

Rainbow: *At this point engage the child in the naming of the colors. Use your fists to make long sweeping half circles across the back beginning below the shoulder blades to the opposite side of the back. Do the sweeping motion for each color and say the name of the color out loud.*

Then something very special happened. The little _____ *(name character)* looked up toward the sky, and the sparkling rainbow began to melt all over *(his/her)* body. All those beautiful colors flowed to every single part of *(his/her)* body.

Melting Rainbow: *At this point try to engage the child in the process of naming where the colors all go and have the child place their own hands on the spots. The places I name are the: top of the head, face (forehead, nose, eyebrows, ears, mouth, checks), throat, shoulders, arms, elbows, hands, each finger, palms, knees, feet, and each toe.*

The last place the beautiful rainbow flowed was to *(his/her)* heart.

Have the child place both of their hands over their heart.

References

Adler, J. (2002). *Offering from the conscious body: The discipline of authentic movement.* Rochester, VT: Inner Traditions.

Aiken, M. (2016). *The cyber effect: A pioneering cyberpsychologist explains how human behavior changes online.* New York, NY: Spiegel & Grau.

Allan, J. (1988). *Inscapes of the child's world.* Dallas, TX: Spring Publications.

Allen, F. H. (1976). Therapeutic work with children. In C. Schaefer (Ed.), *Therapeutic use of child play* (pp. 227–238). New York, NY: John Wiley & Sons.

American Psychiatric Association. (2013). Substance Use Disorders. In *Diagnostic and statistical manual of mental disorders* (5th ed.). Arlington, VA: American Psychiatric Publishing.

Aponte, H. (1976). Under-organization in the poor family. In P. J. Guerin (Ed.), *Family therapy: Theory and practice.* (pp. 432–448). New York, NY: Gardner Press, Inc.

Association for Play Therapy. (2019). *Paper on touch: Clinical, professional & ethical issues.* Retrieved from https://cdn.ymaws.com/www.a4pt.org/resource/resmgr/publications/2019/Paper_on_Touch_2019_-_Final.pdf

Atkins, S., & Snyder, M. (2018). *Nature-based expressive arts therapy: Integrating the expressive arts and ecotherapy.* Philadelphia, PA: Jessica Kingsley Publishers.

Axline, V. (1964). *Dibs in search of self.* New York: Ballantine Books.

Axline, V. (1969). *Play therapy* (Revised edition). New York, NY: Ballantine Books.

Badenoch, B. (2008). *Being a brain-wise therapist. A practical guide to interpersonal neurobiology.* New York, NY: W. W. Norton & Company.

Badenoch, B. (2018a). *The heart of trauma.* New York, NY: W. W. Norton & Company.

Badenoch, B. (2018b). "Safety *is* the treatment." In S. W. Porges & D. Dana (Eds.), *Clinicalapplications of polyvagal theory: The emergence of polyvagal-informed therapies* (pp. 73–88). New York, NY: W. W. Norton & Company.

Bailey, B. (2000). *I love you rituals: Fun activities for parents and children.* New York, NY: HarperCollins Books.

Baldwin, K. M. (2019). *An examination of adolescent maternal-infant attachment relationship outcomes following a FirstPlay Therapy infant storytelling-massage inter-vention: A pilot study* (Unpublished doctoral dissertation). Florida Atlantic University, Boca Raton, Florida.

Bankart, C. P. (1997). *Talking cures: A history of Western and Eastern psychotherapies.* Pacific Grove, CA: Brooks/Cole Publishing Company.

Berger, R., & McLeod, J. (2006). Incorporating nature into therapy: A framework for practice. *Journal of Systemic Therapies 25*(2), 80–94.

Betensky, M. G. (1987). Phenomenology of therapeutic art expression and art therapy. In J. A. Rubin (Ed.), *Approaches to art therapy* (pp. 149–166). Bristol, PA: Brunner/Mazel.

Blum, R. (1987). *The book of runes.* New York, NY: Oracle Book, St. Martin's Press.

Booth, P. (2018). TheraPlay, Part 2: Inspiration and longevity. *Play Therapy, 13*(2), 24–26.

Bowen, M. (1976). Theory in the practice of psychotherapy. In P. J. Guerin (Ed.), *Family therapy: Theory and practice* (pp. 42-90). New York, NY: Gardner Press, Inc.

Bowlby, J. (1988). *A secure base: Parent-child attachment and healthy human development.* New York, NY: Basic Books.

Bowlby, R. (1997). *Attachment: Three educational videos.* Richard Bowlby, Boundary House, Wyldes Close, London NW11 7 JB.

Bratton, S., Ray, D., Rhine, T., & Jones, L. (2005). The efficacy of play therapy with children: A meta-analytic review of treatment outcomes. *Professional psychology: Research and practice, 36*(4), 376–390.

Brody, V. (1995). *Developmental play therapy: A clinical session and interview with Viola Brody.* [DVD]. Center for Play Therapy (Producer). (Available from Center for Play Therapy http://cpt.unt.edu).

Brody, V. A. (1997a). Developmental play therapy. In K. J. O'Connor & L. M. Braverman (Eds.), *Play therapy theory and practice: A comparative casebook* (pp. 160–183). New York, NY: John Wiley & Sons.

Brody, V. A. (1997b). *The dialogue of touch: Developmental play therapy* (2nd ed.). Northvale, NJ: Jason Aronson.

Brown, S. (2009). *Play: How it shapes the brain, opens the imagination, and invigorates the soul.* New York, NY: Penguin.

Brown, S., & Eberle, M. (2018). A closer look at play. In T. Marks-Tarlow, M. Solomon, & D. J. Siegel (Eds.), *Play & creativity in psychotherapy* (pp. 21–38). New York, NY: W. W. Norton & Company.

Burdick, D. (2014). *Mindfulness skills for kids & teens: A workbook for clinicians & clients with 154 tools, techniques, activities & worksheets.* Eau Claire, WI: PESI Publishing & Media.

Burns, R. C. (1987). *Kinetic-House-Tree-Person Drawings (K-H-T-P): An interpretive manual.* New York, NY: Brunner/Mazel Publishers.

Capacchione, L. (2002). *The creative journal: The art of finding yourself* (2nd ed.). Franklin Lakes, NJ: New Page Books.

Carlson, F. (2006). *Essential touch: Meeting the needs of young children.* Washington, DC: National Association for the Education of Young Children.

Centers for Disease Control and Prevention (2019). *The number of women with opioid use disorder at labor and delivery quadrupled from 1999–2014.* Retrieved from www.cdc.gov/media/releases/2018/p0809-women-opiod-use.html

Center on the Developing Child at Harvard University. (2019). Epigenetics and child development: How children's experiences affect their genes. Retrieved from https://developingchild.harvard.edu/resources/what-is-epigenetics-and-how-does -it-relate-to-child-development/#epigenetics

Chapman, L. (2014). *Neurobiologically informed trauma therapy with children and adolescents: Understanding mechanisms of change.* New York, NY: W. W. Norton Publishing.

Coelho, P. (1994). *The alchemist.* New York, NY: HarperCollins Publishers.

Committee on Child Psychiatry (1982). *The process of child therapy.* New York, NY: Brunner/Mazel, Inc.

Courtney, J. A. (2020). *Infant play therapy: Foundations, models, programs, and practice.* New York, NY: Routledge.

Courtney, J. A. (2004, September 12). "Kids need help to work out hurricane stress." Article by Jane Daugherty. *The Palm Beach Post,* West Palm Beach, Florida.

Courtney, J. A. (2008, June) The perfect dollhouse. *Play Therapy, 3*(2), 6–7.

Courtney, J. A. (2012). Touching autism through developmental play therapy. In L. Rubin & L. Gallo-Lopez (Eds.), *Play-based interventions for children and adolescents with autism spectrum disorders* (pp. 137–157). New York, NY: Routledge.

Courtney, J. A. (2013a). *The curative touch of a magic rainbow hug.* TEDx Talk, Delray Beach, Florida. Retrieved from https://www.youtube.com/watch?v=kYZ qyjzuaOw

Courtney, J. A. (2013b). *The magic rainbow hug: Calm & relax.* Palm Beach Gardens, FL: Developmental Play & Attachment Therapies, LLC.

Courtney, J. A. (2015). *FirstPlay parent manual.* Boynton Beach, FL: Developmental Play & Attachment Therapies, LLC.

Courtney, J. A. (2017a). Overview of touch related to professional ethical and clinical practice with children. In J. A. Courtney & R. D. Nolan (Eds.), *Touch in child counseling and play therapy: An ethical and clinical guide* (pp. 3–17). New York, NY: Routledge.

Courtney, J. A. (2017b). The art of utilizing the metaphorical elements of nature as "co-therapist" in ecopsychology play therapy. In A. Kopytin & M. Rugh (Eds.). *Environmental expressive therapies: Nature-assisted theory and practice* (pp. 100–122). New York, NY: Routledge.

Courtney, J. A., & Gray, S.W. (2011). Perspectives of a child therapist as revealed through an image illustrated by the therapist. *Art Therapy: Journal of the American Art Therapy Association, 8*(23), 132–139. doi:10.1080/07421656.2011.599719

Courtney, J. A., & Gray, S. W. (2014). A phenomenological inquiry into practitioner experiences of developmental play therapy: Implications for training in touch. *International Journal of Play Therapy, 23*(2), 114–129.

Courtney, J. A., & Mills, J. C. (2016). Utilizing the metaphor of nature as co-therapist in StoryPlay. *Play Therapy, 11*(1), 18–21.

Courtney, J. A., & Nolan, R. D. (2017). *Touch in child counseling and play therapy: An ethical and clinical guide.* New York, NY: Routledge.

Courtney, J. A., & Nowakowski-Sims, E. (2018). Technology and the threat to secure attachment relationships: What play therapists need to consider. *Play Therapy, 13*(3), 10–14.

Courtney, J. A., & Nowakowski-Sims, E. (2019) Technology's impact on the parent-infant attachment relationship: Intervening through FirstPlay therapy. *International Journal of Play Therapy, 28*(2), 57–68.

Courtney, J. A., & Siu, A. F. Y. (2018). Practitioner experiences of touch in working with children in play therapy. *International Journal of Play Therapy, 27*(2), 92–102. doi:10.1037/pla0000064

Courtney, J. A., Velasquez, M., & Bakai Toth, V. (2017). FirstPlay Infant Massage Storytelling: Facilitating Corrective Touch experiences with a teenage mother and her abused infant. In J. A. Courtney & R. D. Nolan (Eds.), *Touch in child counseling and Play Therapy: An ethical and clinical guide* (pp. 48–62). New York, NY: Routledge.

Courtney, R. C. (1964). The concept of business ethics. In D. N. Delucca (Ed.), *The council on business ethics* (pp. 91–95). Brooklyn, NY: St. Joseph's College.

Cozolino, L. (2014). *The neuroscience of human relationships: Attachment and the developing social brain* (2nd ed.). New York, NY: W. W. Norton & Company.

Crenshaw, D. A., & Stewart, A. L. (2015). *Play therapy: A comprehensive guide to theory and practice.* New York: Guilford Press.

Curry, H. (2000). *The way of the labyrinth: A powerful meditation for everyday life.* New York, NY: Penguin Compass.

Davis King, A., & Woods, D. (2017). The utilization of touch and StoryPlay in preschool bereavement groups. In J. A. Courtney & R. D. Nolan (Eds.), *Touch in child counseling and play therapy: An ethical and clinical guide* (pp. 178–188). New York, NY: Routledge.

Degges-White, S., & Davis, N. L. (2018). *Integrating the expressive arts into counseling practice: Theory-based interventions* (2nd ed.). New York, NY: Springer Publishing Co.

Dhaese, M. J. (2011). Holistic expressive play therapy: An integrative approach to helping maltreated children. In A. A. Drewes, S. C. Bratton, & C. E. Schaefer (Eds.), *Integrative play therapy* (pp. 75–93). Hoboken, NJ: John Wiley & Sons.

Diehl, E. R. M. (2009). Gardens that heal. In L. Buzzell & C. Chalquist (Eds.), *Ecotherapy: Healing with nature in mind* (pp. 166–174). San Francisco, CA: Sierra Club Books.

Doidge, N. (2007). *The brain that changes itself.* New York, NY: Penguin Group.

Donaldson, O. F. (1993). *The vision and practice of belonging: Playing by heart.* Deerfield Beach, FL: Health Communications, Inc.

Dorfman, E. (1965). Play therapy. In C. R. Rogers (Ed.), *Client centered therapy* (pp. 235–277). Boston, MA: Houghton Mifflin Company.

Durrant, J., & Ensom, R. (2012). Physical punishment of children: lessons from 20 years of research. *Canadian Medical Association Journal, 184*(12), 1373–1377. doi:10.1503/cmaj.101314

Edwards, B. (1979). *Drawing on the right side of the brain.* Los Angeles, CA: J. P. Tarcher, Inc.

Elbrecht, C. (2013). *Trauma healing at the clay field: A sensorimotor art therapy approach.* London, UK: Jessica Kingsley Publishers.

Engemann, K., Bøcker Pedersen, C., Arge, L., Tsirogiannis, C., Mortensen, P. B., & Svenning, J. C. (2019). Residential green space in childhood is associated with lower risk of psychiatric disorders from adolescence into adulthood. *Proceedings of the National Academy of Sciences of the United States of America, 116*(11), 5188–5193. doi:10.1073/pnas.1807504116

Epstein, G. (1989). *Healing visualizations: Creating health through imagery.* New York, NY: Bantam Books.

Erikson, E. H. (1963). *Childhood and society* (2nd ed.). New York, NY: W. W. Norton & Company.

Estrella, K. (2005). Expressive therapy: An integrated arts approach. In C. A. Malchiodi (Ed.), *Expressive therapies.* New York, NY: Guilford Press.

Feldman, R. (2011). Maternal touch and developing infant. In M. J. Hertenstein & S. J. Weiss (Eds.), *The handbook of touch: Neuroscience: Behavioral and health perspectives* (pp. 373–408). New York, NY: Springer.

Ferber, S. G., Kuint, J., Weller, A., Feldman, R., Dollberg, S., Arbel, E., & Kohelet, D. (2002). Massage therapy by mothers and trained professionals enhances weight gain in preterm infants. *Early Human Development, 67,* 37–45. Retrieved from https://www.ncbi.nlm.nih.gov/pubmed/11893434

Field, T. (2011). Massage therapy: A review of the recent research. In M. J. Hertenstein & S. J. Weiss (Eds.) *The handbook of touch: Neuroscience: Behavioral and health perspectives.* (pp. 455–468). New York, NY: Springer.

Field, T. (2014). *Touch* (2nd ed.). Cambridge, MA: MIT Press.

Fisher, C. (2019). *Mindfulness and nature-informed creative activities for kids.* Eau Claire, WI: PESI Publishing.

Fitzpatrick, L. (2019, January 24). The monk who taught the world mindfulness awaits the end of this life. *Time.* Retrieved from http://time.com/5511729/monk -mindfulness-art-of-dying

Frank, A. (1952/1993). *Anne Frank: The diary of a young girl.* (B. M. Mooyart, trans.). New York: Bantam Books.

Fromm, E. (1956/1970). *The art of loving.* New York, NY: Harper & Row Publishers.

Gil, E. (1991). *The healing power of play.* New York, NY: Guilford Press.

Gil, E. (1994). *Play in family therapy.* New York, NY: Guilford Press.

Gil, E. (2006). *Helping abused and traumatized children: Integrating directive and nondirective approaches.* New York, NY: Guilford Press.

Gil, E. (2015a). *Play in family therapy* (2nd ed.). New York, NY: Guilford Press.

Gil, E. (2015b). Reuniting families after critical separations: An integrative play therapy approach to building and strengthening family ties. In D. A. Crenshaw & A. L. Stewart (Eds.), *Play therapy: A comprehensive guide to theory and practice* (pp. 353–369). New York, NY: Guilford Press.

Gil, E. (2017). *Posttraumatic play in children: What clinicians need to know.* New York, NY: Guilford Press.

Gillespie, J. (1994). *The projective use of mother-and-child drawings: A manual for clinicians.* New York, NY: Brunner/Mazel, Inc.

Gilligan, S. (2012). *Generative trance: The experience of creative flow.* Williston, VT: Crown House Publishing Limited.

Goldenberg, H., & Goldenberg, I. (2013). *Family therapy: An overview* (9th ed.). Belmont, CA: Brooks/Cole.

Golly, C., Riccelli, D., & Smith, M. (2017). Healing adolescent trauma: Incorporating ethical touch in a movement and dance therapy group. In J. A. Courtney & R. D. Nolan (Eds.), *Touch in child counseling and play therapy: An ethical and clinical guide* (pp. 134–148). New York, NY: Routledge.

Goodyear-Brown, P. (2019). *Trauma and play therapy: Helping children heal.* New York, NY: Routledge.

Gordon, W. (1961). *Synectics.* New York, NY: Harper & Row.

Granieri, A., Luana La Marca, L., Giuseppe Mannino, G., Giunta, S. Guglielmucci, F., & Schimmenti, A. (2017). The relationship between defense patterns and DSM-

5 maladaptive personality domains. *Frontiers in Psychology*. Retrieved from www
.ncbi.nlm.nih.gov/pmc/articles/PMC5673655. doi:10.3389/fpsyg.2017.01926

Green, R. J. (1994). Foreword. In E. Gil. *Play in family therapy* (pp. v–vii). New York,
NY: Guilford Press.

Green, E. J., & Drewes, A. A. (Eds.) (2014). *Integrating expressive arts and play therapy
with children and adolescents*. Hoboken, NJ: John Wiley & Sons.

Green, E. J., & Drewes, A. A. (2014). *Integrating expressive arts and play therapy with
children and adolescents*. Hoboken, NJ: John Wiley & Sons.

Grobbel, R., Cooke, K., & Bonet, N. (2017). Ethical use of touch and nurturing-
restraint in play therapy with aggressive young children, as illustrated through a
reflective supervision session. In J. A. Courtney & R. D. Nolan (Eds.), *Touch in
child counseling and play therapy: An ethical and clinical guide* (pp. 120–133). New
York, NY: Routledge.

Guerney, L. F. (2015). Foreword. In E. Green, J. N., Baggerly, & A. C. Myrick (Eds.),
Counseling families: Play-based treatment. Lanham, MD: Rowman & Littlefield.

Guerney, L., & Guerney, B. (1989). Child relationship enhancement: Family therapy
and parent education. Special issue: Person-centered approaches with families.
Person Centered Review, 4, 344–357.

Haslam, D. (2010). Family sculpting with puppets. In L. Lowenstein (Ed.). *Creative
family therapy techniques: Play, art and expressive therapies to engage children in
family sessions*. Toronto, ON: Champion Press.

Hebb, D. O. (1949). *The organization of behavior: A neuropsychological theory*. New
York, NY: John Wiley & Sons.

Heider, J. (1985). *The Tao of leadership: Lao Tzu's Tao Te Ching adapted for a new age*.
Atlanta, GA: Humanics New Age.

Heider, J. (2000). *The Tao of daily living*. Lawrence, KS: Process Publishing Company.

Heller, L., & LaPierre, A. (2012). *Healing developmental trauma: How early trauma
affects self-regulation, self-image, and the capacity for relationship*. Berkeley, CA:
North Atlantic Books.

Homeyer, L., & Morrison, M. (2008). Play as therapy. *American Journal of Play, 1*(2),
210–228.

Hudak, M. L., & Tan, R. C. (2012). Neonatal drug withdrawal. *Pediatrics, 129*(2).
Retrieved from https://pediatrics.aappublications.org/content/129/2/e540

Iselin, J. (2007). *Heart stones*. New York, NY: Harry N. Abrams, Inc.

Jernberg, A., & Booth, P. (2001). *TheraPlay: Helping parents and children build better relationships through attachment based play* (2nd ed.). San Francisco, CA:
Jossey-Bass.

Jimenez-Pride, C. (2018). *The sun salutation*. Columbia, SC: FreedOM Yoga, Inc.

Jung, C. G. (1963). *Memories, dreams, reflections*. A. Jaffe (Recorded & Ed.), R. Winston & C. Winston (Translators). New York, NY: Vintage Books.

Jung, C. G. (1964). *Man and his symbols*. New York, NY: Dell Publishing.

Kain, K. L., & Terrell, S. J. (2018). *Nurturing resilience: Helping clients move forward from developmental trauma*. Berkeley, CA: North Atlantic Books.

Keith, D. V., & Whitaker, C. A. (2004). Play therapy: A paradigm for work with families. In C. E. Schaefer & L. Carey (Eds.), *Family play therapy*, (pp. 185–204). New York, NY: Rowman & Littlefield Publishers, Inc.

Kellert, S. R. (1993). Introduction. In S. R. Kellert & E. O. Wilson (Eds.), *The biophilia hypothesis* (pp. 18–25). Washington, DC: Shearwater Books/Island Press.

Kestly, T. A. (2014). *The interpersonal neurobiology of play: Brain-building interventions for emotional well-being*. New York, NY: W. W. Norton & Company.

Kestly, T. A. (2016). Presence and play: Why mindfulness matters. *International Journal of Play Therapy, 25*(1), 14–23.

Klepsch, M., & Logie, L. (1982). *Children draw and tell: An introduction to the projective uses of children's human figure drawings*. New York, NY: Brunner/Mazel Publishers.

Knell, S. M. (2011). Cognitive-behavioral play therapy. In C. E. Schaefer (Ed.), *Foundations of play therapy* (2nd ed.). Hoboken, NJ: John Wiley & Sons.

Knill, P. J., Levine, E. G., & Levine, S. K. (2005). *Principles and practice of expressive arts therapy: Toward a therapeutic aesthetics*. Philadelphia, PA: Jessica Kingsley Publishers.

Kopytin, A., & Rugh, M. (2017). *Environmental expressive therapies: Nature-assisted theory and practice*. New York, NY: Routledge.

Landreth, G. L. (2012). *Play therapy the art of the relationship* (3rd ed.). New York, NY: Routledge.

Lane, D. (1994). *Music as medicine*. Grand Rapids, MI: Zondervan Publishing.

Lankton, S. (2004) *Assembling Ericksonian therapy: The collected papers of Stephen Lankton*. Phoenix, AZ: Zeig, Tucker, & Theisen, Inc.

Lankton, C. H., & Lankton, S. R. (1989). *Tales of enchantment: Goal-oriented metaphors for adults and children in therapy*. New York, NY: Brunner/Mazel, Inc.

Leboyer, F. (1976). *Loving hands: The traditional art of baby massage*. New York, NY: Newmarket Press.

LeFeber, M. M. (2014). Working with children using dance/movement therapy. In E. J. Green & A. A. Drewes (Eds.), *Integrating expressive arts and play therapy with children and adolescents* (pp. 125–147). Hoboken, NJ: John Wiley & Sons.

Levick, M. (1986). *Mommy, daddy, look what I am saying: What children are telling you through their art*. New York: M. Evans & Company, Inc. Levick, M. F. (2003). *See what I'm saying: What children tell us through their art*. Hong Kong, China: Regal Printing.

Levine, P. A. (2018). Polyvagal theory and trauma. In S. W. Porges & D. Dana (Eds.), *Clinical applications of the polyvagal theory: The emergence of polyvagal-informed therapies* (pp. 3–26). New York, NY: Norton.

Levine, P. A., & Kline, M. (2007). *Trauma through a child's eyes: Awakening the ordinary miracle of healing.* Berkeley, CA: North Atlantic Books.

Liebman, R., Minuchin, S., Baker, L., & Rosman, B. (1976). The role of the family in the treatment of chronic asthma. In P. J. Guerin (Ed.), *Family therapy: Theory and practice* (pp. 309–324). New York, NY: Gardner Press, Inc.

Lindaman, S., & Makela, J. (2018). The polyvagal foundation of TheraPlay treatment: Combining social engagement, play, and nurture to create safety, regulation, and resilience. In S. W. Porges & D. Dana (Eds.), *Clinical applications of polyvagal theory: The emergence of polyvagal-informed therapies* (pp. 227–247). New York, NY: W. W. Norton & Company.

Linden, D. J. (2015). *Touch. The science of hand, heart, and mind.* London, UK: Penguin Random House.

Linden, S., & Grut, J. (2002). *The healing fields: Working with psychotherapy and nature to rebuild shattered lives.* London, United Kingdom: Frances Lincoln.

Lonegren, S. (2015). Labyrinths: Ancient myths and modern uses. New York, NY: Gothic Image Publications.

Louv, R. (2008). *Last child in the woods: Saving our children from nature-deficit disorder.* Chapel Hill, NC: Algonquin Books.

Lowenfeld, M. (1979). *The world technique.* London, UK: Allen & Unwin.

Lowenfeld, M., & Dukes, E. (1938). Play therapy and child guidance. *The British Medical Journal, 2*(4065), 1150–1151.

Ludwig, E. (2015). *Obituary.* Retrieved from www.legacy.com/obituaries/palmbeach post/obituary.aspx?n=ethyle-kauffman-ludwig&pid=173942316

MacLean, P. D. (1990). *The triune brain in evolution: Role in paleocerebral functions.* New York, NY: Kluwer Academic Publishers.

Macy, J., & Gahbler, N. (2010). *Pass it on: Five stories that can change the world.* Berkeley, CA: Parallax Press.

Malchiodi, C. A. (1998). *Understanding children's drawings.* New York, NY: Guilford Press.

Malchiodi, C. (Ed.) (2005). *Expressive therapies.* New York, NY: Guilford Press.

Malchiodi, C. (2015). *Creative interventions with traumatized children* (2nd ed.). New York, NY: Guilford Press.

Marks-Tarlow, T. (2018). Awakening clinical intuition: Creativity and play. In T. Marks-Tarlow, M. Solomon, & D. J. Siegel (Eds.), *Play and creativity in psychotherapy* (pp. 144–166). New York, NY: W. W. Norton & Company.

Marks-Tarlow, T., Solomon, M., & Siegel, D. J. (2018). Introduction. In T. Marks-

Tarlow, M. Solomon, & D. J. Siegel (Eds.), *Play and creativity in psychotherapy* (pp. 1–12). New York, NY: W. W. Norton & Company.

Maslow, A. H. (1968). *Toward a psychology of being* (2nd ed.). Princeton, NJ: Van Nostrand.

McClure, V. (2000). *Infant massage: A handbook for loving parents* (Revised edition). New York, NY: Bantam Books.

McGilchrist, I. (2009). *The master and his emissary: The divided brain and the making of the Western world*. New Haven, CT: Yale University Press.

McGlone, F., Wessberg, J., & Olausson, H. (2014). Discriminative and affective touch: Sensing and feeling. *Neuron, 82*(4), 737–755. doi:10.1016/j.neuron.2014.05.001

McGoldrick, M., Gerson, R., & Petry, S. (2020). *Genograms: Assessment and intervention*, (4th ed.). New York, NY: Norton.

McNiff, S. (2005). Foreword. In C. A. Malchiodi (Ed.), *Expressive therapies*. New York, NY: Guilford Press.

McNiff, S. (2009). *Integrating the arts in therapy: History, theory, and practice*. Springfield, IL: Charles C. Thomas Publisher, LTD.

McQueen, K., & Murphy-Oikonen, J. (2016) Neonatal abstinence syndrome. *The New England Journal of Medicine, 375,* 2468–2479. doi:10.1056/NEJMra1600879

Michael, T., & Luke, C. (2016). Utilizing a metaphoric approach to teach the neuroscience of play therapy: A pilot study. *International Journal of Play Therapy, 25*(1), 45–52.

Miles, E. (2005). *Tune your brain: Using music to manage your mind, body, and mood*. New York, NY: Authors Choice Press.

Mills, J. (1993). *Gentle willow*. Washington, DC: Magination Press.

Mills, J. C. (2011). *StoryPlay foundations training manual*. Phoenix, AZ: Imaginal Press.

Mills, J. C. (2015). StoryPlay: A narrative play therapy approach. In D. A. Crenshaw & A. L. Stewart (Eds.), *Play therapy: A comprehensive guide to theory and practice* (pp. 171–185). New York, NY: Guilford Press.

Mills, J. C., & Crowley, R. J. (2014). *Therapeutic metaphors for children and the child within* (2nd ed.). New York, NY: Routledge.

Montagu, A. (1986). *Touching: The human significance of the skin* (2nd ed.). New York, NY: Harper & Row.

Montgomery, C. S., & Courtney, J. A. (2015). The theoretical and therapeutic paradigm of botanical arranging. *Journal of Therapeutic Horticulture, 25*(1), 16–26.

Moustakas, C. E. (1959). *Psychotherapy with children: The living relationship*. New York, NY: Harper & Row.

Neiman, B. (2015*). Mindfulness & yoga skills: For children and adolescents*. Eau Claire, WI: PESI Publishing & Media.

Nhat Hanh, T. (2011). *Planting seeds: Practicing mindfulness with children*. Berkeley, CA: Parallax Press.

Norton, B., Ferriegel, M., & Norton, C. (2011). Somatic expressions of trauma in experiential play therapy. *International Journal of Play Therapy, 20*(3), 138–152.

Norton, C., & Norton B. (2008). *Reaching children through play therapy: An experiential approach* (3rd ed.). Denver, CO: White Apple Press.

Oaklander, V. (1988). *Windows to our children*. New York, NY: The Gestalt Journal Press.

O'Brien, M., & Lynch, H. (2011). Exploring the role of touch in the first year of life: Mothers' perspectives of tactile interactions with their infants. *British Journal of Occupational Therapy, 74*(3), 129–136. doi:10.4276/030802211X 12996065859247

Ogden, P. (2018a). Play, creativity, and movement vocabulary. In T. Marks-Tarlow, M. Solomon, & D. J. Siegel (Eds.), *Play and creativity in psychotherapy*, (pp. 92–109). New York, NY: W. W. Norton & Company.

Ogden, P. (2018b). Polyvagal theory and sensorimotor psychotherapy. In S. W. Porges & D. Dana (Eds.), Clinical applications of the polyvagal theory: The emergence of polyvagal-informed therapies, pp. 34-49.

Ogden, P., & Fisher, J. (2015). *Sensorimotor psychotherapy: Interventions for trauma and attachment*. New York, NY: Norton.

Okie, S. (2009, Jan 26). The epidemic that wasn't. *New York Times*. Retrieved from www.nytimes.com/2009/01/27/health/27coca.html

Osofsky, J. D. (2009). Perspectives on helping traumatized infants, young children, and their families. *Infant Mental Health Journal, 30*, 673–677.

Osofsky, J. D., Stepka, P. T., & King, L. S. (2017). *Treating infants and young children impacted by trauma: Interventions that promote healthy development*. Washington, DC: American Psychological Association.

Palmer, D., & Barlow, J. (2017). Teaching positive touch: A child-to-child massage model for the classroom. In J. A. Courtney & R. D. Nolan (Eds.), *Touch in child counseling and play therapy: An ethical and clinical guide* (pp. 189–201). New York, NY: Routledge.

Panksepp, J. (2009). Brain emotional systems and qualities of mental life: From animal models of affect to implications for psychotherapeutics. In D. Fosha, D. Siegel, & M. Solomon (Eds.), *The healing power of emotion: Affective neuroscience, development, and clinical practice* (pp. 1–26). New York, NY: Norton.

Panksepp, J. (2018). Play and the construction of creativity, cleverness, and reversal of ADHD in our social brains. In T. Marks-Tarlow, M. Solomon, & D. J. Siegel (Eds.), *Play and creativity in psychotherapy* (pp. 242–270). New York, NY: W. W. Norton & Company.

Perls, F. (1969). *Gestalt therapy verbatim*. Moab, UT: Real Person Press.

Perry, B. D. (2006a). Applying principles of neurodevelopment to clinical work with maltreated and traumatized children: The neurosequential model of therapeutics. In N. B. Webb (Ed.), *Working with traumatized youth in child welfare* (pp. 27–52). New York, NY: Guilford Press.

Perry, B. D. (2006b). *The boy who was raised as a dog: And other stories from a child psychiatrist's notebook.* New York, NY: Basic Books.

Perry, B. D. (2015). Foreword. In C. Malchiodi (Ed.). *Creative interventions with traumatized children* (2nd ed.). New York, NY: Guilford Press.

Phillips, R. D. (1985). Whistling in the dark? A review of play therapy research. *Psychotherapy, 22*(4), 752–760.

Porges, S. (2018). Polyvagal theory: A primer. In S. W. Porges & D. Dana (Eds.), *Clinical applications of polyvagal theory: The emergence of polyvagal-informed therapies* (pp. 50–72). New York, NY: Norton.

Ramachandran, V. S. (2011). *The tell-tale brain: A neuroscientist's quest for what makes us human.* New York, NY: Norton.

Rappaport, L. (2015). Focusing-oriented expressive arts therapy and mindfulness with children and adolescents experiencing trauma. In C. A. Malchiodi (Ed.), *Creative interventions with traumatized children* (pp. 281–330). New York, NY: Guilford Press.

Rawat, P. (2016). *Splitting the arrow: Understanding the business of life.* Nagano, Japan: Bunya Publishing Corporation.

Ray, D., & Bratton, S. (2010). What the research shows about play therapy: 21st century update. In J. Baggerly, D. Ray, & S. Bratton (Eds.), *Child-centered play therapy research: The evidence base for effective practice.* Hoboken, NJ: John Wiley & Sons.

Reamer, F. G. (2017). Ethical and risk-management issues in the use of touch. In J. A. Courtney & R. D. Nolan (Eds.), *Touch in child counseling and play therapy: An ethical and clinical guide* (pp. 18–32). New York, NY: Routledge.

Reich, W. (1960). *Selected writings: An introduction to orgonomy.* New York, NY: Farrar, Straus and Giroux.

Richardson, C. (2016). *Expressive arts therapy for traumatized children and adolescents: A four-phase model.* New York, NY: Routledge.

Robbins, A. (1998). Introduction to therapeutic presence. In A. Robbins (Ed.), *Therapeutic presence: Bridging expression and form* (pp. 17–35). Philadelphia, PA: Jessica Kingsley.

Rogers, C. R. (1939). *The clinical treatment of the problem child.* New York, NY: Brunner/Mazel, Inc.

Rogers, C. (1954). *Toward a theory of creativity, A review of general semantics, 11*(4), 249–260.

Rogers, C. R. (1965). *Client-centered therapy.* Boston, MA: Houghton Mifflin Company.

Rogers, F. (1986). *Mister Rogers' playbook: Insights and activities for parents and children*. New York, NY: Berkley Books.

Rogers, F. (2005). *Life journeys according to Mister Rogers*. New York, NY: Family Connections, Inc.

Rogers, N. (1993). *The creative connection: Expressive arts as healing*. Palo Alto, CA: Science & Behavior Books.

Rogerson, C. H. (1939). *Play therapy in childhood*. Oxford, UK: Oxford University Press.

Rosen, S. (1989). Foreword. In M. H. Erickson & E. L. Rossi. *The February man: Evolving consciousness and identity in hypnotherapy*. New York, NY: Brunner/Mazel.

Ruefle, M. (2017). *On imagination*. Brooklyn, NY: Sarabande Books.

Russ, S. W. (2004). *Play in child development and psychotherapy: Toward empirically supported practice*. Mahwah, NJ: Lawrence Erlbaum Associates, Publishers.

Sams, J. (1990). *Sacred path cards: The discovery of self through native teachings*. New York, NY: HarperCollins.

Satir, V. (1985). *Meditations & inspirations*. Berkeley, CA: Celestial Arts.

Satir, V. (1988). *The new peoplemaking*. Mountain View, CA: Science & Behavior Books.

Schaefer, C. E. (1993). *The therapeutic powers of play*. Northvale, NJ: Jason Aronson Inc.

Schaefer, C. E. (1976). *The therapeutic use of child's play*. Northvale, NJ: Jason Aronson, Inc.

Schaefer, C. E. (2003). Prescriptive play therapy. In C. E. Schaefer (Ed.), *Foundations of play therapy* (pp. 306–320). Hoboken, NJ: John Wiley & Sons.

Schaefer, C. E., & Carey, L. (2004). *Family play therapy*. Lanham, MD: Rowman & Littlefield Publishers, Inc.

Schaefer, C. E., & Drewes, A. A. (2014). *The therapeutic powers of play: 20 core agents of change* (2nd ed.). Hoboken, NJ: John Wiley & Sons.

Schaefer, C. E., & O'Connor, K. J. (1983). *Handbook of play therapy*. New York, NY: John Wiley & Sons.

Schaefer, C. E., & Peabody, M. A. (2016). Glossary of play therapy terms. *Play Therapy Magazine*. Retrieved from https://cdn.ymaws.com/a4pt.site-ym.com/resource/resmgr/Publications/Glossary_of_Play_Therapy_Ter.pdf

Scharlepp, R., & Radey, M. (2017). Hand are not for hitting: Redefining touch for children exposed to domestic violence. In J. A. Courtney & R. D. Nolan (Eds), *Touch in child counseling and play therapy: An ethical and clinical guide*, (pp. 106–119). New York, NY: Routledge.

Schneider, E. F., & Patterson, P. P. (2010). You've got that magic touch: Integrating the sense of touch into early childhood services. *Young Exceptional Children, 13*(5), 17–27. doi:10.1177/1096250610384706

Schore, A. N. (2012). *The science of the art of psychotherapy*. New York, NY: W. W. Norton & Company.

Schore, A. N. (2019). *Right brain psychotherapy*. New York, NY: W. W. Norton & Company.

Schore, A. N., & Schore, J. R. (2012). Modern attachment theory: The central role of affect regulation in development and treatment. In A. N. Schore (Ed.), *The science of the art of psychotherapy* (pp. 27–51). New York, NY: John Wiley & Sons.

Schore, A. N., & Sieff, D. F. (2015). On the same wavelength: How our emotional brain is shaped by human relationships. In D. F. Sieff (Ed.). *Understanding and healing emotional trauma: Conversations with pioneering clinicians and researchers,* (pp. 111–136). New York, NY: Routledge.

Schwartzenberger, K. (2020). Neurosensory play in the infant-parent dyad. In J. A. Courtney (Ed.), *Infant play therapy: Foundations, models, programs and practice*. New York, NY: Routledge.

Sharfstein, J. M. (2015). Neonatal abstinence syndrome: Déjà vu all over again? *JAMA Forum.* Retrieved from https://newsatjama.jama.com/2015/10/21/neonatal-abstinence-syndrome-deja-vu-all-over-again/

Shibata, M., Terasawa, Y., & Umeda, S. (2014). Integration of cognitive and affective networks in humor comprehension. *Neuropsychologia, 65,* 137–145. doi:10.1016/j.neuropsychologia.2014.10.025

Siegel, D. J. (2012). *The developing mind: How relationships and the brain interact to shape who we are* (2nd ed.). New York, NY: Guilford Press.

Siegel, D. J. (2018). *Mind: A journey to the heart of being human*. New York, NY: Norton.

Siegel, D. J., & Payne Bryson, T. (2012). *The whole-brain child: 12 revolutionary strategies to nurture your child's developing mind*. New York, NY: Bantam Books.

Siegel, D. J., & Payne Bryson, T. (2015). *The whole-brain child workbook: Practical exercises, worksheets and activities to nurture developing minds*. Eau Claire, WI: PESI Publishing & Media.

Smith, G. (1991). Assessing family interaction by the collaborative drawing technique. In C. E. Schaefer, K. Gitlin, & A. Sandgrund (Eds.), *Play diagnosis and assessment* (pp. 599–608). New York, NY: John Wiley & Sons.

Souter-Anderson, L. (2010). *Touching clay, touching what?: The use of clay in therapy*. Dorset, UK: Archive Publishing.

Spock, M. (1985). *Teaching as a lively art*. Hudson, NY: Anthroposophic Press.

Stack, D., & Jean, A. (2011). Communicating through touch: Touching during parent-infant interactions. In M. J. Hertenstein & S. Weiss (Eds.), *The handbook of touch: Neuroscience, behavioral, and health perspectives* (pp. 273–298). New York, NY: Springer.

Stauffer, S. D. (Ed.). (2018). Technology in the playroom [Special issue]. *Play Therapy*, *13*(3), 1–27.

Stewart, A. L., Field, T. A., & Echterling, L. G. (2016). Neuroscience and the magic of play therapy. *International Journal of Play Therapy*, *25*(1), 4–13. doi:10.1037/pla0000016

Stone, J. (2019). Digital games. In J. Stone & C. E. Schaefer (Eds.), *Game play* (3rd ed.). New York, NY: John Wiley & Sons.

Swank, J. M., & Shin, S. (2015). Nature-based child-centered play therapy: An innovative counseling approach. *International Journal of Play Therapy*, *24*(3), 151–161.

Taft, J. (1933/1973). *The dynamics of therapy in a controlled relationship*. Gloucester, MA: Peter Smith Publisher, by permission of Dover Publications, Inc. [Originally published by The Macmillan Company in 1933 and copyrighted in 1962 by Dover Publications, London, UK.]

Terr, L. (1981). Forbidden games: Post-traumatic child's play. *American Academy of Child Psychiatry*, *20*, 741–760. Retrieved from: https://www.jaacap.org/article/S0002-7138(09)60740-8/pdf

Terr, L. (1990). *Too scared to cry: How trauma affects children and ultimately all of us*. New York, NY: Basic Books.

Terr, L. C. (1991). Childhood traumas: An outline and overview. *American Journal of Psychiatry*, *148*(1), 10–20. doi:10.1176/ajp.148.1.10

The Freedom Writers & Gruwell, E. (2009). *The freedom writers diary*. New York, NY: Broadway Books.

Thomson, J. (1994). *Natural childhood*. New York, NY: Simon & Schuster.

Thomson, P. (2004). The impact of trauma on the embryo and fetus: An application of the diathesis-stress model and the neurovulnerability-neurotoxicity model. *Journal of Prenatal and Perinatal Psychology and Health*, *19*(1), 9–64.

Underdown, A., & Barlow, J. (2011). Interventions to support early relationships: Mechanisms identified within infant massage programmes. *Community Practitioner*, *84*(4), 21–26. Retrieved from http://connection.ebscohost.com/c/articles/59535001/interventions-support-early-%20relationships-mechanisms-identified-within-infant-massage-programmes

Uvnäs-Moberg, K. (2003). *The oxytocin factor: Tapping the hormone of calm, love, and healing*. Cambridge, MA: Da Capo Press.

van der Kolk, B. (2014). *The body keeps the score*. New York, NY: Penguin.

Vincent J., Felitti, V. J., Anda, R. F., Nordenberg, D., Williamson, D. F., Spitz, A. M., . . . Marks, J. S. (1998). Relationship of childhood abuse and household dysfunction to many of the leading causes of death in adults. *American Journal of Preventative Medicine*, *14*(4), 245–258. doi:10.1016/S0749-3797(98)00017-8

Walsh, F. (2006). *Strengthening family resilience* (2nd ed.). New York, NY: Guilford Press.

Weber, R. (1991). A philosophical perspective on touch. In K. E. Barnard & T. B. Brazelton (Eds.). *Touch: The foundation of experience* (pp. 11–43). Madison, CT: International Universities Press.

Webb, N. B. (2019). *Social work practice with children* (4thrd ed.). New York, NY: Guilford Press.

Wheeden, A., Scafidi, F.A., Field, T., Ironson, G., Valdeon, C., & Bandstra, E. (1993). Massage effects on cocaine-exposed preterm neonates. *Journal of Developmental and Behavioral Pediatrics, 14,* 318–322. Retrieved from www.ncbi.nlm.nih.gov/pubmed/8254063

Wilson, E. (1993). Biophilia and the conservation ethic. In S. R. Kellert & E. O. Wilson (Eds.), *The biophilia hypothesis* (pp. 31–40). Washington, DC: Shearwater Books/Island Press.

Winnicott, D. W. (1971a). Therapeutic consultations in child psychiatry. New York, NY: Basic Books.

Winnicott, D. W. (1971b). *Play and reality.* New York, NY: Routledge.

Wonders, L. L. (2019). *When parents are at war.* Atlanta, GA: Wonders Counseling Services, LLC.

Yalom, I. D. (2002). *The gift of therapy: An open letter to a new generation of therapists and their patients.* New York, NY: HarperCollins Publishers.

Index

In this index, *f* denotes figure.